GARDEN PESTS

OF BRITAIN & EUROPE

Michael Chinery

A & C Black • London

Published 2010 by A&C Black Publishers Ltd,
36 Soho Square, London W1D 3QY

Copyright © 2010 text by Michael Chinery

ISBN: 978 1408 12283 9

A CIP catalogue record for this book is avai

All rights reserved. No part of this publicati
in any form or by any means – photograph
including photocopying, recording, taping
retrieval systems – without permission of th

This book is produced using paper that is n
managed sustainable forests. It is natural, r
The logging and manufacturing processes
regulations of the country of origin.

Publisher: Nigel Redman
Commissioning Editor: Jim Martin
Project Editor: Lisa Thomas
Copy Editor: Marianne Taylor
Proofreading: Wendy Smith, Marianne Taylor
Picture Research: D&N Publishing
Design by D & N Publishing, Baydon, Wiltshire and Fluke Art, Cornwall
Printed in Spain

10 9 8 7 6 5 4 3 2 1

Visit www.acblack.com/naturalhistory to find out more about our authors
and their books. You will find extracts, author interviews and our blog, and
you can sign up for newsletters to be the first to hear about our latest
releases and special offers.

Photographic acknowledgements

All photographs taken by the author, Michael Chinery, with the exception of the following:

John Baker 231 (top); Nigel Catlin 103; Anneliese Emmans Dean (www.theBigBuzz.biz) 286;
Stan Dumican 17 (top right), 218; Rob Edmunds 262, 289; Peter Eeles 189 (main image), 189 (inset);
Antonio Sanchez Floro 260; Food and Environment Research Agency 72 (right), 81; Joaquim Alves
Gaspar 267; Phil Gates 46; Jozef Grego 53; Csóka György 143 (top), 177, 179, 204 (bottom left), 216
(top & bottom), 244 (top); Rich Hoyer 85; Roger Key 27, 69 (top), 160 (top), 182, 187 (right), 231
(bottom), 250, 254; Guy Knight 287, 293 (main image), 298; Rayanne Lehman (Pennsylvania
Department of Agriculture, Bugwood.org) 84; Jeffrey W. Lotz (forestryimages.org) 143 (bottom);
Chris Manley 204 (top), 235, 240 (left); Ian McLean 120, 174, 243 (inset), 258, 261; Geoff Nobes
200 (lower), 223 (bottom); Charles Olsen (www.forestryimages.org) 265; Trevor and Dilys Pendleton
239; Richard Revels 17 (top left), 26 (top), 50, 61 (left), 73, 116, 121, 129, 133, 154, 159, 161
(bottom), 163, 180 (left), 198, 224 (bottom), 256, 259 (top), 279 (top); Neil Sherman 233, 234;
Shutterstock: 36 (Grandpa), 37 (Michael Pettigrew), 41 (i9370), 63 (Thomas Payne), 94 (Michael
Pettigrew), 95 (Arto Hakola); Dr Dave Skingsley FRES (www.bugbotherer.org.uk) 268; D. Smirnov 67;
Paul Sterry (Nature Photographers Ltd) 65 (top), 70 (top left and right), 171 (top); Barry Stewart 107;
Luc Viatour 132; Robin Williams 65 (bottom), 72 (left), 92 (right), 105, 278, 279 (bottom);
www.j-alemany.com 122 (left); Cor Zonneveld 266.

GARDEN
PESTS
OF BRITAIN
& EUROPE

CONTENTS

PART ONE

YOUR GARDEN AND ITS INHABITANTS

GARDEN HABITATS

People have been creating gardens around their homes for hundreds or even thousands of years. We have vegetable gardens and orchards to provide us with food, flower gardens and shrubberies for sheer enjoyment, hedges and walls for privacy, and lawns for games and relaxation. In all of these habitats we lovingly cultivate a wide variety of plants, including both native and exotic species, and those that we cultivate are usually joined by a host of uninvited plant species that we normally refer to as weeds. We spend a lot of time and effort – and money – trying to get rid of these unwanted plants, although many of them, notably the daisies

Even a small garden can contain many different micro-habitats, including trees and shrubs, hedges and walls, and a range of herbaceous plants. Don't be too eager to remove weeds from the bottom of a hedge: they can shelter many useful creatures.

Old walls can support a wide range of wild and cultivated plants, which in turn attract insects. Solitary bees and wasps excavate their nesting chambers in the soft mortar.

on the lawn and the dandelions under the hedge, are actually quite attractive.

Encouraging diversity

Although we create our gardens for our own benefit, to provide food or pleasure or both, they are rapidly colonised by a wealth of animal life that takes full advantage of the food and shelter provided by the vegetation. In fact, gardens exhibit a greater diversity of animal life than many natural environments simply because of the variety of habitats that we create in relatively small areas. And when you take into account the huge areas covered by our gardens – one recent estimate was about 380,000 hectares in Britain alone – it is easy to see that they are extremely important as wildlife habitats. A recent survey of bumblebee nests, carried out by Rothamsted Research, clearly demonstrated the importance of gardens for these insects, which have suffered an alarming countrywide population crash during the last few years. Over 700 gardens were studied in the survey and were found to have an average of 36 bumblebee nests per hectare – a considerably higher density than that found in many parts of the countryside.

Long-established gardens are likely to be the richest in terms of resident wildlife species simply because the animals and plants have had more time to colonise there, but several other factors are involved in the make-up of the garden community, with the gardener playing a major role by way of the number of habitats that he or she creates in the garden and the variety of plants grown in these habitats. A garden consisting of a neatly manicured lawn and a patio with a few pots will obviously attract fewer insects and other animals than one full of flowers and shrubs. The gardener who is too eager to use the lawn mower and the hedge trimmer or too ready to reach for the insecticide will also have a less interesting garden than a slightly less fastidious neighbour!

Soil and location

The soil can have a considerable influence on a garden's wildlife. Soil acidity determines what plants, including weeds, can flourish in the garden and indirectly affects the animal life because many creatures, especially the insects, are restricted to certain food-plants. The soil also has a direct effect on some animals. Some snails, for example, require plenty of lime in the soil in order to form their shells, and if the required concentration of lime is not there – in sandy soils, for example – the snails will also be missing.

The location of a garden certainly affects the amount and variety of its resident wildlife. Urban gardens and those in the middle of large housing estates tend to be less well endowed because the plant and animal life has further to travel from the surrounding countryside. Much of the wildlife will get there in time, although air pollution, particularly by sulphur dioxide, may prevent some species from taking up residence. Many lichens, for example, and several mosses are unable to cope with much sulphur dioxide in the air and are never found in industrial regions or other heavily built-up areas, so the insects and other animals that depend on them are also absent. Sulphur dioxide is produced during the burning of various fuels and much of it is converted to sulphuric acid in the atmosphere before falling as acid rain. As well as having a direct effect on the vegetation, this rain increases the acidity of the soil and reduces its fertility, thus influencing to some extent the type of vegetation that can grow in an area.

TOP TIP

Encourage bumble-bees to settle down in your garden by providing artificial nest chambers. An easy way is to bury flower pots in sloping ground with the basal hole exposed. If you can stuff them with some used mouse bedding from a local pet shop, the bees will be even happier. Try burying a pot in your compost heap, where the warmth will be much appreciated by the bees.

Large gardens with a range of different habitats can obviously support more resident wildlife than smaller gardens, but size does not necessarily worry the casual visitors, which make up a considerable proportion of the wildlife that can be seen in our gardens. If a garden contains something to interest them they will surely find it. Gangs of Long-tailed Tits, for example, may invade the smallest of gardens if there is a shrub or two to be investigated, and Pied Wagtails will scour the tiniest patch of grass, but they soon move off to pastures new. Similarly, Red Admirals and several other butterflies flock to garden buddleias, but for most of these creatures our gardens are simply feeding grounds and not permanent homes.

The Red Admiral butterfly (*Vanessa atalanta*) is a common visitor to gardens with plenty of flowers. It is particularly fond of michaelmas daisies and the ice plant pictured here. It also enjoys a drink from over-ripe fruit, but its caterpillar feeds on stinging nettles, so the insect is not likely to breed in many gardens. In common with many other butterflies, it is protected by its bold warning colours (see p. 28).

The Hummingbird Hawkmoth (*Macroglossum stellatarum*) is a day-flying visitor to many gardens, plunging its long tongue into a wide variety of flowers to obtain nectar.

THE INHABITANTS

The vast majority of our garden residents are completely neutral as far as the health and well-being of our gardens and gardeners are concerned. We rarely even notice them. For example, scores of different moths make their homes in a typical garden and harmlessly sip nectar from the flowers. Most of them are nocturnal, so we don't often see them in action, and we don't see them much in the daytime because many have a marvellous ability to select just the right background on which to rest. So good is the camouflage of some moths that even experienced entomologists have difficulty in spotting them. Many species spend the daylight hours on tree trunks and fences, while others bed down on foliage or among dead leaves on the ground. Some moths may actually make a conscious choice of background colour, by comparing it with their own colours, but it is likely that a genetic factor is at work in most species – in other words the moths have been programmed to seek out particular colours. The caterpillars of our garden moths nibble various plants – weeds as well as our cultivated crops and flowers – but their numbers are seldom high enough to cause any appreciable damage, and we rarely see the caterpillars themselves because, in common with the adults, many are beautifully camouflaged. They blend in with the foliage on which they feed and some bear uncanny resemblances to twigs.

Although most of the uninvited guests that settle in our gardens are inconspicuous and neutral to our interests, there are still many species that do come to our notice in one way or another. Some are good and commonly listed as the gardener's friends in older gardening books. Many are bad and regarded as pests – the gardener's foes – and quite a few, both good and bad, have the misfortune to be ugly.

TOP: The Dotted Chestnut moth (*Conistra rubiginea*) is extremely well camouflaged on a piece of wood. A good way to find out which moths live in your garden is to look carefully at tree trunks and fences early in the morning, before the sun gets on them. If the moths get too warm they will move away.

ABOVE: The caterpillar of the Early Thorn moth (*Selenia dentaria*) adopts a rigid pose when at rest and, in common with many other caterpillars, it is very difficult to distinguish from the twigs on which it rests.

The good guys

The garden good guys are mostly carnivorous creatures that help us by eating a variety of pests. Welcome in the garden, they are commonly referred to as the gardener's friends, although the distinction between friend and foe is not always as clear-cut as some of the early gardening books suggested. Centipedes, for example, feed on a wide variety of small creatures, including many garden pests **(see p. 71)**, and are basically good guys – but not always because they also eat lots of their own kind and thus undo some of the good.

Spiders

The Wasp Spider (*Argiope bruennichi*) spins a more or less vertical orb web among long grass and other low-growing vegetation and catches a wide range of insects, although not all of these are pests. Many bees and wasps are caught in spiders' webs, but they don't all perish: the spiders often cut them out and set them free – almost as if they know that the insects can hurt them! Although common on the continent, this spider has only recently established itself in the British Isles.

Spiders, although disliked by many people, are definitely among the good guys. We are all familiar with the circular orb webs that adorn our fences and window frames as well as the vegetation. Huge numbers of flies and other annoying insects come to a sticky end in these webs. Harmless insects, including butterflies and grasshoppers, are also caught by these non-selective traps, but on balance the spiders are certainly valuable allies of the gardener. Not all spiders actually spin webs to catch their prey. Our gardens contain numerous wolf spiders and other hunters that chase their prey, which usually consists of small flies and various crawling insects. And then there are the crab spiders – squat creatures that sit on flowers and grab unwary insects with their sturdy front legs. Many of these crab spiders can change colour to blend in with different flowers, and they often blot their copy books by catching bees.

The harvestmen, which got their name because they are particularly noticeable in the autumn, are related to the spiders and often called harvest spiders, although there are some significant differences between the two groups. Harvestmen, for example, have no venom and do not produce silk. They are largely nocturnal creatures and they feed on a range of small invertebrates,

both living and dead. Although they are good in the sense that they destroy quite a number of pests, they have no obvious effect on the garden community and could equally be regarded as non-aligned.

ABOVE LEFT: This crab spider, *Thomisus onustus,* has caught a bluebottle. They paralyses victims by injecting venom behind the head.

ABOVE RIGHT: Harvestmen are distinguished from spiders because the body is not divided into two sections.

Ladybirds and their allies

Where would we gardeners be without the colourful **ladybirds**? Most people are familiar with the adult insects, but fewer people recognise the steely blue larvae and many of these useful little creatures are destroyed in the belief that they are up to mischief! In fact, they are extremely useful. Both adults and larvae are voracious predators, and during its lifetime a ladybird will eat hundreds of aphids. Numerous kinds of ladybirds inhabit our gardens, with the **Seven-spot Ladybird** (*Coccinella septempunctata*) being the commonest species in most places. Delicate **lacewings** and their larvae join forces with the ladybirds to mop up the aphids and other plant pests, including scale insects **(see p. 138)**, and if we leave them to get on with it they will do much of our pest control for us without the need for expensive and

BELOW: Ladybirds often hibernate in large clusters, using the same site each year. These Seven-spot Ladybirds (*Cocinella septempunctata*) have just woken from a winter sleep.

The larva of a Seven-spot Ladybird (*Cocinella septempunctata*) is often mistaken for a pest – but it is an important ally of the gardener.

possibly harmful insecticides. By providing these helpful creatures with winter accommodation we can ensure that there are plenty of them around to make early inroads into the pests in the spring. Suitable accommodation can be bought from many garden centres or made at home from a simple wooden box – a bit like a bird-box but with numerous entrance holes up to a centimetre across. Packed with corrugated cardboard or egg-boxes and placed in a thick hedge or a bush, it will provide comfortable winter quarters for the insects. Despite their colourful appearance, the ladybirds are rarely bothered by birds because they have a bitter or acrid taste – pick one up and you will find a sickly yellow fluid oozing from its joints and staining your hands. Birds soon get the message and leave the insects alone. This is a good example of warning coloration **(see p. 281)**. Many other garden creatures are protected in the same way, including various caterpillars **(see p. 225)** and some adult moths as well.

RIGHT: Green lacewings are voracious predators of aphids.

BOTTOM LEFT: Lacewing larvae use their large, curved jaws to suck fluid from their aphid prey.

BOTTOM RIGHT: The larvae of some green lacewings camouflage themselves by sticking the empty skins of victims onto their backs.

Ground beetles

The **ground beetles,** belonging to the family Carabidae, include many long-legged, fast-running predators, with numerous representatives in our gardens. Largely nocturnal, they are often found resting under logs and stones in the day-time. Many of these beetles are flightless and some have their front wings (elytra) fused together, giving the insects good protection as they tunnel in the soil or scurry through the surface debris. Adults and larvae destroy large numbers of slugs and snails **(see p. 47)** and other pests, such as leather-jackets **(see p. 250),** and they are also attracted to carrion, although some ground beetles are herbivorous.

The Violet Ground Beetle (*Carabus violaceus*), easily recognised by the violet or purple sheen around its wing cases, is one of the largest ground beetles in the garden.

Amphibians, reptiles, birds and mammals

Frogs and **toads** are very happy to take up residence in our gardens, especially if there is a suitable pond in which they can breed, and they repay our hospitality by snapping up large numbers of slugs and snails and other invertebrates. **Slow-worms**, which are actually legless lizards, also enjoy our gardens, particularly those with warm slopes and areas of rough grass. They feed largely on slugs and are well worth encouraging in the garden by leaving the odd plank or sheet of wood under which they can shelter.

The **Hedgehog** is another of the gardener's friends, gobbling up large numbers of slugs and snails as well as leatherjackets, cutworms **(see p. 220)** and other pests. It also eats plenty of earthworms, although it probably has little effect on the population of these abundant and useful crea-tures **(see p. 45).**

Most people like to see birds in the garden and positively encourage their visits by putting out a variety of foods, often on elaborate bird tables. But even without the additional provisions, many birds visit our gardens to find food. Some of these visitors may settle down and breed in the garden, especially if we provide them with nestboxes. Woodpigeons can be a nuisance on the vegetable patch and House Spar-rows seem to delight in wrecking crocuses to get at the nec-tar in the spring, but most of our bird visitors are helpful in

The Slow-worm (*Anguis fragilis*) enjoys patches of rough grass, where it snaps up slugs and other soft-bodied creatures.

The Common Frog (*Rana temporaria*) has smooth skin and a more or less round pupil.

The Common Toad (*Bufo bufo*) has very warty skin and a horizontal pupil.

that they catch and destroy lots of pests. Even the finches and other seed-eating species turn to insects and other invertebrates in the breeding season, when succulent caterpillars form the bulk of the diet of both adults and nestlings. Wrens, tits and Robins all pluck insects from the vegetation with their slender, tweezer-like bills and are pretty good at removing aphid eggs from twigs in the winter. **Song Thrushes** are particularly welcome because of their liking for snails. They have learned how to extract the juicy bodies from the shells, and it is fun to watch their technique as they bash their victims on stones to break them open.

ABOVE LEFT: The Blue Tit (*Cyanistes caerulus*) rids our gardens of huge numbers of caterpillars, aphids and other pests.

ABOVE: The Robin (*Erithacus rubecula*), one of our favourite garden birds, feeds mainly on insects and spiders.

The Hedgehog (*Erinaceus europaeus*) is fun to watch as it scours the garden for slugs and snails and other invertebrates. It also enjoys fallen fruit and beetles, including some of the useful ground beetles.

Rejuvenators and pollinators

But not all the good guys are carnivorous flesh-eaters. There are many **friendly herbivores** in the garden, subsisting on a variety of vegetable foods without harming our cultivated plants or reducing crop yields in any way. In fact, many of them actually increase the productivity of our gardens. Hordes of tiny creatures work unseen in the soil and in our compost heaps to break down dead plant matter and recycle the nutrients. Earthworms also play a major role in recycling nutrients and maintaining soil fertility **(see p. 45)**. And we would certainly go hungry without the numerous bees and other insects that pollinate our crops. Lured by the bright colours and scents, the insects feed mainly on the sugary nectar produced by the flowers, and while feeding they inadvertently pick up pollen grains on various parts of their bodies. And here is the clever bit: evolution has arranged that the pollen is scattered on just the right part of the body for it to be brushed onto the stigmas of the next flower that the insect visits. Bees also collect a lot of pollen as food for their offspring, but the flowers produce far more than is needed for pollination and it is their way of paying the bees for their pollination services. Other important pollinating insects include many butterflies and moths, numerous hoverflies and

This bumblebee is plunging its long tongue into a fading apple flower to obtain the last drop of nectar. At the same time the stamens brush their last few pollen grains on to the bee's tongue and head. Many bees tend to stick to one kind of flower on each journey, thus increasing the efficiency of pollination.

A queen wasp drinks nectar from a currant flower in spring. Although wasps can be a nuisance later in the year, they play a major role in pollinating fruit blossom in the spring. The insects need the nectar from the flowers to provide the energy necessary to establish their colonies.

a wide variety of beetles. Fruit crops, including apples and plums and all our soft fruits, are particularly dependent on bees and flies for pollination, while many of our garden flowers and vegetables would fail to set seed without the aid of various insects.

The baddies

Gardening can be great fun and very rewarding, but we don't have things all our own way: numerous other creatures enjoy our gardens and many of them are only too ready to muscle in and steal our crops or cause other damage. Gardening is thus undoubtedly a competition, and this book aims to describe our main competitors – the pests and how they live and how we can, and perhaps must, live with them, keeping them under control so that we can literally enjoy the fruits of our labours.

Just like the good guys, the baddies include members of many different groups. Some gardeners even have to put up with deer and badgers, although most garden pests are considerably smaller. Mice and voles, for example, can play havoc in the seed bed, while squirrels and birds destroy vast amounts of fruit, but it is the even smaller creatures that do most of the damage, and it is these creepy-crawlies or mini-beasts that occupy much of the rest of this book. These plant-feeding pests include the slugs and snails **(see p. 47)**, hordes of insects and armies of microscopic mites **(see p. 72)**. Between them, they attack every kind of plant, and no part of the plant, from the roots to the fruits and seeds, is safe from their onslaught. Millipedes **(see p. 66)** and woodlice **(see p. 63)** also join the fray, although the damage they do is relatively slight.

Is it a chewer or a sucker?

The majority of herbivorous insects feed on leaves, but not all of them attack the leaves in the same way. They are essentially either chewers or suckers. The chewers include grass-hoppers **(see p. 88)**, many adult and larval beetles **(see p. 153)**, the caterpillars of butterflies and moths **(see p. 184)** and the larvae of most sawflies **(see p. 286)**. They all have biting jaws, with sharp and often toothed edges, that work rather like a pair of salad servers, although instead of merely picking up the food they slice through it. The action can be seen very easily by watching a caterpillar at work on a leaf.

Holding the edge of a leaf in its front legs, a caterpillar uses its cutting jaws to carve up the succulent tissues. Only the tough central veins are left, and some caterpillars even chew these as well.

Although the feeding activities of a few caterpillars may not do much harm in itself, the damaged tissues can be invaded by disease-causing germs and these *can* cause serious damage.

Many larvae scrape away either the upper or lower surface layer of the leaf to reach the nutritious tissues in the middle, and leave the opposite surface intact in the form of translucent windows. These window-feeders include the larvae of various beetles and sawflies as well as the caterpillars of many butter-flies and moths, especially during their earliest stages. Many adult beetles feed in the same way. The windows are often more obvious than the insects themselves and, because each species tends to carve out windows of a particular shape, looking for the windows is the easiest way to find some of these insects.

Leaf-miners

Leaf-miners attack leaves from the inside. Mostly the larvae of tiny flies and moths, they chew their way through the soft tissues between the upper and lower surfaces of the leaves, and their presence is usually indicated by pale streaks or blotches on the leaf surface. Blotch mines result when larvae make extensive excavations in one part of a leaf, while ser-pentine or gallery mines are produced by larvae that travel from one part of a leaf to another. Gallery mines are very narrow and often close to the leaf margin at first, but they become wider as the larvae get bigger. It is usually possible for a specialist to identify a miner just from the host plant and the shape of the mine. Some leaf-miners pupate in their

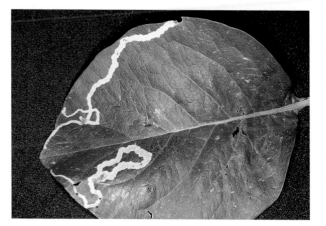

These serpentine mines on a honeysuckle leaf are possibly those of the larva of the fly *Chromatomyia lonicerae*. Each mine starts as a very slender tunnel at the edge of the leaf and can then go almost anywhere, although it rarely crosses the tough mid-rib. The mines get wider as the grub gets bigger, and often end in a little 'trap-door' through which the insect escapes. Many mines peter out after a short distance because the grub dies for some reason.

mines, but others leave to pupate elsewhere on the plants or in the soil beneath. Leaf-miners rarely cause serious damage to their host plants, although the Horse Chestnut Leaf-miner **(see p. 238)** has been causing major damage to Horse Chestnut trees in many parts of Europe in recent years.

Aphids and other suckers

The suckers are represented mainly by the bugs of the order Hemiptera **(see p. 95)**. These include the shield bugs or stink bugs, the cicadas and froghoppers, and the teeming hordes of aphids – better known to the gardener as 'greenfly' and 'blackfly'. All have sharp piercing beaks that puncture the plants and draw out the sap. Sap-sucking bugs feed mainly on leaves and tender shoots, but some aphids feed on roots **(see p. 113)** and some also feed on petals, which are essentially modified leaves. The simple removal of sap does little harm to the plants, unless the insects are present in large numbers, as often happens with aphids **(see p. 114)**, and the most serious damage is done by the disease-causing microorganisms carried by the insects and pumped into the plants with their saliva. Aphids and various other bugs carry the viruses responsible for sugar beet yellows, potato leaf roll and many other serious diseases of farm and garden plants.

Thickly clustered on a young shoot of guelder rose, these are Black Bean Aphids (*Aphis fabae*), which attack a wide range of woody and herbaceous plants. There are many similar species of black aphids or blackfly, but most of them are restricted to particular host plants. Dense populations like this can easily weaken and distort the plants.

Attacking stems, roots and fruit

Herbaceous stems are attacked by slugs and snails and chewed by numerous beetles and caterpillars. Woody stems also have their enemies, mostly the larvae of moths and beetles that tunnel unseen through the tough tissues, often for several years. Wood is difficult to digest and it is not very nutritious: it contains plenty of carbohydrate material, but relatively little protein, so most wood-feeding insects grow quite slowly and take several years to mature. Records suggest that some buprestid or jewel beetles may survive as larvae for over 25 years, although this is probably exceptional. The Currant Clearwing Moth, one of the commoner wood-borers in the garden **(see p. 197)**, is an exception in completing its life cycle in a single year.

Roots are targeted by a wide range of insects, especially the young stages. Familiar examples are the leatherjackets **(see p. 250)**, the wireworms **(see p. 160)** and the grubs of the Carrot-fly **(see p. 256)**. Slugs and millipedes also enjoy our root crops.

Juicy fruits evolved primarily to attract birds and other animals that eat the flesh and scatter the seeds, often in new areas far from their original homes, but many insects also find ripe fruit attractive and, unlike the pollen-feeders, they

Fruit attracts many insects, including the Hornet (*Vespa crabro*), pictured here on a bunch of grapes, and other wasps. Unfortunately, the wasps often attack the fruit before it has ripened to our own satisfaction, and a whole crop can be lost in that way.

TOP TIP

Harvest greengages and other plums before they are fully ripe and let them complete the ripening process indoors. In this way you will get to eat at least some of your fruit.

BELOW: Robin's pincushion galls, or bedeguar galls, are the work of the gall wasp *Diplolepis rosae*. The fluffy 'hairs' conceal a woody core containing numerous gall wasp grubs, each in its own little chamber.

BOTTOM: A spruce twig bears two 'pineapple galls', the work of the aphid *Adelges abietis*.

give nothing in return. Social wasps are notorious fruit-eaters at the end of the summer, when they have finished rearing their young **(see p. 273)**. A single wasp can demolish a whole greengage in a morning, and even if it does not eat the lot it spoils the look and taste of the fruit. And wasps can, of course, make harvesting the fruit an unpleasant task.

Other insects work undercover, nibbling their way through the fruit unseen until they are ready to leave. Common garden pests in this category include the larvae of Raspberry Beetles **(see p. 163)**, Codling Moths **(see p. 230)**, and the Mediterranean Fruit-fly **(see p. 267)**. Seed pests are less important in the garden than in agriculture, where grain weevils and related insects can cause enormous losses to grain crops, both in the field and in store, although Pea Moths **(see p. 231)** and Pea Beetles **(see p. 173)** sometimes cause problems.

The creation of galls

Feeding insects, especially the sucking varieties, commonly distort the leaves and other parts of their host plants but some have an even greater effect on the plants – they cause the plant tissues to swell and form the elaborate growths known as **galls**. Gall formation begins either when an insect lays its eggs in the plant or, more often, when the young insects start to feed. Saliva from the feeding insects causes the plant tissues to proliferate and produce the galls, with each insect species inducing the formation of its own particular kind of gall. Some of these galls are little more than folded leaves or swollen buds, but others are quite bizarre structures showing little resemblance to any of the normal plant tissues. The nutritious gall tissues provide the insects with all of their food and they may completely enclose the insects. Aphids induce galls on a wide range of woody and herbaceous plants, and some of their galls, notably the red candle-like galls on the terebinth trees of southern Europe, are truly spectacular. You will not find many aphid-induced galls in a normal garden, but if you have the traditional Norway spruce as a Christmas tree and plant it in the garden afterwards you might well find that it develops 'pineapple galls'.

These are the work of aphids belonging to the genus *Adelges*, and they form when the bases of adjacent needles swell and cluster tightly together around the aphids. The galls open to release the aphids in the summer.

Gall wasps are responsible for many galls on our oaks, and also for the 'robin's pincushion', which is common on hedgerow roses. Sawflies induce various galls on willows (see p. 299), while tiny gall midges affect a wide variety of wild and garden plants, including violets (see p. 251) and day-lilies (see p. 253), and can cause severe damage. Some gall-causing insects pupate in their galls, while others leave when fully grown and pupate elsewhere. Mites are also responsible for many plant galls (see p. 72).

ABOVE: New adult gall wasps leave the pincushion galls in the spring and lay their eggs in the opening buds, as pictured here. Males are extremely rare in this species and females can lay fertile eggs without mating.

The ugly ones

Ugliness, like beauty, is in the eye of the beholder and, although some of our garden minibeasts certainly lack a certain amount of glamour and many people probably do consider them to be ugly, scary is perhaps a better description. Despite their small size, they do scare a lot of people. As far as the garden is concerned, some are good and some are bad, but the majority are harmless and completely neutral: they get on with their lives without any noticeable effect on our crops.

The **Devil's Coach-horse** (*Ocypus olens*) is one of the scariest of our garden beetles, especially when it is alarmed and displays its huge jaws. At the same time, it raises its rear end in a threatening manner − an attitude that gives the beetle its alternative name of 'cock-tail'. This scorpion-like pose, backed up by a repellent odour discharged from glands in the abdomen, is quite enough to deter most would-be predators, and any that try to press home an attack are likely to receive a painful bite from the jaws. Handle the beetle and you might also feel the power of its jaws, but it is otherwise quite harmless to people. It lives mainly under logs

and stones and emerges at night to feed on worms, leatherjackets and various other soft-bodied invertebrates. So it is really quite a useful beast to have in the garden.

The male **Stag Beetle** (*Lucanus cervus*) is another scary creature on account of its noisy flight and enormous, antler-like jaws. But it is harmless: its jaws have outgrown the muscles that operate them and, despite their threatening appearance, they are quite incapable of biting. They are used only to wrestle with other males in disputes over the females. The small-jawed female is much more likely to bite, although only if handled. Stag Beetles grow up in rotting wood and are most likely to be seen in rural and suburban gardens containing old fence posts. Although quite common on the Continent, they are now rare in the British Isles and confined to the southern counties of England and Wales.

The female **Horntail** or **Wood Wasp** (*Urocerus gigas*) is really scary, partly because of its wasp-like colours but mainly because of the fearsome spike protruding from its rear end. It is completely harmless, however, and the spike is

ABOVE: The Devil's Coach-horse (*Ocypus olens*) in threatening pose, with tail raised and powerful jaws wide open. It belongs to the large family of rove beetles, all of which have short front wings (elytra). This is why the beetle is able to raise its rear end.

BELOW: The male Stag Beetle (*Lucanus cervus*) is up to 6 cm long, including its immense antler-like jaws. It looks scary as it flies around at head height at dusk, but is harmless.

merely its egg-laying equipment or ovipositor. It is one of the sawflies **(see p. 286)** and grows up in the trunks and branches of pine trees. Whereas most sawflies have tiny saw-like ovipositors with which they slice open their host plants, the horntail uses its ovipositor like a drill to lay its eggs deep in the timber. It is not really a garden insect, but its grubs take several years to grow up and they often survive the sawmill to continue their development in building timbers – only to emerge in new houses and conservatories a year or two later. The male Greater Horntail has no drill and is a smaller and darker insect.

The aptly named **Dark-edged Bee-fly** (*Bombylius major*) causes consternation in the garden in spring because its long, rigid beak is often thought to be some kind of sting. It is, of course, nothing more sinister than a 'drinking straw' used for sucking nectar from deep-throated flowers. Lungwort is one of its favourites. When not feeding, the flies often bask on the ground. The females scatter their eggs over the soil as they glide to and fro just above the surface, and the resulting grubs make their way into the nests of various solitary bees where they live as parasites on the bee grubs.

The female Greater Horntail or Giant Wood Wasp (*Vrocerus gigas*) is up to 4 cm long, including its sturdy ovipositor.

The Dark-edged Bee-fly's (*Bombylius major*) furry coat gives it a remarkable similarity to a bumblebee, but the insect has a much faster, darting flight than the bumblebees. It also hovers and emits a high-pitched whine. This species has a body about a centimetre long. Its rigid tongue is nearly the same length. There are several other similar species of bee-fly.

The spider **Dysdera crocota** is certainly one of the uglier of our garden inhabitants, and one of the very few spiders in our gardens that can dish out a painful bite, although you will have to provoke it – by picking it up or sitting on it! It normally reserves its venom for woodlice, which it catches with its enormous jaws. Keep an eye out for it in and around sheds and log-piles, and anywhere else with a good population of woodlice.

Scorpion-flies (*Panorpa* species) get their name for the swollen, up-turned tip of the male abdomen and, although

Dysdera crocota, commonly known as the Woodlouse Spider, is easily recognised by its coloration and its enormous jaws. It is about 1.5 cm long.

the insects are not unattractive, they can certainly cause alarm, especially when they land on a sweaty arm for a drink! But they are completely harmless. They are scavenging creatures, feeding on a variety of dead plant and animal material, including rotting fruit, which they nibble with jaws at the tip of a long, stout 'beak'. They even steal prey from spiders' webs, often removing it after dissolving the silk with their own saliva. The arachnids rarely attack them because the saliva also repels most spiders.

This male scorpion-fly clearly shows the characteristic beak, with jaws at the tip, and also the up-turned abdomen that gives the insects their name. These harmless insects are up to 2 cm long.

The origins of our garden pests

It is quite natural for gardeners and others to wonder where all our garden pests came from: were they around before we started gardening, and if so, what did they do? Many of them are, of course, 'home-grown' pests – native creatures that originally fed harmlessly on wild plants and became a nuisance only when we started to cultivate suitable food plants. Good examples include the 'cabbage white' butter-flies **(see p. 184)** and various aphids. Lots of tasty food plants growing close together in our fields and gardens suited the insects down to the ground: they did not have to spend time and energy searching for food, so they could spend more time actually feeding and breeding. Populations build up quickly in such conditions and pests are 'born'. This does not happen in the wild because it is rare for large numbers of plants of the same kind to grow close together. The plant-feeding creatures have to spend more time searching for the right food-plants and may also have to face 'hostile' vegetation – plants that harbour predators or that actually repel some of the vegetarian species. It is worth remembering this when planning your garden: several studies have shown that gardens in which crops are intermingled are more productive than those with large stands of a single crop, so try a bit of companion planting **(see p. 32)** to keep the pests down.

Aliens and stowaways

Many other garden pests are aliens. These were usually brought from other parts of the world as stowaways in consignments of fruit and vegetables or on plants imported for the horticultural trade and, free from their natural enemies, they were able to multiply rapidly and establish themselves in their new homes. The Woolly Aphid of apples **(see p. 124)** and the Fuchsia Gall Mite **(see p. 81)** are both American species now well established in Europe, but perhaps the most damaging import for European crops was the Grape Phylloxera, although this aphid now causes little trouble **(see p. 134)**. Alien pests are becoming increasingly common as a result of air travel and the greater mobility of people, and also through the great increase in horticultural trade. Global warming is another important factor in the spread of garden pests, allowing many southern European species to establish themselves in the British Isles and other parts of northern Europe. The Green Vegetable Bug **(see p. 98)** is a good example of a pest that has recently been able to get a foothold in Britain after accidental introduction, while the Rose Jewel Beetle **(see p. 158)** has been making its own way up through Europe, and if, as seems likely, climate change continues the beetle may well appear in the British Isles before long.

On the basis that prevention is better than cure, the best way to deal with alien pests is to keep them out with the help of strict plant health and quarantine laws. Such regulations work well with commercial imports and have kept the

United Kingdom essentially free from the Colorado Beetle, although they cannot prevent the natural movement of pests from one country to another.

Colorado Beetles (*Leptinotarsa decemlineata*) are native to North America, but are now serious pests of potatoes in many parts of the world (see p. 168).

CONTROLLING THE PESTS

Total eradication of garden pests is an impossible dream, and not really desirable in terms of the balance of nature. Every creature, in our gardens as well as in the wild, has a role to play in the food web, and removal of any one species alters the balance and has a knock-on effect on the other creatures. Complete removal of all the slugs and snails, for example, may force the local hedgehogs to eat more earthworms, which could lead to water-logged lawns and a loss of soil fertility **(see p. 45)**. Similarly, loss of all the caterpillars and aphids would drive away most of our garden birds. The aim is to control the pests and limit their numbers to levels at which they do not cause any serious damage. This can be achieved in several different ways, employed singly or in harness in what is known as integrated pest control.

As mentioned above, the way in which we plan our gardens and go about our day-to-day gardening activities can have a marked effect on pest populations. This is sometimes called **cultural control** and crop-rotation is one of its most important aspects. By not growing susceptible crops year after year on the same patch of ground we can prevent the build-up of harmful creatures. Carrot-flies, for example, spend the winter as larvae or pupae in the soil, and if the adults find no suitable food-plants on hand when they emerge in the spring many will die without laying their eggs, although some will, of course, find carrots growing elsewhere. Another advantage of crop-rotation is that different crops make different demands on the soil, so by moving your crops around the garden you will give the soil a chance to recover. This in itself will help you to produce vigorous and healthy crops, and healthy crops are better able to resist pests. Regular watering in dry weather, together with good supplies of manure or fertiliser, will also help to keep the crops stress-free and better able to cope with the pests.

Companion planting

Companion planting is another popular cultural method of outwitting pests without waging direct warfare. The idea is based on the assumption that some plants repel certain insects and other pests, and if these plants are grown close to the susceptible crops the damage will be reduced. Not all garden experts are convinced that it works, but it does seem to work for some garden crops. Maybe it is more a matter of confusing the pests than actively repelling them, causing them problems when trying to find the food-plants on which to lay their eggs. Companion planting was mentioned by Pliny nearly 2,000 years ago when he wrote that planting hyssop among grape vines encouraged the latter to perform well. Hyssop certainly seems to discourage certain aphids and is worth planting among susceptible crops. Garlic is another useful companion, well worth planting in the rose bed to keep the aphid population down. Chives are equally good in this respect and more colourful. Sage, dill, lavender, thyme and mint all have similar effects on aphids, while sage and lavender also repel many of the midges that annoy us in the garden **(see p. 247)**. Dried lavender hung in the house deters flies there as well, and the use of dried lavender

TOP TIP

Plants of the onion family nearly all give out a strong odour that is believed to deter a variety of insect pests. Growing such plants, especially chives, as companion plants among your roses can protect them from aphids. Onions are also said to keep the Carrot-fly away from carrots.

flowers to keep clothes moths away from the wardrobe is a very ancient practice.

Planting hemp among your cabbages will keep the caterpillars at bay according to Cuthbert Johnson's *Farmer's Encyclopedia and Dictionary*, published in 1844, while marjoram is also said to repel 'cabbage white' butterflies, although it is strongly attractive to several other butterflies, such as the Gatekeeper. African and French marigolds (*Tagetes* species) are said to afford cabbages some protection from whitefly attack, and they are great companions for many other flowers and vegetables on account of the chemicals exuded from their roots. These chemicals include a compound called thiopene which repels nematode worms and some subterranean slugs, thus making the marigolds good companions for various root crops. The secretions also inhibit root growth in several stubborn weeds, including ground elder and bindweed.

Companion plants can also be used as decoys to draw pests away from various crops, and here again the African and French marigolds can help. Although they repel a number of pests, they are very attractive to snails, and we can turn this to our advantage by planting them around or among the crops. The marauding molluscs are easily gathered from the marigolds at night or after rain and can then be destroyed – but don't expect the marigolds to last very long! This kind of 'ring-fencing' can also be used to reduce aphid attack on

Lavender is a good companion for many other plants. Although the flowers attract bees and butterflies and many other insects, the strong scent repels aphids and various flies and it is well worth planting a few clumps of lavender among roses and under vines as a natural deterrent.

African and French marigolds (*Tagetes*) are excellent companion plants in the garden. These are African marigolds. Try planting some at the ends of rows of brassicas to reduce the whitefly population. Their roots also secrete various chemicals that have a deterrent effect on subterranean pests and also inhibit the root growth of bindweed and some other weeds.

various crops. Feverfew, for example, planted around the edge of a broad bean patch will trap invading 'blackfly', and when the aphids are well ensconced on the feverfew it can be uprooted and destroyed, leaving a relatively unharmed bean crop. Nasturtiums work equally well around the beans. A variation on this decoy theme can also be used to protect your brassicas from the 'cabbage white' butterflies **(see p. 184)**. The butterflies find their food-plants by scent and can be tricked into laying their eggs on the wrong plants by making the surrounding plants smell like cabbages! This can be done very easily by liquidising half a dozen cabbage leaves and then diluting the liquid with up to ten times its volume of water before spraying it onto the vegetation around your brassicas. At least some of the butterflies will be fooled into laying their eggs there, but the resulting caterpillars will find no suitable food and will die. But don't make the spray too strong: when caterpillars nibble the brassicas the leaves give out their characteristic odour, and if this is too strong the butterflies will move away in the belief that the plants are already overloaded with caterpillars. The treatment needs to be repeated every week or so during the butterfly season, especially after rain.

Attracting the good guys

Beneficial creatures can also be attracted by planting various flowers among your vegetables. The flowers will attract hoverflies, which might then lay their eggs on any neighbouring aphid-infested crops. The resulting larvae will then mop up many of the aphids. It is for this reason that many European vineyards have roses at the ends of the vine rows.

It has been known for some time that the sound of a wasp buzzing in the vicinity causes many caterpillars to drop to the ground, thereby escaping their predators. Recent research in Germany has shown that caterpillars react to bees in the same way. So here is another reason for planting flowers among your vegetables, especially among the cabbages. It will not eradicate the caterpillars, but if they spend a lot of time on the ground they will not be defoliating your crops.

Plant breeders are continually coming up with new varieties, aiming for bigger and more colourful flowers or bigger and tastier vegetables. Resistance to pests or diseases is another major aim and many of our vegetables do now have varieties resistant to some of the major pests. Planting these varieties can clearly help with pest control and lead to better harvests. Several potato varieties, for example, are resistant to slug attack **(see p. 50)** and, although they may not crop as heavily as some others, you can expect to lift clean, undamaged tubers. Similarly, you can grow carrot varieties that are resistant to the Carrot-fly **(see p. 256)** and blackcurrant bushes that resist the big-bud mite *Cecidophyopsis ribis* **(see p. 73)**. Consult the catalogues to see what other pest-resistant plants are available.

Keeping a clean garden

Good **garden hygiene** can play a significant role in pest control. Regular hoeing, for example, disturbs pests in the soil and may well expose them to birds and other predators.

> ### TOP TIP
>
> *You can draw cabbage white butterflies away from brassicas by liquidising a few cabbage leaves and spraying a dilute solution of the liquid onto other plants. The butterflies may be fooled into laying their eggs on these treated plants, but the resulting caterpillars will starve in the absence of their correct food-plants.*

Poppies are full of pollen that attracts numerous hover-flies. Well-fed, the flies turn their attention to egg-laying and seek out nearby greenfly colonies on which the fly larvae can feed. So it is well worth allowing a few poppies to grow among your vegetables and other plants.

Removal of old cabbage stumps and other debris after harvest is essential to prevent the build-up of cabbage aphids and other pests. Weeds can harbour a wide range of pests and diseases and should be kept away from the vegetables, but it is possible to be too tidy! A few old leaves left around a row of lettuces will be more attractive to the slugs than the growing crop, and you can then gather them up and dispose of them. Clumps of grass and other wild plants left at the base of a hedge or a wall may shelter useful predators as well as a few unwanted guests, and can also add a bit of colour to the garden. Take care when buying plants that you do not bring pests home with you as well: you might not be able to look at the roots before you buy, but you can give the aerial parts a good going over for aphids and caterpillars.

Physical barriers and **traps** can be used to protect many crops. Horticultural fleece, which is a very light material, is excellent for covering low-growing plants, such as carrots, and can be used over seedlings of all kinds. It keeps the flying insects away, although it does not offer any protection from soil-living pests. Baited pitfall traps can be used to catch slugs **(see p. 48)**, while sticky traps, similar to the old fashioned fly-papers, are particularly useful for catching insects flying in the confined space of the greenhouse. They might not intercept more than a small proportion of the pests flying around, but they can give timely warning of any

Regular hoeing keeps the weeds down and also reveals leatherjackets and other soil-dwelling pests, which are quickly snapped up by the birds.

build-up of whitefly or other inconspic-uous pests, allowing you to step in with some other action if necessary. Sticky traps are easily made from pieces of card coated with a slow-drying glue, or even honey. You can use card of any pale col-our, but yellow is the best colour because most insects seem to be attracted to yellow.

Pheromone traps or lures are now be-coming more widely available for con-trolling insect pests, especially moths. These are usually based on manufactured versions of the mating scents given out by the females, and they can attract large numbers of males. The latter usually emerge and scatter a short while before the females appear, so they are usually caught before they mate – leaving most of the females unable to find mates and lay fertile eggs. Because each species has its own scent, you need to buy a separate lure for each pest.

Biological control

Biological control is the control of a pest with another liv-ing organism – usually one of its natural enemies. In this respect, squashing with your fingers is a form of biological control! This is very easy and one of the best methods for dealing with aphids and other soft-bodied pests, but it is not much good against hidden pests or tiny ones that are scat-tered here and there. And not everyone wants to do it any-way. Luckily, there are other helpful creatures in the garden ready and willing to do the job for us. Ladybirds and lacew-ings, for example, mop up loads of aphids and scale insects **(see p. 138)**. Some of these predators can be obtained from commercial outlets for release in our gardens and green-houses, and many more parasites and predators are now coming onto the market. Red spider mites **(see p. 82)** can be controlled by *Phytoseiulus* mites – bright red predatory mites that work well indoors and out although they need a temperature of about 20°C for at least part of the time.

Ladybirds are among the gardener's most valuable allies. Adults and larvae (pictured here) all eagerly seek out greenfly and other aphids. One ladybird will eat hundreds of aphids during its lifetime. Most ladybirds live for about a year, although they spend the winter months in a dormant state, tucked up in a secluded spot.

Whiteflies **(see p. 135)** can be controlled in greenhouses by a tiny parasitic wasp called *Encarsia* that lays its eggs in the young whiteflies. The wasp grubs then destroy the pests from the inside. Microscopic nematode worms have recently become available to fight a variety of garden pests, including slugs, leatherjackets, chafer grubs, 'cabbage white' caterpillars, cutworms **(see p. 220)** and the dreaded Vine Weevil. One of these nematode species can also be used to get rid of ants when these are causing problems on rockeries and in raised beds **(see p. 284)**. The worms are supplied in a dry form, usually with several million in a pack, and are then watered into the ground or onto the vegetation, where they become active and seek out their hosts. Once inside the hosts, the worms release toxic bacteria and death of the hosts follows within a few days. The worms continue to live and breed in the dead bodies for a while and then leave to carry the deadly bacteria to fresh victims.

For many years a bacterium called *Bacillus thuringiensis* did sterling work in controlling various caterpillar pests. Because it killed a wide range of caterpillars and was harmless to almost all other animals, it was widely used in forestry and agriculture as well as in the garden and in food stores. Unfortunately, it is no longer available for garden use in the United Kingdom, although it is still approved for use by commercial growers.

Biological control has several important advantages over chemical control. The predators or parasites employed attack only a narrow range of pests and do no harm to other creatures in the garden, including other useful predators. The fact that biological agents leave no toxic residues on the plants or in the soil is especially important for other wildlife and also for us humans. Biological agents can also reach targets that might be beyond the reach of chemical sprays – in folded leaves, for example, or high in the trees. In addition, the pests are unlikely to develop any appreciable resistance to the control agents, although some insects have developed a certain amount of immunity to *Bacillus thuringiensis*.

Chemical control

A quick look at the shelves in any garden centre will show that **chemical control** of pests is big business. You can find pesticides to get rid of wasps, ants, aphids, caterpillars, slugs

Garden centre shelves are laden with pesticides. Some are wide-spectrum products, often labelled bug-killers, for use against a wide range of pests, while others are formulated to deal with particular pests, such as wasps and ants. All such pesticides have been thoroughly tested for toxicity, to ensure that they are safe when properly used, but gardeners must always follow the instructions.

and snails, and just about any other pest that you might find in your garden, including the weeds. Control of insects with chemicals really took off towards the middle of the 20th century, when the insecticidal power of DDT was discovered. First used against malaria-carrying mosquitoes, it certainly saved thousands of lives during the Second World War, and because it was thought to be relatively safe for humans, it was used to combat a wide range of medically important insects, including lice and fleas. Agricultural and horticultural use soon followed, and DDT was hailed as a miracle material. Populations of insect pests dwindled rapidly at first, but the euphoria did not last. The insects began to develop resistance to the insecticide, so it had to be used in larger quantities and before long it became obvious that all was not well in the natural world. Birds were dying in their thousands, along with many other animals, and investigations revealed that their bodies contained large amounts of DDT – much of it derived ultimately from the insects that they or their prey had eaten. The insecticide was also found in the soil and in rivers and seas, often far from where it had been applied. It was even turning up in human milk, having got there via the food that people were eating. DDT was obviously being passed along the food chains and was proving to be almost indestructible, with residues showing up almost everywhere. In 1962, Sir Julian Huxley wrote in the foreword to Rachel Carson's classic book *Silent Spring*: '…though chemical control can be very useful, it too needs to be controlled and should be permitted only when other methods are not available'. It is now very obvious that chemical pesticides, although they may be successful for a short while, can cause more problems than they cure.

Chemical pesticides under attack

DDT is now banned in many countries and, although it is still used for mosquito control in some areas where malaria is rife, the United Nations recently announced a plan to outlaw use of the pesticide completely by 2020.

Scores of different pesticides have appeared over the last 50 years or so, including many DDT-like compounds, collectively known as chlorinated hydrocarbons. Most of these have now been withdrawn because of their detrimental environmental effects. Organo-phosphorous insecticides joined the war against insect pests in the 1940s, often proving more effective than DDT and its relatives and having the advantage that they broke down fairly quickly in the environment. But the organo-phosphorous compounds turned out to be much more dangerous to people and most of them have now been banned. Several other groups of insecticidal chemicals have come and gone over the years, having been found to be dangerous in one way or another, but one group of insecticidal compounds has stood the test of time and these are the pyrethrins and their derivatives.

Pyrethrum-based insecticides

It has been known for a long time that pyrethrum flowers contain powerful insecticidal compounds, and 'insect powder' derived from the flowers was in widespread use by the middle of the 19th century – and probably a good deal earlier. The active ingredients, known as pyrethrins, act on the insects' nervous systems, disabling and killing them very quickly. Although lethal to many insects, the pyrethrins have a very low toxicity to humans and most other vertebrates and have often been stated to be harmless! This is what has made them so valuable, but the natural pyrethrins do have one drawback – they are rapidly destroyed by sunlight so, although they work well when applied directly to the insects, they are less effective when sprayed on to foliage. This problem began to be addressed in the middle of the 20th century, when chemists started to make artificial pyrethrins. These new compounds have the same basic structure as the natural ones but with slight modifications: they have the same insecticidal activity and most of them have the same low toxicity to humans, but they are more stable and do not break down quite so quickly. They can thus be applied to plants to kill pests coming along later, although they do break down after a while – usually within a few days.

These artificial pyrethrins are known as pyrethroids, and most of the insecticides that you find on the garden centre shelves today, although sold under numerous different trade names, contain one or more of these materials, with names ending mainly in '…ethrin' or '…enthrin'. Natural pyrethrins are still used, however, especially in sprays to give a quick 'knock-down' of flying insects. They are also acceptable to organic gardeners, who wish to use only natural materials for pest control.

Pyrethrum flowers belong to the daisy family and are quite closely related to chrysanthemums. Native to south-east Europe, they have long been used as a source of insecticide and are now cultivated on a large scale, especially in East Africa.

Nicotine, obtained from tobacco plants, was used as an insecticide for many years, but it is a dangerous material and has now been replaced by a number of much safer synthetic insecticides with a similar composition. They target the insects' nervous systems and produce a quick kill when ingested or simply when the insects come into contact with them. Thiacloprid, imidacloprid and acetamiprid are the best known of these and can be used against a wide range of garden pests, both above and below ground. Imidacloprid is also widely used to control fleas on cats and dogs, to kill cockroaches in the house and to control termites, although it has been banned in France because it is believed to be responsible for the decline in bee populations. It has also been banned for some agricultural uses in Germany.

Insecticidal vegetable oil

Many other plants contain their own insecticides – compounds that render them poisonous or unpalatable to various insects – and several of these compounds are now marketed as insecticidal vegetable oils. Neem oil, derived from the seeds of the Indian Neem tree, works well against many insects and also kills spider mites without harming other animals. It interferes with the pests' hormonal systems and, among other effects, it prevents the nymphs and larvae from moulting and growing up. It is therefore most useful against immature insects. Neem oil is extremely safe as far as people are concerned and is used in a variety of pharmaceutical products, including toothpaste! Several plant oils are now being incorporated into winter washes, which are sprayed or painted onto shrubs and tree trunks to kill the resting stages of Codling Moths and other insects in the winter months. These washes are the modern equivalents of the tar washes that were used in bygone days but are no longer available.

Horticultural oil is a highly refined petroleum product that can be used to kill a range of soft-bodied insect pests. It works mainly by blocking the insects' breathing pores, so has to be sprayed directly onto the insects. It is most useful against insects living on mature stems, as younger plant tissues can be damaged by the oil.

Insecticidal soaps are the modern equivalents of the soapy water that gardeners once used to get rid of aphids and various other soft-bodied insect pests. They consist of various plant and animal oils combined with sodium or potassium compounds and they work by damaging the outer coverings of the insects and causing them to lose vital water. These insecticides are harmless to most other creatures, but they must be applied directly to the pests as they do not work once they have dried on the plants.

Choosing the right formulation

Most modern insecticides are available in several different formulations, which act in different ways to kill the insects, although they may contain the same active ingredients. Contact insecticides kill the insects on contact, being absorbed through the skin and usually attacking the nervous system. Most of them break down and lose their activity quite quickly and have to be applied directly to the insects, so they are ideal for treating clusters of aphids or caterpillars. Residual insecticides have a somewhat longer active life and when sprayed onto foliage they form a coating that remains active and can kill caterpillars and other chewing insects that come along and eat the leaves later. If they are not washed away by rain, some residual formulations can remain active for several weeks, although many break down more quickly. Systemic insecticides reach the pests in a different way. They are absorbed by the leaves or roots and carried to all parts of the plants in the sap, so they cannot be washed away by rain. They can kill any insect that feeds on the treated plants, although they are most useful in combating aphids

TOP TIP

Always choose the right formulation when selecting an insecticide. Contact insecticides, in the form of dusts and sprays, can be used to kill exposed clusters of aphids or caterpillars, but systemic insecticides, which are absorbed by the plant, are more useful against pests that are concealed in buds or crumpled leaves.

and other sap-sucking creatures and are especially valuable for getting at those insects that hide among crumpled leaves where they are not touched by dusts and sprays. Systemic insecticides are also useful against root-feeding pests, but tend not to be recommended for use on food crops because the active ingredients stay in the plants for some time.

You can buy insecticides in the form of liquids, aerosols, dusts, smokes and pellets. Each preparation has its uses but the most convenient for the gardener are certainly the ready-to-use sprays in trigger-operated containers. Aerosols are useful for treating individual plants, especially indoors or in the greenhouse, although they are generally too expensive for large-scale use in the garden. Dusts, which are mostly contact insecticides, leave deposits that many gardeners consider unsightly and they cannot be used effectively in windy conditions. Insecticidal smokes are a bit like fireworks, but without the bangs: the insecticides are released when the canisters are ignited, and they can be used to get rid of all the pests in greenhouses and conservatories. Pellets are used primarily against soil-dwelling pests and are often added to potting composts. The active ingredients are released slowly and they work for a long time. Pellets containing systemic insecticides can be used to protect pot-plants from all kinds of insect pests. Many slug and snail killers – molluscicides – also come in the form of pellets.

Although today's insecticides are relatively safe to us and our pets when used in the correct way, they are not without problems. There will always be some residual material on crops, and this is why we are advised to leave a certain period of time between treatment and harvesting. Useful and harmless species succumb to the insecticides as well as the pests. Pyrethrins and the synthetic pyrethroids, for example, are particularly lethal to bees, so the gardener needs to be very careful when using them around the flower garden and the orchard, spraying in the evening, when the bees have gone to bed. And then there is the problem of resistance, with insects gradually becoming tolerant of the poisons. This has been a major problem ever since we started to use insecticides, and hundreds of insect species are now resistant to insecticides that once kept them nicely under control.

The development of resistance has been a natural evolution based on the survival of the fittest. In every generation, insects exhibit slight variations in their ability to deal with poisons just as they vary in other respects, such as size and colour. Some individuals can therefore break down poisonous insecticides better than others. These chemically better-endowed specimens are the ones that survive and breed. With variability present in each generation, the ability to deal with the poisons gradually spreads through the population until it is entirely resistant, and this can happen within just a few decades with those pests that have several generations each year. To start with we tried to overcome the problem simply by using larger and larger quantities of insecticides, but this caused a variety of environmental and health problems, not least among the workers engaged in applying the poison, and the search was on for newer and safer chemicals – a search that continues today. One exciting line of research involves looking at the genetic make-up – the genome – of various pests, as this could lead to the development of pesticides active only against specific pests.

Chemicals – a last resort

Chemical control of your garden pests should really be considered a last resort, if cultural and biological methods fail. Take stock of the situation: will insecticidal treatment really increase yields or improve appearance sufficiently to make it worthwhile? If you must use chemicals, it is essential to follow the instructions carefully. These include instructions for use and for disposal. All of the pesticides that you can find in the supermarkets and garden centres have been certified as being safe for use in the home and in the garden, but they remain poisons, and the containers should carry clear instructions on how to use them. Many other products have been approved for use by farmers and other commercial organisations and must be used only by those who have had the appropriate training. Professional products tend to be stronger and should never be used by the amateur gardener.

We can now have a look at some of the commoner garden pests and find out how to deal with them.

PART TWO

KNOW YOUR PESTS

WORMS

The earthworms that appear almost every time we bring up a forkful of soil do nothing but good in our gardens, although the lawn fanatic and green-keeper may disagree when they see a fresh crop of worm casts on the grass. By tunnelling through the soil, the worms help with aeration and drainage. They also help to fertilise the soil by their ploughing action, bringing nutrient-rich soil (worm casts) from the depths to the surface layers where it can nourish the plant roots. Gilbert White was not wrong in 1777 when he wrote:'…men would find that the earth without worms would soon become cold, hardbound and void of fermentation; and consequently sterile'. Writing about earthworms 100 years later, Charles Darwin doubted whether any other animals have played such an important part in the history of the world! But there are worms in our gardens that we could well do without.

The earthworm is one of the gardener's greatest friends and the number of earthworms in the soil is an indication of its quality and fertility.

New Zealand Flatworm

Looks: Purple-brown and very flat

Food: Attacks beneficial earthworms

When: All year

Where: Much of Britain, especially cooler areas

TOP TIP

New Zealand Flatworms like undisturbed sites and are most likely to be found lurking under stones and large pots. If you do find one, there will be others in the area. To trap them, lay a plank of wood, a length of old carpet or black plastic sheeting on the soil. Lift it regularly and squash any worms you find. Their mucus has an irritant quality, so do not to pick them up with bare hands. Keep an eye open for the worms' egg sacs in the summer and squash them as well. They are smooth and shiny and look like squashed blackcurrants.

NEW ZEALAND FLATWORM
Arthurdendyus triangulatus

This slimy creature, is purple-brown on top, pointed at both ends, and very flat, and it shows no sign of the rings that are such a conspicuous feature of the earthworm's body. It is about 1 cm wide and when fully extended it can be up to 30 cm long, although it is usually much shorter than this. At rest, the worm's body is wound into a tight, flat coil. It is regarded as a pest because it preys on the useful earthworms, wrapping itself around them and covering them with digestive juices before sucking up the resulting 'soup'. Accidentally introduced into the British Isles in the 1960s, this flatworm is now abundant in many gardens, especially in cooler and wetter parts of Scotland, Northern Ireland and northern England. Reports of its effect on earthworm populations vary, although earthworms do seem to have declined in some places where the flatworm is established, with damage to soil structure and fertility. But it is not all bad and sometimes eat the eggs of slugs and snails.

The alien New Zealand Flatworm can reach lengths of 30 cm.

AUSTRALIAN FLATWORM
Australoplana sanguinea

A more recent introduction, this species was recorded in the Isles of Scilly in 1980, but is now quite widespread in south-west and north-west England and in North Wales. It has also been recorded from Scotland and from Northern Ireland. A little smaller than its New Zealand cousin, it is usually pale brown or pink, but it behaves in a similar way.

Australian Flatworm

Looks: Pale brown or pink

Food: Attacks beneficial earthworms

When: All year

Where: Western and northern British Isles

SLUGS AND SNAILS

These animals are probably the most disliked of all garden creatures. They belong to the large group of molluscs called gastropods, a name meaning 'belly-foot' and referring to the way in which the animals slither around on their muscular bellies – although this part of the body is technically known as the foot and its underside is, understandably, known as the sole. The latter pours out copious amounts of mucus or slime that lubricates the animals' passage, and this can be seen as silvery trails when the animals have passed. Slugs and snails are nearly all vegetarians and they rasp away at our plants with the aid of a tongue resembling a strip of sandpaper. Not all of our garden species are harmful, for many prefer dead and decaying vegetation to healthy leaves and some snails are out and out carnivores, but most gardeners find that some degree of control is necessary to protect their crops from damage by slugs and snails. Tender young plants are particularly susceptible. Total elimination of the pests is not possible – and not desirable as far as our Hedgehogs are concerned – and the aim should be to reduce the population to a level at which damage is slight. This can be achieved by a variety of methods.

Safe control of slugs and snails

Until recently, chemical control of slugs and snails was achieved mainly with pellets containing metaldehyde. The pests die quickly in a mass of slime after sampling the pellets, but metaldehyde is dangerous stuff and very harmful to Hedgehogs and birds that might eat the poisoned molluscs. Pets and small children can also be harmed if they ingest the pellets, so metaldehyde pellets must be used with great care. If you feel you must use them, put them in small heaps around the plants that you want to protect and cover each heap with a cage of wire netting, firmly fixed into the ground so that Hedgehogs cannot reach them. The mesh should also be small enough to prevent the Hedgehogs from getting their heads stuck in it. Don't forget that free-roaming Hedgehogs will destroy a lot of slugs and snails for you free of charge.

A liquid formulation of metaldehyde sprayed on to the soil is less dangerous as far as other wildlife is concerned because it is unlikely to be ingested, but there are now several much safer, environmentally friendly alternatives. Crystals and powders based on aluminium sulphate are relatively non-toxic and widely used, as are pellets containing iron phosphate. These pellets kill slugs and snails but are harmless to other wildlife, pets and children. A great advance on earlier slug killers, they are safe to handle and can be used to protect all kinds of plants, including vegetables ready for harvest. Having sampled the bait, the slugs and snails crawl away and die, so there are no piles of slimy bodies around the plants. Uneaten bait quickly disintegrates, leaving the iron phosphate to nourish your plants.

Physical protection

Pot plants can be protected by smearing petroleum jelly around the rims of the pots. Matting impregnated with copper salts can be placed under pot plants and around other particularly valuable plants to deter slugs, and various moisture-absorbent minerals can be used in the same way. They work by absorbing the animals' slime and preventing them from moving properly. All of these products are readily available from garden centres, but you don't have to use toxic chemicals: there are plenty of other ways of reducing slug damage.

One popular method is to bury a jam jar in the soil and half fill it with beer. Slugs will be attracted from a wide area, and there's no escape for them once they have sampled the brew. The rim of the jar should be at least 3 cm above soil level to prevent ground beetles from tumbling in. Surrounding your plants with coarse, sharp-edged grit effectively deters many of the pests because they find crossing it too uncomfortable. Vermiculite also works very well, and some gardeners advocate surrounding prize plants with hair – bags of which are easily obtained from your local hairdresser. If you need to protect just one or two small plants from surface-roaming slugs you can use plastic lemonade bottles: cut off the bottoms and remove the caps and then fix the bottles into the soil around the plants. Root-feeding subterranean slugs will, of course, still have access to your plants. You can use the same method to protect individual plants against cutworms **(see p. 220)**, but again it will not provide complete protection.

Ordinary table salt is lethal to slugs, but overuse is detrimental to plants and other creatures. It is probably best to

TOP TIP

Slugs and snails are active mainly in the cooler air of the night and they hide under any available shelter during the daytime. Old wooden planks or strips of black polythene laid between your plants make inviting shelters for slugs, and you can lift them each morning and destroy the pests – or scatter them on a convenient patch of waste ground if you prefer.

collect your slugs and drop them into a container of salt, rather than sprinkling it around the garden. Vinegar is another readily available slug-killer, and less harmful to the soil than salt. You can spray the pests with a 50-50 vinegar-water mixture, or you can use the vinegar in your jam-jar traps, with or without the beer.

Slugs and snails are active mainly in the cooler air of the night and they hide under any available shelter during the daytime. Old wooden planks or strips of black polythene laid between your plants make inviting shelters for slugs, and you can lift them each morning and destroy the pests – or scatter them on a convenient patch of waste ground if you prefer. Empty grapefruit and melon skins placed among your plants also attract slugs looking for daytime retreats. The less squeamish gardener can, of course, take a torch into the garden at night and simply pick off the marauding creatures – a good example of biological control! Hand-picking is also one of the best methods of reducing your snail population.

Biological control

There is now a safe and efficient biological method of slug control that will not endanger any other garden wildlife. It uses a tiny nematode worm that is a naturally occurring slug parasite. About a third of the slug population seems to be naturally infected, although the parasite is not normally numerous enough to kill many of them. Sold as a dried product, the worms quickly become active when mixed with water. Sprayed over the ground a week or so before planting or before slug damage would normally be expected, the nematodes seek out and enter the slugs. Heavily infested slugs swell up like little balloons and die in about a week, but the parasites continue to breed in the corpses and the young nematodes simply move off to find new hosts, carrying with them the toxic bacteria that actually kill the slugs **(see p. 38)**. The big advantage of this method of control is that it targets the subterranean slugs as well as those that roam over the surface. In theory, it is possible to kill all the slugs in a small garden, but it is unlikely that the nematodes, which are less than a millimetre long, will move into the surrounding areas at the densities required for slug-killing, so Hedgehogs, Slow-worms and other slug-eating predators are unlikely to go hungry.

The Yellow Slug (*Limax flavus*), easily identified by its yellow body and blue tentacles, is up to 10 cm long. Rarely found away from human habitation, it is quite common in gardens and also in damp sheds and cellars, but it feeds mainly on fungi and rotting vegetation and does little harm to our plants.

Gardeners are often advised to remove all dead leaves and other debris from around their plants in order to reduce damage by slugs and snails, but this is not necessarily good advice: without any of this decaying material to eat, the pests will be forced to nibble the growing plants. The odd bits of debris will also shelter ground beetles and other useful creatures that may control some of your pests free of charge, so being *too* tidy in the garden is not always a good thing! A bit of long grass here and there, especially at the bottom of a wall or a hedge, can support quite a lot of useful creatures, including slug-eating Slow-worms as well as Hedgehogs, and if you can't accommodate such a habitat it is well worth leaving a pile of logs or brushwood in a corner. Hedgehogs will appreciate it and repay you by eating a lot of slugs and snails.

Finally, if your potatoes suffer from slug damage you might find it advantageous to grow a different variety, for not all potatoes are equally susceptible to slugs. Pink fir apple, which is an excellent salad potato, is one of the best for slug resistance. Several new varieties, including Valor and Kestrel, also have good resistance. Early potatoes seem to suffer less than second-earlies and main-crop varieties.

Some troublesome slugs

Slugs are commonly described as snails without shells, and their German name – *Nacktschnecken* – literally means 'naked snails'. They have evolved from snails through the gradual reduction and loss of the shell and the incorporation of all the internal organs into the foot, although the various families of slugs have evolved from different families of snails.

NETTED SLUG OR GREY FIELD SLUG
Deroceras reticulatum

The commonest slug in most gardens and one of the gardener's worst enemies. No more than about 5 cm long, it ranges from cream to light brown or grey and has a short keel on the rear of its body. It exudes a colourless or milky white slime when disturbed. It is a surface dweller and, in common with our other garden slugs, is active in all but the coldest weather. Few garden plants escape damage, although young leaves are its favourite foods. Lettuces are particular favourites: whole rows of seedlings can be destroyed overnight and the slugs often chew their way into the hearts of mature plants. **Deroceras caruanae** is a very similar slug, native to south-western parts of Europe but occurring in gardens in many other regions. It is found mainly in the west of the British Isles.

Netted Slug

Looks: Cream to light brown or grey with keel at rear

Food: Young leaves

When: All but very cold weather

Where: Throughout the British Isles

The Netted Slug is one of the most troublesome garden slugs. Look for the short keel on the rear of the body. The dark circle near the middle of the body is the opening of the lung. In the keeled slugs this is always near the rear of the mantle – the thick 'cloak' of skin covering the front region of the body. Round-backed slugs have the lung opening near the front of the mantle. The lung opening of the very similar *Deroceras caruanae* has a more defined pale ring around it.

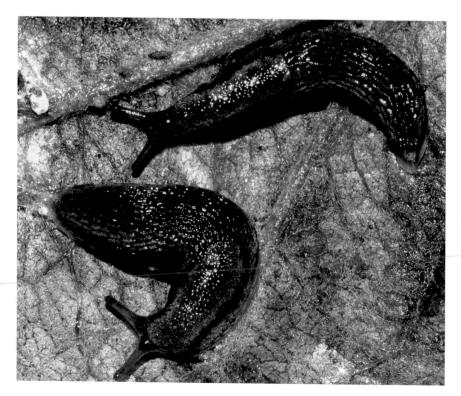

The Garden Slug is readily distinguished from other blackish slugs in the garden by its orange sole.

GARDEN SLUG
Arion hortensis

This is one of the round-backed slugs, with no trace of a keel on the back. Up to about 4 cm long, it is bluish-black with a darker line on each side. The orange sole distinguishes it from other dark slugs in the garden, and it also exudes an orange or yellow mucus when disturbed. This slug is not far behind the Netted Slug in terms of the damage it can do in the garden. It attacks almost any herbaceous plant and strikes both above and below ground. Together with the next two species, it is often found in potato tubers when they are lifted.

Garden Slug

Looks: Bluish-black with orange sole

Food: Eats leaves and roots of most kinds of herbaceous plants

When: All but very cold weather

Where: Found all over British Isles

Sowerby's Slug has a yellowish keel running from the mantle to the rear end of the body. It is usually less slimy than other slugs.

SOWERBY'S SLUG
Tandonia sowerbyi

A greyish-brown slug, up to 7.5 cm long, it is heavily speck-led with black. It has a yellowish keel running the length of its body and it secretes yellow mucus when handled. The sole is uniformly pale. The slug spends most of its time in the soil, feeding on the roots and tubers of a wide range of plants. It is a serious pest of potatoes and other root crops. The **Smooth Jet Slug** (*Milax gagates*) is similar, but it has a dark keel and white or colourless mucus. Both species are confined to the British Isles and neighbouring parts of the continent. The Mediterranean region is home to *Milax nigricans*, which is darker with a brown sole.

Sowerby's Slug

Looks: Large, speckled, greyish brown; yellow keel runs length of body

Food: Various root crops

When: Most of the year

Where: Western Europe

BUDAPEST SLUG
Tandonia budapestensis

This slug resembles Sowerby's Slug in having a yellowish keel along the back, but it is slightly smaller and its sole is pale with a darker band through the centre. Its mucus is colourless. Whereas Sowerby's Slug and most other garden slugs contract to a more or less hemispherical lump when disturbed, the Budapest Slug adopts a typical comma-shaped position instead. It is a soil-dweller and a serious pest of various root crops.

Budapest Slug

Looks: Yellow keel along back; pale sole with dark central band

Food: Most root crops

When: Most of the year

Where: British Isles and scattered over much of Western Europe

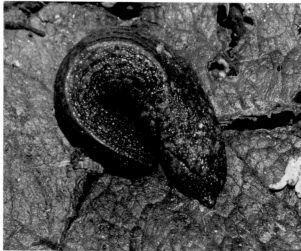

The Budapest Slug has a yellowish keel, but its mucus is colourless and when at rest is curls into a semi-circular or comma-like shape (right) instead of contracting to a hemisphere.

LARGE BLACK SLUG
Arion ater

Reaching lengths of 15 cm or more, this is one of our largest slugs but, although quite common in the garden, it does not do much damage. It prefers dead and decaying vegetation to green leaves and can often be seen on the compost heap or mopping up freshly cut grass after rain. Despite its name, it is not always black: chestnut brown and orange forms are found in the south, and some are fawn or grey but all have an orange fringe to the pale sole. There is no keel, although the back is conspicuously ribbed. When disturbed, the slug contracts to a hemisphere and may sway rhythmically from side to side. Its colourless mucus is extremely sticky.

Large Black Slug

Looks: Very large, can be black, chestnut and orange; some are even lighter in colour

Food: Decaying vegetation

When: Most of the year

Where: British Isles and much of Europe apart from the far north

This pale form of the Large Black Slug is laying a batch of soft, pearly white eggs, which are usually concealed in the earth. The eggs emerge from a pore just behind the head on the right side of the animal. An individual slug can lay up to 300 eggs, usually in batches of 10–30, and the eggs hatch in about 10 days during summer, although in cooler weather they may take longer. The new slugs mature in a few months and can live for two or more years.

Slugs with shells

Although most of our slugs have lost their shells, a few species have tiny shells, shaped rather like finger nails, perched on the rear ends of their bodies. Three of these shelled slugs can be found in our gardens. In fact, they are rarely found away from parks and gardens and other cultivated, well-manured lands with plenty of earthworms. The slugs feed on the useful earthworms and that is their only claim to be pests, although they are not common enough to have any serious effect on the earthworm population. They are almost pear-shaped at rest, but when on the move they become long and thin and they can actually follow the worms along their tunnels. When the slug makes contact with a worm it pushes out its toothy tongue and the backward-pointing teeth dig into the prey. There is no escape and the worm is gradually sucked into the slug's body. Rarely seen above ground, the shelled slugs can sometimes be found in compost heaps and under paving slabs laid on the garden. The commonest of the three species is ***Testacella haliotidea***, which is pale yellow or fawn with a white sole and reaches 12 cm in length when extended. The similar ***T. scutulum*** has an orange sole, while ***T. maugei*** is much darker and also has a pink or orange sole. All three species become dormant in the winter after burrowing deeply into the soil or the compost heap.

Testacella halliotidea

Looks: Pear-shaped at rest; long and thin when moving. Tiny shell on rear of body

Food: Beneficial earthworms

When: Spring to autumn

Where: Southern half of the British Isles and scattered locatilities in Western Europe

Testacella haliotidea, one of the shelled slugs. The tiny shell can be seen perched on the rear end of the body.

Two-way sex

Most of the snails and all of the slugs in our gardens are hermaphrodite creatures, meaning that each animal possesses both male and female organs. Each one can thus lay eggs, but not until it has paired up and received sperm from another individual. This is quite a good system for these relatively slow-moving creatures, because it means that any other mature individual of the same species is a potential mate, so time and energy is not wasted on looking for a member of the opposite sex.

Courtship can be complex and prolonged, and that of the great grey or leopard slug (Limax maximus) is truly amazing. Having met and got acquainted by crawling around each other on the ground, the pair climb a fence-post or other vertical object and each then exudes copious amounts of thick, sticky mucus. This forms a rope on which the slugs gradually lower themselves, and here, perhaps a couple of metres above the ground, the amorous couple extrude their shiny white genitalia (as shown here) and exchange sperm. This aerial mating may take an hour or two, and then one slug drops to the ground. The other usually climbs back up the rope and, reluctant to waste anything, it consumes the mucus as it goes.

Back on the ground, the slugs go their separate ways and eventually lay their pearly white eggs. With a length of 20 cm or more, it is a good job that this species pays little attention to our crops: it prefers decaying vegetation and is most likely to be found in and around the compost heap.

Problem snails

GARDEN SNAIL
Helix aspersa

This snail has a more or less spherical shell, mottled grey and yellow and up to 4 cm across. The snail is active mainly at night and few low-growing plants escape its nocturnal foraging. By day it hides under sprawling plants, especially at the bases of walls, with dozens of individuals often sharing the same site and returning to it every morning. Mating pairs are often seen low down on walls on damp mornings, with their white genitalia still visible. Close examination may well reveal the 'love-dart' that each snail fires into its partner to stimulate the final stages of mating. This species is one of the worst offenders in the garden, largely on account of its size. If you are really plagued by them and not keen to poison them, you could try the ultimate biological control and eat them yourself! These snails are the much-esteemed escargots of France. If you want to sample your snails it is wise to starve them for a few days and wash them regularly in running water to get rid of their gut contents, although

These two Garden Snails are getting to know each other before firing their 'love darts' into each other.

a number of people recommend feeding them on dill during this time to give them a bit more flavour. The snails should then be kept dry for two or three days before they are killed by dropping them into boiling water.

Song Thrushes also love all snails **(see p. 17)**. If you don't have a rockery or a concrete path, put a few large stones in your garden to act as anvils on which the birds can break open the snails' shells to get at the tasty contents. This is fun to watch and cheaper than chemicals. Recent research has found that snails respond to the presence of ground beetles **(see p. 15)** by moving away. This could well be in response to smell and the researchers are trying to replicate the beetles' chemicals and use them as a deterrent.

Unlike most of our slugs, our Garden Snails usually pass the winter in a dormant state. Large clusters of Garden Snails can often be found sleeping in log piles or in abandoned flower pots, their shells glued together with hardened slime – and then it is very easy to collect and dispose of them.

Garden Snails spend the colder months in hibernation, their shells glued to stones or to each other with hardened mucus. They usually select concealed spots. This group of snails, cemented to the bottom of a wall, were hidden by a dense clump of iris leaves.

Garden Snail

Looks: Mottled grey and yellow shell; up to 4cm across

Food: Leaves of most low-growing plants

When: Spring to autumn

Where: British Isles and much of Europe apart from the far north

ROMAN SNAIL
Helix pomatia

Roman Snail

Looks: Pale shell; up to 5cm across

Food: Most garden plants; vines

When: Spring to autumn

Where: South-east Britain; Continental Europe

This is one of the largest European snails, it has a pale shell that can be as much as 5 cm in diameter. It is confined to lime-rich soils and, although widely distributed in Europe, it is restricted to the south-east corner of Britain, south of a line from Norfolk to the Severn Estuary. This snail will rasp its way through all kinds of garden plants and regularly makes a nuisance of itself in vineyards, but in most parts of Europe it is seen as a free source of food rather than a pest!

The Roman Snail is closely related to the Garden Snail, but is usually much bigger and easily recognised by its thick, pale shell. It is more of a problem in continental vineyards than in most British gardens.

BROWN-LIPPED SNAIL
Cepaea nemoralis
Frustratingly variable, its top-shaped shell, usually about 2 cm across, almost always has a dark brown lip, but the rest of the shell may be yellow, pink or brown. Up to five brown bands of varying width spiral around the shell, although many individuals have no bands at all. The body is uniformly dark grey. Brown-lipped Snails attack a wide range of low-growing vegetation in the garden, although they prefer dead and dying leaves and do not do much harm to our flowers and vegetables. They are most commonly found under sprawl-ing plants such as aubrieta. Grass cuttings left on the lawn are also very attractive to them and huge numbers can be seen on recently mown roadside verges, especially in damp weather. Handfuls of grass cuttings placed here and there on your herbaceous borders will draw out the snails so that they can be picked up and destroyed.

WHITE-LIPPED SNAIL
Cepaea hortensis
Very similar to its brown-lipped cousin, it has a shell a little smaller and it normally has a white lip. The body is pale grey, often tinged with brown, and there is a yellowish patch at the rear of the foot. The habits of this snail are just like those of the brown-lipped species, but it is usually more common in gardens and probably does a little more damage.

Lip colour is not an infallible guide to the identity of these two snails for, just to make matters even more complicated, the Brown-lipped Snail occasionally has a white lip and the White-lipped Snail sometimes has a brown lip! The only sure way to distinguish them is to look at their 'love darts' – and not many gardeners will want to do this.

LEFT: The Brown-lipped Snail can usually be distinguished from the White-lipped Snail (RIGHT) by the colour of the lip. When living in gardens and hedgerows, both species tend to be strongly banded, while those living in grassland often have no bands. Those living on woodland floors tend to have pinkish-coloured shells.

Brown-lipped Snail

Looks: Shell has dark brown lip; variable colour

Food: Low-growing vegetation; dead leaves

When: Spring to autumn

Where: British Isles and most of Continental Europe

White-lipped Snail

Looks: Shell with white lip; body pale grey

Food: Low-growing vegetation; dead leaves

When: Spring to autumn

Where: British Isles and most of Continental Europe

Strawberry Snail

Looks: Small, with flattened, ridged shell. Body dark grey or black

Food: Lettuces, strawberries, raspberries

When: Spring to autumn

Where: Much of Britain and western Europe

The Strawberry Snail has a very dark body. Its shell is dark reddish or purplish brown, with a slight keel around the edge of the outer whorl.

STRAWBERRY SNAIL
Trochulus striolatus

The commonest snail in many gardens, its flattened shell, up to 1.5 cm across, is usually reddish-brown, often tinged with purple, and it has prominent growth lines crossing each whorl. The lip is pale, with a white ring just inside it, and the body is dark grey or black. Young shells are quite bristly. The snail spends the daytime lurking in low-growing plants or under logs and stones. By night it wreaks havoc among the lettuces and other tender-leaved plants. It can also cause severe damage to strawberries and is quite capable to climbing the canes to attack raspberries. Flower beds do not escape, and the snail is also abundant on rockeries, where mat-forming plants provide plenty of shelter. The **Hairy Snail** (*Trichia hispida*) can be confused with the Strawberry Snail but it usually has a large umbilicus – the hollow at the base of the shell – and the shell is usually somewhat hairy or bristly, especially in and around the umbilicus. The outer edge of the Strawberry Snail shell is very slightly keeled or angled, whereas that of the Hairy Snail is smoothly rounded. The two snails often live together and have similar diets, but the Hairy Snail is less common in the garden.

WOODLICE

Woodlice, also known as 'slaters', are land-living crustaceans and more closely related to crabs and shrimps than to the insects with which they are often confused. Up to about 2 cm in length, they are covered by a clearly segmented coat of armour, but this coat is not waterproof and the animals have not entirely thrown off their watery origins: they cannot survive for very long away from their damp homes under logs and stones or perhaps in the compost heap. Generally grey in colour, often with paler markings, they have seven pairs of walking legs and a pair of fairly stout antennae. Some are able to roll into a ball – hence the name 'pill-bug' commonly given to these fascinating little creatures. They also have scores of other local names, including 'cud-worms', 'bibble bugs', 'sow-bugs' and 'cheese-pigs'.

Despite their name, woodlice do not attack wood unless it is already pretty rotten – a habit that presumably led to their being called 'coffin-cutters' in Ireland. They feed mainly on rotting vegetation, hence their fondness for the compost heap. They may nibble soft fruits and chew a few tender seedlings, but it is rarely necessary to do battle with them. In fact, they are really quite useful because they speed up the decay of organic material and its return to the soil as plant food. Only in the greenhouse are woodlice likely to be more than a minor nuisance – and only then if you leave piles of debris for them to hide in. You can buy proprietary woodlouse killers for use here, and in the house if the animals find their way indoors, but these chemicals must not be sprayed onto your plants.

Lifting an old piece of wood or a stone frequently reveals a host of woodlice.

Woodlice exposed by turning over an old log. The three shiny specimens are *Oniscus asellus* and the other two are *Porcellio scaber*. Woodlice disturbed in this way soon scuttle off to find another dark, damp resting place. They move rapidly in sunlight and dry air, but slow down when they reach damper spots.

Species of woodlice

Several species of woodlice inhabit our gardens, including the tiny pink compost-inhabiting **Rosy Woodlouse** (*Androniscus dentiger*), but only two or three normally come to our notice.

Porcellio scaber

Every garden probably holds some of these woodlice. About 1.8 cm long, this species is normally steely grey with numerous 'warts' and is less shiny than most other woodlice. It can be found in the woodpile and in the drier parts of the compost heap, and also under loose bark on tree trunks. It often climbs trees and walls at night to browse on algae.

Oniscus asellus

About the same size as *P. scaber*, it is much shinier. There are pale patches, especially along the sides, and it has no 'warts'. This woodlouse probably lives in every garden, but it needs slightly damper habitats than *P. scaber* and it is rarely found on tree trunks. It likes the wetter parts of the compost heap and is also common under logs and large stones.

Porcellio scaber

Looks: Steel grey and rather warty

Food: Rotting wood, dead leaves, the occasional seedling

When: Most of the year

Where: Much of Britain and Continental Europe

Oniscus asellus

Looks: Shiny with pale patches

Food: Rotting wood, dead leaves, the occasional seedling

When: Most of the year

Where: Much of Britain and Continental Europe

Pill woodlice can be distinguished from pill millipedes by the small skeletal plates at the rear.

PILL WOODLOUSE
Armadillidium vulgare

This is one of a number of species that can roll into balls when disturbed. It is about the same length as the previous two species, but its body is strongly domed. Its coat is very shiny and also somewhat thicker than that of the other species. This latter feature, combined with the ability to roll up, slows the rate of evaporation from the body and thus enables the Pill Woodlouse to tolerate slightly drier conditions than the other woodlice. In the garden it is most often found at the base of old walls, where crumbling mortar provides the calcium needed for its tough coat. Elsewhere, it is confined largely to calcareous soils, but it is rare in the northern half of the British Isles. The Pill Woodlouse is easily confused with pill millipedes **(see p. 70)**, especially when it is rolled up, but the millipedes are blacker and shinier with many more legs.

Pill Woodlouse

Looks: Domed body with well-defined, small skeletal plates at the rear

Food: Rotting wood, dead leaves, the occasional seedling

When: Most of the year

Where: Much of Britain and Continental Europe

Growing up in the woodlouse world

Female woodlice usually breed when they are about two years old. Each one lays up to 250 eggs, which are carried in a pouch under the body for about a month. When the eggs hatch, the tiny babies gradually leave the pouch and then they have to fend for themselves. They take a couple of years to reach maturity and they may survive for a further two years if they escape enemies such as shrews and toads, ground beetles, and the woodlouse-hunting spider. As they grow, they have to change their coats periodically, but instead of stripping off completely as insects do, woodlice do it in two stages. It is not uncommon to find woodlice that are half grey and half white. The rear half of the old coat is shed first and for a few days the woodlouse has a grey front half and a soft, creamy white rear. But the new coat soon hardens and becomes grey, and then the process is repeated with the front half of the body. The animals hide while moulting but are often discovered when moving logs.

Porcellio scaber half-way through a moult, with the shed rear half of its coat lying by its side. The coat on the front half has become thin and is about to be shed.

MILLIPEDES

If the millipedes lived up to their name, they would have 1,000 feet, but no millipede ever has quite that number, and most European species have less than 100. Only distantly related to insects and woodlice, the millipedes belong to a group called Diplopoda – a name that refers to the two pairs of legs on nearly every segment of the body. Those found in the garden are mostly dark, worm-shaped creatures up to 4 cm in length and they are commonly mistaken for little black worms, although closer inspection will reveal their numerous short legs. Most millipedes live in the soil and leaf litter, tunnelling through it with surprising force: although their legs are individually short and slender, together they can generate all the thrust needed to drive the animal forward. If you hold even a small millipede in your clenched fist you will appreciate the power with which it attempts to escape between your fingers. It is not surprising that the animals are known as 'bulldozers' in some places!

Species of millipedes

Piles of dead leaves and rotting vegetation are an ideal habitat for millipedes, and for millipedes.

Millipedes feed largely on dead and decaying vegetable matter and, with one or two exceptions, they are harmless in the garden. It can be argued that they aid the gardener by breaking down organic material and returning minerals to the soil.

The Spotted Snake Millipede lives almost entirely in the soil, especially in moist, well-manured areas. It can be a real pest of potatoes. The red spots are poison-filled defensive glands.

SPOTTED SNAKE MILLIPEDE
Blaniulus guttulatus

One of the commonest garden species, and one that can certainly damage crops, this is named for the red spots on each side of its pale body. These spots are actually glands full of various poisons that effectively deter many, although not all, of the millipede's enemies. Most millipede species possess repellent glands of some kind, but our European species pose no danger to the gardener. The Spotted Snake Millipede lives almost entirely underground and, although common, it is rarely seen except when it attacks our potato crops. It prefers moist, heavy soils that have been well-manured – just the conditions that the gardener needs for a good potato crop. But even then the millipede does not usually invade healthy potatoes: it has to wait for some other organism to damage the tubers before it can get in and start nibbling. Damage is often most severe in dry spells, when the millipedes are probably seeking moisture rather than food.

Spotted Snake Millipede

Looks: Long body with red glands

What: Potatoes

When: Most of the year becoming a pest mainly in dry spells

Where: Much of Britain and Continental Europe

White-legged Millipede

Looks: Pale legs and darker body

Food: Potatoes, the occasional soft fruit seedling

When: Throughout the year

Where: Much of Britain and Continental Europe

The White-legged Millipede on the move and (INSET) coiled up in typical fashion. This millipede is especially fond of strawberries and other soft fruit. It is most common in alkaline soils.

WHITE-LEGGED MILLIPEDE
Tachypodoiulus niger

Our gardens harbour several other snake millipedes, named for their cylindrical bodies. One of the commonest and most widespread is the White-legged Millipede whose pale legs contrast strongly with its shiny black body. Up to 4 cm long, it coils up like a watch spring when disturbed and it is perhaps the typical millipede for most people. Most often found under logs and stones and under loose bark, it does little harm although it may find its way into potatoes and, in common with many other species, it may nibble the occasional seedling and sample the soft fruit. Strawberries are particularly susceptible, but are easily protected by sitting the ripening fruit on mats of dry straw. Even raspberries are not immune, for the millipedes will readily climb the canes for a nocturnal snack.

Portuguese Millipede

Looks: Black or dark grey

Food: Melons and similar crops

When: All year

Where: South-west Europe

PORTUGUESE MILLIPEDE
Ommatoiulus moreletii

This is a very common black or dark grey snake millipede in south-west Europe, where it occasionally damages melons and other crops. Unlike most other millipedes, it is attracted to lights and it may invade houses, but cannot do any harm and curls up and dies in the dry atmosphere.

Flat-backed millipedes are often mistaken for centipedes because, although their bodies are essentially cylindrical, the top of each segment has a broad flange on each side, giving the animals a flat-topped appearance. Look at the legs to distinguish the two groups – the millipede always has two pairs on most segments. Flat-backed millipedes generally live in leaf litter and are not uncommon in compost heaps, where they help to break down the rotting vegetation. They are also regularly found under decaying logs.

Polydesmus angustus

One of our commonest species, it is up to 2.5 cm long and may join the White-legged Millipede in the strawberry bed. It is not uncommon in the greenhouse, where it may attack seedlings and have a go at old wooden seed trays and other rotting wood – which has no place in a tidy greenhouse!

Oxidus gracilis

A much more sinister inhabitant of the greenhouse, this is an alien species introduced to Europe from Asia many years ago. Recognised by its shiny chestnut brown body about 2 cm long, it will injure the roots and foliage of almost any plant. It can also live in large compost heaps, where the heat of decay keeps it happy but, luckily for the gardener, it cannot survive out in the open garden.

Polydesmus angustus

Looks: Small, brown

Food: Strawberries, seedlings and rotting vegetation

When: Much of the year

Where: Much of Britain and Continental Europe

Oxidus gracilis

Looks: Small, chestnut brown

Food: Roots and foliage of most plants

When: All year in heated greenhouses

Where: Much of Britain and Continental Europe

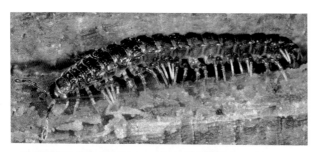

Polydesmus angustus clearly shows the two pairs of legs present on most of its segments. Only the segments at the very front and back have just a single pair of legs or none at all.

Oxidus gracilis is an Asiatic millipede that is now well-established in greenhouses in many parts of Europe. It is considerably more damaging than our other garden millipedes.

Glomeris marginata is the commonest of our pill millipedes. It can be distinguished from the Pill Woodlouse as it has a single large plate at the rear end instead of several small ones (see p. 65). When it is not rolled into a ball, you can also see that it has many more legs than a woodlouse.

Glomeris marginata

Looks: To 2 cm; rolls into ball with several large plates showing

What: Roots and foliage of most plants, leaf litter

When: Spring to autumn

Where: Much of Britain and Continental Europe

TOP TIP

Placing damp wood or sacking close to where millipedes congregate will attract them and allow you to remove them elsewhere.

Pill millipedes are short, squat creatures and are easily mistaken for woodlice. But if you take a closer look you will find far more than the seven pairs of legs on which the woodlouse scurries about. Look also at the rear end: pill millipedes have a single shield-like plate, whereas the Pill Woodlouse **(see p. 65)** has several small plates. In common with their woodlouse look-alikes, the pill millipedes can roll themselves into balls, and this, together with their thick coats, enables them to survive in somewhat drier habitats than other millipedes. In the garden, they are most likely to be found in hedge bottoms and at the bases of old walls, where they feed mainly on leaf litter. Our commonest species is **Glomeris marginata** which is up to 2 cm long

It is rarely necessary to do anything in the way of controlling millipedes in the open garden, but it is worth squashing any that you find while preparing your potato patch. If they are a nuisance elsewhere in the garden you can leave a few pieces of moist sacking or short lengths of wood on the soil. The millipedes will congregate under these and can then be removed. Over-ripe fruit can also be used as bait to deflect the animals from growing crops, especially in the greenhouse. Some people advocate the use of insecticides containing pyrethrins or synthetic pyrethroids **(see p. 40)**. These will certainly kill millipedes if applied directly to the animals, and may be useful in the greenhouse, but they are unlikely to have much effect on the subterranean millipede population.

Millipede or centipede?

These two groups are superficially similar in having long, thin, segmented bodies and lots of legs, but they differ in that the millipedes have two pairs of legs on each segment while the centipedes have only one pair per segment – and they never have the 100 legs suggested by their name. Many centipedes have only 15 pairs of legs. Centipede legs are also longer and more obvious, and the animals are considerably faster over the ground in connection with their carnivorous nature: millipedes are vegetarians and do not have to chase prey, so they don't need to be able to run.

Centipedes are basically friends of the gardener because they eat slugs and a variety of other harmful creatures. But they also eat worms and spiders and many other useful things, including other centipedes – so they are not entirely on our side! Prey is caught and poisoned by the large claws that curve around the centipede head. Some of the large centipedes living in southern Europe can dish out painful bites, but our garden species are not large enough to do us any harm. Several European centipedes are known to nibble roots in addition to eating small soil-dwelling creatures, possibly in order to get additional moisture, although damage is serious only when the centipedes are very numerous.

Stigmatogaster subterranea

A slender, yellowish centipede, this is the commonest of the nibblers and the only British species showing much interest in plants. Up to 7 cm long, with between 77 and 83 pairs of legs (there is always an odd number of pairs in centipedes), this well-named creature spends nearly all of its life tunnelling through the soil and leaf litter and rarely comes to the surface, although it can often be seen gliding away when we lift stones or logs.

Stigmatogaster subterranea

Looks: Slim and yellow

What: Most plant roots

When: All year

Where: Much of Britain and Continental Europe

Stigmatogaster subterraneanea is most often seen when we are digging our gardens or lifting half-buried stones and logs. It is one of the few centipedes that nibble plant roots: most species are entirely carnivorous.

MITES

True to their name, the mites are extremely small and inconspicuous creatures, many of them visible only with the help of a microscope. Related to the spiders, most of them have rounded or oval bodies and four pairs of legs when adult, but they are extraordinarily variable in appearance and also in their behaviour. Take a spoonful of material from your compost heap and look at it with a strong lens or, better still, a microscope, and you will come face to face with an assortment of bristly 'monsters' that match anything from science fiction. Hundreds of different kinds of mites live in the garden, as scavengers, predators and herbivores. Most of them are completely harmless, but there is one group whose behaviour certainly brings them into conflict with the gardener. These are the gall mites, individually microscopic yet capable of causing conspicuous and sometimes damaging galls on a wide range of plants.

The dreaded gall mites

BELOW LEFT: A beetle mite, one of many minute species that are found in the compost heap.

BELOW RIGHT: A typical gall mite, greatly magnified. Unlike the other mites, gall mites have only four legs.

Gall formation is triggered by chemicals secreted by the feeding mites **(see p. 24)**. Gall mites actually look more like maggots than mites, for they have elongated bodies and just four legs at the front. Mite-induced galls are amazingly varied and include swollen buds, leaf blisters and an assortment of colourful pimples. Many others take the form of dense mats of hair, known as erinea, which usually develop on the undersides of leaves **(see p. 74)**.

Big-bud disease of black currant, caused by the gall mite *Cecidophyopsis ribis*. The swollen buds contain thousands of mites and should be destroyed as soon as they are noticed.

TOP TIP

To control big-bud mites and other garden gall mites, remove all infected buds and burn them. Heavily infested bushes should be destroyed, especially if reversion disease is present, and replaced with fresh stock from a reputable nursery. Mite-resistant varieties are becoming available and these should gradually reduce the incidence of big-bud.

Cecidophyopsis ribis

Big-bud disease of blackcurrants is caused by this gall mite. The infested buds are larger and more spherical than normal buds and they contain hundreds, or even thousands of the microscopic mites. Because the mites cause the buds to swell up and provide food and shelter for them, the swollen buds are regarded as plant galls **(see p. 24)**. They do not open to produce either leaves or flowers, so even a moderate infestation can seriously reduce the yield of fruit. The mites live in the swollen buds throughout the winter and leave just as the flowers are beginning to open elsewhere on the bushes. These migrating mites head for the tiny buds developing at the bases of the new leaves, and that is where they will live and feed for the next year. The mites can't move far under their own steam and many stay on the original plants, but they can be carried to new plants by the wind. When disturbed, by a slight breeze for example, the mites can leap a few millimetres into the air, and that is enough for them to be swept away by the breeze. The mites also hitch lifts to new plants by clinging to the hairs of visiting insects. As well as causing direct damage to the host plants, the mites carry reversion disease. This is a very common disorder caused by a virus. The symptoms may not be very obvious, but they include smaller and more deeply divided leaves, fewer flower clusters and sometimes sterile flowers – all of which lead to a reduction in fruit yield.

Cecidophyopsis ribis

Looks: Infested buds appear larger and more rounded

Food: Blackcurrants

When: Mites live in buds through winter

Where: Much of Britain and Continental Europe

Walnut foliage heavily infested with the gall mite *Aceria erinea*. Each blister-like gall has a corresponding hollow on the underside of the leaf and this is where the mites live.

Aceria erinea

Walnut leaves are commonly disfigured by yellowish blisters, caused by this gall mite. These blisters are galls and they sometimes cover most of the upper surface. The mites live on the underside of the leaves, in the hollows below the blisters. These hollows have a pale brown, velvety lining formed from modified hairs, and it is on these sap-filled hairs that the mites feed. Although heavy infestations may look unsightly to the gardener, the mites do not seem to damage the trees' health or their ability to produce fruit.

Colomerus vitis

Vines growing on the continent are frequently attacked by this gall mite, which causes blister-like swellings (galls) on the leaves. The upper surface of the swelling is often a little paler than the rest of the leaf, while the concave lower surface is coated with fine hairs, among which the mites live and feed. The hairs are creamy white at first but they become rusty brown as the galls mature towards autumn. The mites then leave the galls and spend the winter tucked up in tiny bark crevices or between the bud scales. The galls appear to have little effect on the productivity of the vines unless the infestation is particularly heavy, in which case the affected leaves tend to fall early. There is no effective treatment for the condition. Although uncommon in the British Isles at present, the mite could well increase with climate change, especially if this encourages gardeners to grow more vines.

Colomerus vitis

Looks: Blister-like swellings on leaves

Food: Vine leaves

When: Mites live in the galls in the summer and in buds in the winter

Where: Mainly Continental Europe; rare in Britain

Vine foliage galled by the mite *Colomerus vitis*.

Aceria genistae

Looks: Ball-shaped growths to 3 cm

Food: Brooms

When: Mites live in the galls all year

Where: Britain, Continental Europe

Looking a little like flower clusters from a distance, these pinkish grey growths on broom are actually the galls of the mite *Aceria genistae*.

Aceria genistae

Gardeners who grow the common broom and its various cultivars will probably find pale, furry, ball-shaped growths on the stems from time to time. Up to 3 cm across, these growths are galls caused by this gall mite. Each consists of a cluster of stunted leaves covered with grey or purplish hairs. Each gall is full of mites feeding on the succulent hairs and tissues, although you will need a powerful lens or even a microscope to see them. A few such galls do no harm to the plants, but heavier infestations, which are fortunately rare, can interfere with growth and flowering. Large numbers of galls can also look unsightly, especially when they get old and brown, for old galls can remain on the twigs for several years. Removal of the affected twigs or the individual galls is the only way to combat the mite.

TOP TIP

Remove badly infested leaves to reduce the density of the mite population on the tree.

A pear leaf bearing numerous young, blister-like galls of the mite *Eriophyes pyri*. Later in the year the blisters become black.

PEAR LEAF BLISTER MITE
Eriophyes pyri

This is a white or pinkish gall mite that causes blisters to develop on pear leaves. The adult mites overwinter in the buds and emerge to feed on the undersides of the young leaves in the spring. This causes the formation of blister–like galls which can be seen on both leaf surfaces. The blisters are greenish–yellow at first, but then turn pink or red and become brown or black later in the year. Eggs are laid in the blisters and the young mites live there until they are mature and ready to start the process again. Two or three generations may be produced during the summer months and young fruits may be attacked as well as the leaves. Badly infested leaves can be removed to reduce the density of the population, but mature trees are unlikely to be damaged by this mite. Infestation seems to be worse in trees grown against walls – possibly because of the extra warmth.

Pear Leaf Blister Mite

Looks: Yellow, later reddish, then black blisters on leaves

Food: Pear trees

When: Mainly summer

Where: Britain; Continental Europe

The underside of an apple leaf extensively galled by the Apple Leaf Mite. The galls consist of mats of soft hairs and are often called felt galls, although they are technically known as erinea.

APPLE LEAF MITE
Phyllocoptes malinus

Apple leaves, especially those of crab apples, sometimes develop irregular, velvety, rust-coloured or blood-red patches on the undersides during the summer. These are caused by various gall mites, the commonest of which is the Apple Leaf Mite. The patches, known as erinea, are composed of tiny woolly or globular hairs, amongst which the mites live and feed. Badly affected leaves may fall in late summer, but the mites have no serious effect on the trees. Eating apples seem to suffer more than cooking apples in the garden, although Bramleys sometimes carry heavy infestations. The mites pass the winter in a dormant state under loose bark or in crevices, or perhaps in the buds, and attack the young leaves in late spring, although populations build up quite slowly and the galls are not obvious until well into the summer.

Apple Leaf Mite

Looks: Velvety red or rusty patches on leaves

Food: Apple and crab apple trees

When: Mainly summer

Where: Britain; Continental Europe

These nail galls on lime leaves are caused by the mite *Eriophyes tiliae*. Each 'nail' is full of tiny mites, but such infestations do not seem to harm the trees in any way.

Eriophyes tiliae

Red or pinkish spikes springing from the upper surface of lime leaves are due to the activity of this gall mite. Each spike, commonly called a nail gall, is full of hairs, among which live numerous mites. The latter escape through a hairy opening on the lower leaf surface in late summer and pass the winter in bark crevices, especially around the bases of the buds. Surviving females initiate new galls when the leaves open in the spring.

Aceria lateannulatus

This closely related mite induces similar galls, but these have rounded tips instead of the pointed tips of the *E. tiliae* galls. The galls do not seem to harm the trees and the gardener need not worry about them. Some people even consider them to be decorative, but if you don't like the look of them you can simply remove the affected leaves.

Eriophyes tiliae

Looks: Red or pink spikes on upper surface of leaf

Food: Lime trees

When: Late summer

Where: Britain; Continental Europe

Aceria lateannulatus

Looks: Red or pink spikes with rounded tips on upper surface of leaf

Food: Lime trees

When: Summer

Where: Britain; Continental Europe

Galls of the mite *Eriophyes similis* on a greengage leaf.

Eriophyes similis

Looks: Oval, green swellings on edges and middle of leaf

Food: Plum trees and blackthorn hedges

When: Mites escape in late summer

Where: Britain; Continental Europe

Eriophyes similis

Plum leaves, especially those of the greengage, often bear oval green swellings around the edges and sometimes on the midrib. These are the work of the gall mite *Eriophyes similis*. The galls are also abundant on blackthorn hedges, where they tend to be pink or purplish. The galls are full of mites, which escape through slits on the upper surface in late summer. Winter is passed between the bud scales or in tiny bark crevices. Badly affected leaves can be removed and destroyed, but no other control measures are recommended. Galls on the leaves do not seem to have any effect on crop yields, but when they are abundant the mites may spread to the fruits and disfigure them.

Galls of the mite *Eriophyes similis* usually develop around the edges of blackthorn leaves. They are abundant in many hedgerows, but do not appear to do the plants any harm.

The Fuchsia Gall Mite deforms the shoots and flowers of fuchsias. A recent arrival from America, it is regarded as a serious threat to fuchsia growing.

FUCHSIA GALL MITE
Aculops fuchsiae

Fuchsia plants that exhibit reddening and distortion of the leaves, particularly at the tips of the shoots, could well be suffering from attack by the Fuchsia Gall Mite. This American mite was first noticed in Europe in France in 2003, but has already spread to several other countries, including Great Britain, and is regarded as a serious threat to fuchsia growing, although some cultivars are known to be resistant to it. Infested plants become deformed at the tips and may stop growing. Flowers may also be deformed. Garden fuchsias and indoor plants are equally susceptible to the mite, although it cannot survive out of doors where winter temperatures drop below about 5°C. The pest is very difficult to control with sprays because it is so well hidden among the distorted leaf clusters, although neem oil **(see p. 41)** is said to be effective and systemic products should also be useful. Predatory mites such *Amblyseius californicus* may provide a degree of biological control, but destruction of affected plants is the best way to combat the pest and this is legally required in some parts of France. Suspected infestations in the United Kingdom must be reported to the local plant health authority.

TOP TIP

Destroying the affected plants is the best way to combat Fuchsia Gall Mites.

Fuchsia Gall Mite

Looks: Reddening and distortion of leaves

Food: Fuchsia plants

When: Spring to autumn

Where: USA, spreading to France, UK and elsewhere in Europe

FRUIT TREE RED SPIDER MITE
Panonychus ulmi

This is a fairly typical mite, with a dark red, oval body and eight legs. Adults are up to 0.4 mm long and just about visible to the naked eye. They live on many trees of the rose family and are particularly troublesome on fruit trees such as apples, plum and cherries. The mites swarm over the undersides of the leaves and cover them with mats of fine silk – which is why the creatures are called spider mites. They puncture the leaves and feed on the sap, causing the leaves to take on a mottled yellow appearance. Badly affected leaves may fall early, with consequent reduction in growth and fruit quality. Fewer fruiting buds are formed, leading to a reduction in fruit quantity in the following year. Several generations of mites develop on the leaves in summer and in the autumn the adult mites leave to lay their rust-coloured eggs on the twigs – occasionally in such numbers that the twigs appear red from a distance. The mite is not often a serious problem in gardens with just a few trees, especially if these are not sprayed, because carnivorous bugs and other predators keep it fairly well under control. It is much more of a pest in orchards which are sprayed against aphids and other pests because the mite has become resistant to many pesticides and, with its enemies wiped out, it can multiply rapidly. The simplest thing to do in the garden is just to remove and destroy the most severely affected leaves, but small trees can be sprayed with neem oil **(see p. 41)** to obtain effective control of the mite. Some trees and varieties, including the Bramley apple, seem to be more resistant to the mite than others.

GREENHOUSE RED SPIDER MITE
Tetranychus urticae

This mite, which attacks a wide range of flowers and vegetables both in and out of doors, resembles the previous species but for much of the year it is yellowish-green with two dark spots. Only in the autumn does it become red. It is sometimes called the Two-spotted Spider Mite. Leaves are attacked and clothed with silk, and if the infestation is heavy the leaves shrivel and die. Whole plants may also be killed. Although it is primarily a greenhouse and indoor pest, thriving in a warm atmosphere, the mite often moves into the garden in hot summers. Tomatoes, strawberries, cucumbers and other cucurbits, chrysanthemums, carnations and

---

TOP TIP

• *In the garden, remove and destroy affected leaves.*

• *Spray small trees with neem oil for control of the pest.*

Fruit Tree Red Spider Mite

Looks: Undersides of leaves covered with mats of silk; leaves appear yellowish

Food: Roses and several fruit trees

When: Summer to autumn

Where: Britain; Continental Europe

polyanthus are among its many targets, although there are plenty of predators in the garden and the mite is rarely much of a problem out of doors. Not surprisingly, it prefers plants growing in sunny spots. The species has become resistant to many pesticides, but it can be controlled in the greenhouse with the aid of the predatory mite *Phytoseiulus persimilis*, which can be obtained through garden centres. This predator destroys eggs and active stages, but it requires a temperature of around 20°C for best results and is less successful in the garden. It will not attack the Fruit Tree Red Spider Mite. Neem oil **(see p. 41)** is also useful in the greenhouse, but spraying the greenhouse with water on a regular basis can control this warmth-loving spider mite simply by keeping the temperature down. Wet leaves also make it difficult for the mites to spin their webs.

Greenhouse Red Spider Mite

Looks: Undersides of leaves covered with mats of silk; may shrivel

Food: Wide range of flowers and vegetables in and out of doors

When: Spring and summer

Where: Britain; Continental Europe

Polyanthus leaves dying in the face of a heavy infestation of the Greenhouse Red Spider Mite, which spins its silk mainly on the underside of the leaves.

CLOVER MITE
Bryobia praetiosa

This minibeast is more of a nuisance than a pest, although large populations can certainly damage the lawn. Dark brown and nearly 1 mm long, it is one of the larger mites and easily seen with the naked eye. It can be distinguished from most other mites by its long front legs. It feeds on clovers and grasses and many other low-growing herbaceous plants, including many weeds as well as cultivated plants. Polyanthus seem particularly susceptible to this mite, which causes the leaves to develop silvery spots and streaks. Unlike the spider mites, it prefers the upper surfaces of the leaves and does not produce any silk. The mite passes the winter in the egg stage, safely tucked into bark crevices and other hidey-holes, and young mites start to appear with the early spring sunshine. Large populations can build up during the summer, and this is when they can cause the grass to wilt and turn yellow. But it is in the autumn that the mites are most likely to be a nuisance, swarming off the vegetation to look for egg-laying sites. They often invade houses and outbuildings, especially in areas with lots of grass and no trees, and, although they do no damage in such situations, any that get crushed leave unwelcome red stains behind. The best way to remove the mites is to get out the vacuum cleaner! Garden plants rarely need to be treated, but pyrethroid-based sprays can be used if necessary.

TOP TIP

Use your vacuum cleaner to hoover away infestations of Clover Mites quickly and easily.

Clover Mite

Looks: Leaves have silvery spots; mite is dark, 1 mm

Food: Clovers and grasses

When: Most often seen in autumn

Where: Britain; Continental Europe

Distinguished from most other garden mites by their long front legs, Clover Mites feed on a wide range of herbaceous plants.

GRASSHOPPERS AND CRICKETS

These insects, of the order Orthoptera, are jumping creatures with enlarged back legs. With or without wings, all have strong biting jaws. Grasshoppers are mainly vegetarians, while crickets are more omnivorous and a few are carnivores. There are about 25 species in the British Isles, but only the Greenhouse Camel Cricket is a pest – and it is an alien confined to greenhouses and indoor habitats. Grasshoppers enjoy grassy places, and if you have an orchard or leave patches of long grass you will probably have some. You will hear the cheerful chirps of the males even if you don't see them. They do no harm, and might even keep the grass down. The only crickets likely to occur in British gardens are the House Cricket – although this prefers to stay indoors except in very warm weather – and various bush crickets living in hedges or shrubberies

GREENHOUSE CAMEL CRICKET
Tachycines asynamorus

A wingless insect, up to 1.5 cm long, with long legs and extremely long antennae. Originally from China, it is now found all over the world, although it cannot survive out of doors in Britain or in other temperate regions. It normally occurs only in heated greenhouses in these areas, although colonies have occasionally been found in zoos and warehouses. The insect nibbles various plants, but probably makes up for the damage by eating a variety of other insect pests. Colonies rarely last more than a few years.

Greenhouse Camel Cricket

Looks: 1.5 cm, brown with long legs and antenna

Food: Various plants

When: All year in suitable places; mainly in greenhouses in Europe

Where: Worldwide

The Greenhouse Camel Cricket, a cosmopolitan pest of greenhouse plants, is strictly nocturnal.

HOUSE CRICKET
Acheta domesticus

A nocturnal scavenger, this insect eats our discarded food and a wide range of other dead plant and animal matter. The male advertises his presence with a shrill, bird-like chirping, so you will soon know if you have it in your house or garden. Originally from North Africa and the Middle East, the insect has been established in the British Isles for several centuries, but is normally restricted to indoor habitats, especially permanently heated buildings such as bakeries, hospitals and greenhouses. It can also colonise land-fill sites and other rubbish dumps, where the fermenting refuse provides it with both food and warmth. In hot summers the insect can move outside and take up residence in compost heaps and hedgerows. Although primarily a scavenger, the House Cricket will chew plants in our greenhouses, but it is rarely abundant enough to be a real problem. Good housekeeping in the greenhouse should achieve adequate control. The insect is certainly less common than it was in the past and seems to have disappeared altogether from Ireland.

House Cricket

Looks: Brown or grey; 1.5–2 cm long

Food: Mostly dead plant and animal matter

When: Most of year

Where: Worldwide

The House Cricket is a scavenger, found mainly in buildings. It is up to 2 cm long. This female shows the long, needle-like ovipositor that is typical of the true crickets.

The Migratory Locust, up to 8 cm long, is a fairly rare visitor to Britain and Northern Europe, where all specimens are of the solitary phase, characterised by the domed thorax clearly seen here. The gregarious or swarming phase, rarely seen in Europe, lacks this dome.

MIGRATORY LOCUST
Locusta migratoria

Not to be confused with the much more destructive Desert Locust of warmer climates, this is a large grasshopper resident over an extensive area of southern Europe. It rarely forms large swarms and, although it migrates to many parts of Europe in the summer and attacks a wide variety of plants, it is rarely common enough to do much harm away from its southern breeding grounds. Migrating individuals occasionally reach the British Isles and some also arrive as stowaways in imported vegetables.

Migratory Locust

Looks: Large winged insect up to 8 cm; greenish body

Food: Various plants

When: Can have two to three generations annually

Where: Most of world; not a problem in Britain

EGYPTIAN GRASSHOPPER
Anacridium aegyptium

Superficially similar to the Migratory Locust, this insect is easily distinguished by its striped eyes. The young stages are either bright green or orange. The species can be a nuisance in gardens and vineyards in southern Europe. Although it rarely reaches the British Isles under its own steam, the Egyptian Grasshopper occasionally arrives with consignments of green vegetables.

Egyptian Grasshopper

Looks: Large winged insect up to 8cm; striped eyes

Food: Chews various plants

When: Spring to autumn

Where: Mainly southern Europe

The Egyptian Grasshopper, up to 8 cm long, is a pest in many gardens in southern Europe, but rarely reaches the British Isles.

Grasshopper or cricket?

Grasshoppers have fairly stout antennae that are always much shorter than the body. They like fairly open habitats and are active only in sunshine. They chirp by rubbing their hind legs against their wings. Crickets have hair-like antennae that are much longer than the body. Many are active at night and they chirp by rubbing their wing bases together. Female bush crickets have formidable, sword-like but harmless egg-layers at the rear of the body, while the female house cricket has a more slender, needle-like egg-layer. The young insects look very much like the adults except that they do not have fully-developed wings, and they gradually turn into adults without any chrysalis stage.

BELOW: A Common Green Grasshopper; BOTTOM: A female Great Green Bush Cricket, showing the long ovipositor and very long antennae

Barbitistes fischeri

This fairly small bush cricket, up to 2.5 cm long and densely speckled with black, is rarely common enough to do much damage, but it can be a nuisance in vineyards and gardens in its native south-west Europe. The female has a saw-like tip to her ovipositor (egg-laying organ) and she uses this to rip open plant stems prior to laying her eggs.

Barbitistes fischeri

Looks: Speckled and almost wingless, to 2.5 cm

Food: Vines and garden plants

When: Spring, summer

Where: Mainly a pest in south-west Europe

Barbitistes fischeri nibbles a wide range of plants in southern Europe but, being flightless, it cannot migrate.

Ephippiger ephippiger

One of several fairly similar, rather stout bush crickets living in southern and central Europe, this insect appears to be wingless, but it has just enough of its front wings to be able to rub them together to make its characteristic two-syllable call of *tizi*. In France the insect is commonly called '*le tizi*'. Green or brown, it has a good appetite and readily attacks a wide range of cultivated plants, including vines.

Ephippiger ephippiger

Looks: Large, with sturdy body; brown or green

Food: Vines and garden plants

When: Late spring to autumn

Where: South and central Europe

Ephippiger ephippiger, commonly known as 'le tizi', is a stout bush cricket of central and southern Europe. Up to 3.5 cm long, excluding the ovipositor, it has both green and brown forms.

Ephippiger provincialis

Looks: Very large, sturdy body; long ovipositor

Food: Particularly vines

When: Spring, summer

Where: Serious vineyard pest in southern Europe

Mole Cricket

Looks: To 5 cm with 'shovel-like' forelimbs

Food: Roots of vines, strawberries

When: All year, but usually dormant in winter

Where: Southern England and Channel Islands; Continental Europe

ABOVE LEFT: *Ephippiger provincialis* lives on a variety of shrubs in southern Europe and causes a good deal of damage to grape vines in some years.

ABOVE RIGHT: The Mole Cricket is a sturdy burrowing insect up to 5 cm long. It has short front wings, but can is still fly well on its flimsy hind wings. It is an omnivorous creature, eating other insects as well as plant roots and foliage.

Ephippiger provincialis

With a body up to 5 cm long and an ovipositor up to 3 cm long, this is a veritable monster and one of Europe's largest insects. It is a serious vineyard pest in the south, although it varies a lot in abundance and in some years, luckily for the wine-growers, it hardly puts in an appearance. Species of the genus *Ephippiger* pass the winter in the egg stage deep in the soil. The eggs hatch in the spring and the insects mature towards the end of the summer. If bush crickets are causing serious damage they can be controlled by spraying the foliage with pyrethroid-based insecticides.

MOLE CRICKET
Gryllomorpha gryllomorpha

This insect is not closely related to the other crickets and bush-crickets and, true to its name, it spends much of its life tunnelling through the soil, just like a mole, with the aid of its huge front legs. It can fly, however, and often does so on warm evenings. The male attracts a mate with a churring 'song' produced while sitting in the funnel-shaped entrance to his burrow – a shape that acts like a megaphone to amplify the sound. Mole Crickets eat roots and assorted soil-dwelling invertebrates. The species is almost extinct in British Isles, with just a few colonies in southern England and the Channel Islands, but it is still common in southern Europe, where it causes a good deal of damage to the roots of vines. It also wrecks strawberry beds in some places, nibbling the fruit as well as destroying roots and foliage.

EARWIGS

Earwigs, belonging to the order Dermaptera, are much-maligned insects, disliked by a great many people but fascinating creatures nevertheless. They are easily recognised by the forceps at the rear end – strongly curved in most males and more or less straight in the females – and it is probably the appearance of these forceps that is responsible for the insects' undeserved reputation as destroyers of eardrums. The forceps are used largely for defence and can be raised in a threatening attitude: they will give you a little nip if you handle them roughly, although they are not strong enough to hurt.

Not serious pests

Earwigs are omnivorous scavengers and they do sometimes nibble flowers and fruit, but they are not serious pests and probably make up for the little damage that they do by eating aphids and other harmful insects. They are mainly nocturnal and like to spend the daytime in narrow crevices. The tubular florets of dahlias and chrysanthemums are favourite spots, as are the dimples around the stalks of apples, especially where two or three apples cluster together. Although accumulated earwig droppings do not enhance the appearance of the apples, they are easily removed with a damp cloth. Only rarely do the insects bite into sound apples – mainly the thinner-skinned varieties – and they are most likely to be found enlarging the wounds caused by birds or other creatures. Earwigs also hide among leaves that have been curled and damaged by other creatures. Their use of human ears as resting places is rare, but not unknown!

Earwigs are among the best mothers in the insect world. The female usually lays her eggs in the winter in a little chamber hollowed out under logs or stones and she guards them carefully, licking them regularly to keep them free from mould. When they hatch, she feeds the youngsters with regurgitated food and they all stay together for several weeks. The youngsters are much paler than their mother and have straight, slender pincers. They grow into adults without any chrysalis stage. You may find some that are white or cream, but these are not different species: they are simply youngsters that have just changed their skins and are waiting for the new coats to harden. All insects, along with spiders and other arthropods, have to change their skins several times as they grow up because their tough, outer coats are not composed of living material and they do not grow.

Trapping earwigs

Common Earwig

Looks: Small, dark brown with 'pincers' on abdomen

Food: Variety of flowers and vegetables

When: All year, but usually dormant in winter

Where: Britain, most of Europe and Asia

Lesser Earwig

Looks: Yellowish-brown, only 6mm long

Food: Mainly decaying plant matter

When: All year

Where: Most of world

Unless you are trying to grow prize flowers or fruit, it is not really necessary to do anything to control earwigs: you can live alongside them without any worries. Trapping is the best way to get rid of them if you must, the traditional way being with up-turned flower pots stuffed with straw and fixed to sticks placed among your flowers. The insects bed down in the straw and you can then release them away from your garden. An old cloth draped over the branch of an apple tree will also offer the earwigs a comfortable roost.

We have four native earwigs in the British Isles and a few aliens occasionally colonise greenhouses, but only the **Common Earwig** (*Forficula auricularia*) is likely to be noticed in the garden. The only other widely distributed species is the yellowish-brown **Lesser Earwig** (*Labia minor*). This species often lives in compost heaps but, being no more than 6 mm long, it rarely comes to one's attention.

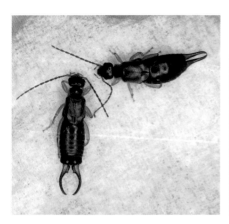

A pair of Common Earwigs, the male on the left exhibiting its characteristically curved pincers or forceps. Up to 1.5 cm long, the insects have a pair of rather square, horny front wings that hide the flimsy hind wings. The insects can fly but rarely do so.

The Lesser Earwig, a common but rarely seen insect. It is the smallest British earwig and, unlike the other species, it readily takes to the air. It lives mainly in compost heaps and other rotting material.

TERMITES

The name termite conjures up visions of huge mounds dotting the tropical grasslands, but not all termites go in for such extravagant housing: many species spend their entire lives tunnelling in dead wood. Several of these destructive species are native to southern Europe, and an American species has established itself in buildings in several areas. **Reticulitermes grassei** is native to Spain and Portugal and has spread northwards to Paris and other French towns, probably in consignments of timber. This insect also cropped up in Devon in the 1990s and, although that infestation has probably been stamped out, further outbreaks are by no means impossible. As well as being transported in timber, the termites can be carried in soil moved around in the horticultural trade.

Wood on the menu

Although they do little or no harm to our crops, these wood-feeding termites can certainly do a lot of damage in the garden, and even more in the house. In some parts of Europe it is not possible to sell a house without a certificate proving that

Reticulitermes grassei

Looks: Pale, soft bodies, just a few millimetres long

Food: Wood

When: Most of year; only seen when reproductive forms swarming

Where: Spain, Portugal, and France

Part of a colony of the termite *Reticulitermes lucifugus*, living in an old log. Most are youngsters, some with developing wings destined to become kings and queens. There are also a few workers, and a large-jawed soldier near the centre. Most of these termites are only 3-4 mm long, but the queens, whose bodies are swollen with eggs, can reach 8 mm.

A close-up shot of *Reticulitermes lucifugus* showing the soft, pale bodies. The insects grow up without passing through a chrysalis stage.

Reticulitermes lucifugus

Looks: Pale, soft bodies, just a few millimetres long

Food: Wood

When: Most of year; only seen when reproductive forms swarming

Where: Mediterranean region

it is free from termites. Tree stumps and large logs are favourite nesting sites, but garden sheds, decking and fence posts are all readily attacked, especially at or below ground level. Vineyards in southern Europe frequently have to replace the posts used to support the vines, and the vines themselves are not immune to attack by the termites. The insects excavate their living quarters with their jaws and digest the timber as they go, and all this goes on virtually unseen – until it is too late to do anything about it. In areas known to harbour termites, all building timbers should be treated with a good, long-lasting insecticide.

Termites have pale, soft bodies, rarely more than a few millimetres long, and are often called white ants, although they are not related to ants. They belong to an order called Isoptera and their closest relatives are the cockroaches. All termites are social insects, living in colonies that each consist of a king and a queen, a few large-jawed soldiers and a host of workers. Some tropical colonies contain millions of termites, all the offspring of the queen, but those of the European species rarely have more than a few thousand insects.

Unless their home is broken into, the insects are seen only when young reproductive forms – new kings and queens – swarm into the air on their flimsy wings. They do not remain airborne for long and they pair up on the ground after breaking off their wings. Couples that avoid being eaten by birds and other predators then search for places in which to start new colonies. New colonies can also develop by fragmentation, when a group on the edge of an existing colony moves away and rears a new king and queen. Only king and queen termites ever have wings.

BUGS

Although 'bug' is commonly used for any insect or other
creepy-crawly, the name should really be used only for
members of the large insect order called the Hemiptera. There
are over 7,000 European species and they are incredibly varied,
ranging from tiny aphids and scale insects to shield bugs and
giant predatory bugs up to 8 cm in length. They include
both winged and wingless species. Shield bugs and many of
the other larger species are often mistaken for beetles, but
they can usually be distinguished from the latter because the
front wings overlap and have membranous tips. The front
wings of beetles are tough and horny and usually meet in
the mid-line with no overlap. The most significant difference between the two groups lies in their feeding habits:
beetles have biting jaws, while bugs have piercing beaks and
feed by sucking liquids from plants or other animals.

Bugs that are pests

Our garden pests are the herbivorous species that feed on
sap. Some have toxic saliva that damages the areas around
the feeding sites, often producing conspicuous white spots,
and many, especially aphids, carry viral diseases from plant
to plant. Bugs all grow up without passing through a pupal
or chrysalis stage. The young stages, known as nymphs, are
quite like the adults, although they have no wings at first.
The wings gradually develop on the outside of the body,
getting larger at each moult or skin change until the adult
stage is reached. Systemic insecticides **(see p. 42)** are
particularly useful for controlling these sap-sucking insects.

The Common Green Shield
Bug is a typical bug in both
its form and habits.

The omnivorous Forest Bug, up to 1.5 cm long, lives mainly on trees and shrubs and, although it may attack fruit, it does little harm in the garden.

FOREST BUG
Pentatoma rufipes

This bug is common in many gardens throughout the summer, but especially in those with fruit trees or shrubberies or those surrounded by hedges. It is one of the shield bugs, which are so-called because of their general shape, and it can be recognised by its rather square 'shoulders' and the bright orange or yellow spot at the tip of the triangular scutellum (a plate on the hindmost parts of the thorax). Shield bugs are also known as stink bugs because many of them release pungent fluids from glands on the sides of the body when they are molested. The often sickly smell and taste deter birds that attempt to peck at the bugs, and some people experience nausea and headache after coming into contact with the insects. The Forest Bug is an omnivorous insect and, although it sometimes plunges its beak into cherries and other fruit for a drink, it does no real damage and more than makes up for any mischief by destroying caterpillars and other harmful insects on the trees and shrubs. The bugs spend the winter as nymphs, hibernating under loose bark and other such secluded spots, often in garden sheds.

Forest Bug

Looks: Square 'shoulders'; orange or yellow spot on centre of body

Food: Some fruits

When: Spring, summer

Where: Britain and Continental Europe

Graphosoma italicum is a common shield bug of southern and central Europe and particularly attracted to carrots and other umbelliferous plants. About 10 mm long, its bold coloration indicates that it has a foul taste (see p. 14).

Graphosoma italicum

This is a very striking shield bug of southern and central Europe, where it causes a certain amount of damage to carrots and other umbelliferous plants by sucking out large quantities of sap. Its bold black and red colours warn of a seriously unpleasant taste and birds usually give it a wide berth. On the plus side, however, the colours make the bug easily visible to the gardener, and if numbers are high they can be removed by hand and destroyed. But be prepared for the smell, for these insects are among the worst of the stink bugs. Wear rubber gloves if you plan to remove them by hand. The bug is active for much of the year, but becomes dormant in the coldest winter months.

Graphosoma italicum

Looks: Black and red striped body

Food: Carrots and other umbellifers

When: Spring, summer

Where: Mainly southern and central Europe

ABOVE LEFT The Green Vegetable Bug, a recent arrival in British gardens, can be distinguished from the Common Green Shield Bug by its pale, transparent wing-tips. Both insects are about 10 mm long.

ABOVE RIGHT: The colourful nymph of the Green Vegetable Bug. The red spots around the abdomen are the stink glands.

GREEN VEGETABLE BUG
Nezara viridula

Also called the Southern Green Shield Bug, this is another smelly shield bug and one that is hard to see as it sits quietly removing sap from our plants. The adult is usually bright green all over, although some individuals have a pale brown or yellowish head and thorax. The nymph is much more conspicuous, with white spots and a bright red border to its abdomen. The bug attacks a wide range of flowers and vegetables and can be especially damaging to peas and potatoes. It is also a minor nuisance to citrus growers in southern Europe. It hibernates as an adult or a fully grown nymph and can produce two or three generations each year. It is widely distributed over the southern half of Europe and has recently become established in the south of England after arriving with imported produce. Although it cannot survive prolonged frost, it may spread further north if the climate continues to warm up.

Green Vegetable Bug

Looks: Bright green; nymph has white spots and red border to abdomen

Food: Especially damaging to peas and potatoes

When: Spring, summer

Where: Southern Britain; southern and central Europe

A mating pair of Common Green Shield Bugs. The wing-tip membranes are brown and often quite opaque, in contrast to the transparent membranes of the Green Vegetable Bug.

COMMON GREEN SHIELD BUG
Palomena prasina

The adult is very similar to the Green Vegetable Bug but has a brown and quite opaque membrane at the wing-tip. The nymph has a more or less circular outline and is green all over. Adults assume a bronzy green colour before going into hibernation in the autumn and revert to their bright green colour when they wake in the spring. The bug feeds on a wide range of woody and herbaceous plants and can often be found on garden raspberries, although it rarely causes any damage in British gardens and control measures are not necessary. It is a minor pest of beans and other leguminous plants on the Continent.

Common Green Shield Bug

Looks: Bright to bronze green with opaque brown membrane at wing tip

Food: Various food plants including peas and raspberries

When: Spring, summer

Where: Britain and Continental Europe

The pale patches on the Brassica Bug range from white or cream to orange and red, but the bug can be distinguished from *Eurydema dominulus* (below) by its thoracic pattern and its more rounded rear end. Both bugs are about 8 mm long.

BRASSICA BUG
Eurydema oleracea

This is an extremely variable bug. The dark areas are usually shiny blue or green, while the pale spots range from cream through yellow and orange to red. The bug feeds mainly on plants of the cabbage family and is a serious pest of brassicas on the Continent, but it is uncommon in the British Isles and causes no damage. Another brassica pest is ***Eurydema dominulus***, which is usually black and red, although the red may be replaced by yellow or cream and the dark areas may be metallic green. The insect then resembles the Brassica Bug. Although common on the continent, it is quite rare in the British Isles.

Brassica Bug

Looks: Shiny blue or green with cream, yellow or orange spots

Food: Brassicas

When: Spring, summer

Where: Britain and Continental Europe

Eurydema dominulus

Looks: Striking; usually black and red but can be yellow or cream and green

Food: Brassicas

When: Spring, summer

Where: Britain and Continental Europe

Eurydema dominulus is a common pest of cabbages and other brassicas on the Continent. Most specimens have red patches instead of yellow.

PEAR LACEBUG
Stephanitis pyri

Yellow mottling of pear and apple leaves often indicates the presence of the Pear Lacebug. Not to be confused with the useful and unrelated lacewings **(see p. 14)**, it is a pretty little insect with conspicuously netted and largely transparent wings, although it is only about 3 mm long and you need a good lens to appreciate its beauty. Several lacebug species may live in our gardens, but the Pear Lacebug can be recognised by the relatively huge 'cut-glass' dome on its thorax. It lives on the undersides of the leaves, draining the sap from them and spattering them with its brown droppings, which at first sight might be mistaken for spider mites. Badly affected leaves may become completely yellow and then turn black before falling prematurely. Two or three generations are produced during the year, with adults of the autumn generation hibernating in bark crevices and leaf litter. Although called the Pear Lacebug, the insect is often more common on apples on the Continent and it also attacks cherries and plums and other rosaceous trees. Abundant in France, it has only recently appeared in the British Isles, but it could well become established as a pest here if the climate continues to warm up. Insecticidal soaps or pyrethroid-based sprays can be used against heavy infestations, making sure that the spray reaches the undersides of the leaves.

The Pear Lacebug is a common pest of pears and apples, living on the undersides of the leaves and causing severe mottling. Its see-through wings help to camouflage it on the leaves. It can be distinguished from other similar lacebugs by the glassy dome on the thorax, clearly seen in the right-hand picture.

Pear Lacebug

Looks: Fairly transparent 'netted' wings; 3 mm. Cut-glass dome on thorax

Food: Apples, pears, cherries, plums

When: Spring, summer

Where: Much of southern Europe. A recent arrival in Britain

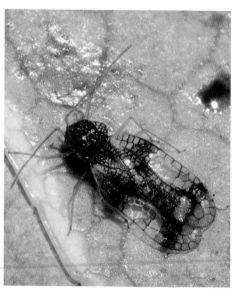

ABOVE RIGHT: The Pieris Lacebug has a very dark thorax. It lives on the undersides of pieris leaves, removing sap and causing the leaves to become streaked and spotted with yellow (ABOVE LEFT).

PIERIS LACEBUG
Stephanitis takeyai

Another alien, that arrived in Europe from Japan in the 1990s, this is much darker than the Pear Lacebug and it has a dark thoracic dome. The black bands on the wings combine with the body to produce a vaguely human-like shape. The insect feeds mainly on *Pieris* shrubs, causing severe yellowing of the leaves and premature leaf-fall if the infestation is heavy. Less often, it attacks rhododendrons. Eggs are laid in the leaves during the summer and they hatch in the following spring, so removal of the worst-affected leaves in late summer or autumn will get rid of a lot of eggs and lessen the problem for the following year. Infestations on small plants can be reduced by removing the insects by hand – or even shaking the branches to dislodge them. Adults will fly back to the plants, but many of the flightless nymphs will perish on the ground. Larger plants are best treated with horticultural oil or a systemic insecticide. The insect is now well established in gardens in southern England and is most common on plants growing in exposed places – possibly because these plants support fewer spiders and other predators than those growing in shadier places.

Pieris Lacebug

Looks: Two black bands on wings; dark thoracic dome

Food: Mainly *pieris* shrubs, sometimes rhododendrons

When: Spring, summer

Where: Continental Europe, southern England

RHODODENDRON LACEBUG
Stephanitis rhododendri

Resembling the Pear Lacebug, this insect is equally attractive when seen through a magnifying glass, although it has a dark thoracic dome and only a single dark band on the front wings. It can be a troublesome pest of rhododendrons and azaleas, especially those growing in dry and sunny positions. Under 4 mm long, it feeds on the undersides of young leaves during the summer and causes yellow or bronze mottling of the upper surface. In common with the Pear Lacebug, it covers the lower leaf surfaces with brown droppings. Badly affected leaves should be removed in the autumn: this should reduce the population because these leaves are most likely to be carrying the eggs. The latter are inserted into the mid-rib or into young shoots towards the end of the summer and brown, corky tissue usually develops around the egg-laying site. The eggs hatch in the spring. The bug was introduced to Europe from North America early in the 20th century and was very common for a time in the British Isles – as is the case with many introductions before their natural enemies catch up with them – but it is now much less common and is not a problem. It rarely, if ever flies, so re-infestation of plants after its removal is unlikely. Not all rhododendron cultivars are equally susceptible, and the wild *R. ponticum* rarely seems to be affected.

Rhododendron Lacebug

Looks: Dark thoracic dome; one dark band on front wings

Food: Rhododendrons and azaleas

When: Spring, summer

Where: Continental Europe, rarely a pest in Britain

Tarnished Plant Bug

Looks: Hairy; wings dull yellow mottled with brown

Food: Many wild and cultivated plants

When: Spring, summer

Where: Britain and Continental Europe

TARNISHED PLANT BUG
Lygus rugulipennis

Feeding on a wide variety of wild and cultivated plants, it attacks leaves, flowers and fruits and causes them to develop white spots around its feeding punctures (**see p. 95**). Affected flowers may be distorted. Damage is not usually serious, however, and there is no need to fight the bug. The insect is rather hairy and its wings are normally dull yellow with brown mottling. There is a prominent pale triangle towards the tip of each wing. Adults can be found throughout the year although they spend the winter in a dormant state in leaf litter and other similar debris.

The Tarnished Plant Bug, which is 4–5 mm long, feeds on a wide variety of plants but rarely causes any serious damage.

The Lucerne Bug feeds mainly on leguminous plants, but sometimes causes distortion in chrysanthemum flowers. Up to 10 mm long, it can be recognised by the pale, often greenish triangles near the rear end and also by the two black spots on the thorax.

LUCERNE BUG
Adelphocoris lineolatus

The Lucerne Bug is usually recognised by the pale triangle towards the tip of each front wing and also by the two black spots just behind the head. It also has very spiny legs. Adults can be found throughout the summer, feeding on the leaves, flowers and young fruits of a wide range of herbaceous plants, although they prefer leguminous species. Garden chrysanthemums are sometimes attacked and the flowers may be distorted by the bugs' feeding activities, but serious damage is rare.

Lucerne Bug

Looks: Pale triangle on front wings; two black spots behind head

Food: Leguminous plants; also chrysanthemums

When: Spring, summer

Where: Britain and Continental Europe

COMMON GREEN CAPSID
Lygocoris pabulinus

Abundant in all kinds of vegetation, this bug is a frequent, although not very serious, pest in the garden. It is one of several quite similar oval green bugs, but can be distinguished from most by the greyish-brown membrane at the wing-tip and also by the pale brown spines on its legs. The insect passes the winter in the egg stage on various trees and shrubs, and then feeds on them in the spring. Many individuals move to potatoes and other herbaceous plants as spring turns into summer. Leaves, flowers and fruits are all acceptable to the bugs, and infested areas are commonly distorted. Leaves often develop small holes around the feeding punctures, while flowers such as chrysanthemums and dahlias often fail to open properly if the bugs have attacked the buds. Raspberries are favourite targets, the bugs piercing the developing drupelets and often causing them to shrivel. The fruit then has dry brown patches. Insecticidal sprays can be used if bugs are noticed on crops.

Common Green Capsid

Looks: Oval green bug; greyish brown membrane at wing tip; spines on legs

Food: Most plants, esp. potatoes, raspberries

When: Spring, summer

Where: Britain and Continental Europe

The Common Green Capsid abounds in many gardens, feeding on a wide range of leaves and fruits, although it does not cause serious damage. It is 5–7 mm long. The greyish brown membrane at the tip of each front wing distinguishes it from several superficially similar green bugs.

The Potato Capsid can be a nuisance in the potato patch, but it is in no way confined to potato plants. It is often responsible for the distortion of strawberry fruits. The two black spots on the thorax help to identify this species, which is up to 8 mm long.

POTATO CAPSID
Calocoris norwegicus

Usually distinguished from the very similar Common Green Capsid by the two black dots just behind the head, although these are not always visible, this bug feeds on a wide range of wild and cultivated herbaceous plants in the summer and can be a nuisance in the potato patch, causing distortion of the leaves as well as necrotic spots and small holes **(see p. 95)**. It can also damage the flowers, although this has no effect on crop yields. Chrysanthemums and strawberries can also suffer, and if the strawberry flowers are attacked the fruit may be severely distorted. If the insect becomes a problem on potatoes it can be controlled by spraying or dusting. A pyrethroid–based insecticide is best for strawberries.

Potato Capsid

Looks: Green with two black dots behind head

Food: Particularly potatoes

When: Spring, summer

Where: Britain and Continental Europe

APPLE CAPSID
Plesiocoris rugicollis

This bug is responsible for many of the corky patches commonly found on the skins of apples. The insect is very like the two previous species but lacks the black spots of the Potato Capsid and has a fairly rough thorax compared with the smooth and shiny surface of the Common Green Capsid – although you will need a lens to spot the difference here. The Apple Capsid also *may* have a good deal of yellow on the head and thorax. The adult insect occurs mainly around midsummer, when eggs are laid on the bark. The eggs do not hatch until the following spring, when the young bugs attack the opening leaves and cause them to develop brown spots around the feeding punctures. They soon turn their attention to the young fruits and feed there for the rest of their lives. The bug is less common in the British Isles than in the past and rarely causes extensive damage.

Apple Capsid

Looks: Rough surface to thorax; may have yellow on head and thorax

Food: Apples

When: Most damage caused in spring

Where: Continental Europe; less common in British Isles

The Apple Capsid feeds on apple leaves as soon as they open in the spring, but soon turns its attention to the young fruits. Corky patches may develop on affected fruit, but the damage is rarely important. It is 5–6 mm long.

The unmistakable Potato Leafhopper is up to about 8 mm long. It feeds on a wide range of herbaceous plants in the summer.

Potato Leafhopper

Looks: Variable black and yellow pattern

Food: Potatoes, mint

When: Summer

Where: Britain and Continental Europe

POTATO LEAFHOPPER
Eupteryx aurata

Although it has a variable black and yellow pattern, this species is not likely to be confused with any other bug. It can be found throughout the summer on a wide range of herbaceous plants, including stinging nettles and mints as well as potatoes. In common with many other bugs, it has toxic saliva that kills the leaf cells around its feeding sites, so infested leaves exhibit numerous pale spots and these often open up into holes as the leaves expand. Heavily infested plants may become pale all over as the insects' feeding sites link up.

ROSE LEAFHOPPER
Edwardsiana rosae

This largely yellow hopper behaves like the Potato Leafhopper but lives on roses, especially those growing against walls and fences. Fatty acids and pyrethroid-based insecticides will control these pests when necessary, but numbers are rarely high enough to justify insecticidal treatment. Several other leafhopper species live on apple trees and other members of the rose family. Turn over almost any leaf in late summer and you will see these little pale green or yellowish insects hopping or flying for cover. Again, despite their large numbers, they do not do any appreciable harm to the trees.

Rose Leafhopper

Looks: Mainly yellow

Food: Roses

When: Summer

Where: Britain and Continental Europe

Philaenus spumarius

Blobs of white froth on the vegetation in early summer are the work of young froghoppers, the commonest of several species being *Philaenus spumarius*. The insects pass the winter in the egg stage and when the eggs hatch in the spring the tiny nymphs plug their beaks into the host plants and start to suck out the sap. They soon surround themselves with froth, which they produce by pumping air into a fluid discharged from the rear end. The froth keeps the little green nymphs moist and also protects them from some of their enemies – although some wasps know exactly what is hiding beneath it and regularly prey on the nymphs. Because it appears in the spring at about the same time as the Cuckoo, the froth is commonly known as 'cuckoo-spit', while the insects themselves are often called 'spittlebugs'. Remove the 'spit' with your fingers if you don't like the look of it, but the insects inside it rarely cause any damage. The adult insects, frog-like in their appearance and jumping ability, live freely on all kinds of plants in the summer and, although very common, they do no harm to our garden plants.

Philaenus spumarius

Looks: Like a miniature frog: brown with variable pale markings

Food: Many plants

When: Spring and early summer

Where: Britain and Continental Europe

Cuckoo-spit, which occurs on a wide range of shrubs and herbaceous plants in the spring, has nothing to do with Cuckoos! It houses the nymphs of various froghoppers, notably those of *Philaenus spumarius* (inset), which lives up to its name in both appearance and jumping ability. It is about 7 mm long and, apart from perhaps spoiling the look of our plants with its froth, it does no harm in the garden.

The Rhododendron Leafhopper, up to 10 mm long, is an unmistakable insect, often seen basking on the tops of rhododendron leaves.

Rhododendron Leafhopper

Looks: Adult is green with red spots and streaks on wings

Food: Rhododendrons

When: Summer and autumn

Where: Britain and Continental Europe

RHODODENDRON LEAFHOPPER
Graphocephala fennahi

This colourful bug is unlikely to be confused with any other insect although the adult's red and green coloration makes it quite difficult to spot on the rhododendrons. The pale yellowish-green nymphs live under the leaves but the adults, around for much of the summer and autumn, often bask on top of the leaves. They lay overwintering eggs in the flower buds and this is when they do the damage: a fungus can enter the slits cut by the egg-laying females and this causes the disease known as 'bud blast' which can kill the buds and sometimes whole twigs. The insects are not usually common enough for their feeding activities to harm the plants directly. Removal of dead and dying buds will control both the leafhopper and the fungus, but spraying with a systemic insecticide in late summer, before the eggs are laid, is probably more efficient on large areas.

The Buffalo Treehopper at rest. Up to 10 mm long, it is easily recognised by its bright green colour and the sharp spine at the rear of its thoracic shield.

BUFFALO TREEHOPPER
Stictocephalus bisonia

This American insect is now established in many parts of western Europe although not in the British Isles. The bright green adult is recognised by the two horns at the front and the sharp spine towards the rear. It feeds on a wide range of woody and herbaceous plants, including vines, taking sap from soft shoots. Feeding damage is not serious, but young woody shoots can be harmed when females cut slits in them for their eggs. Winter is passed in the egg stage and adults can be found throughout summer. Buffalo Treehoppers jump and fly well, but when disturbed, hide by scuttling round to the far side of the stem.

Buffalo Treehopper

Looks: Bright green with two horns and sharp spine

Food: Many plants including vines

When: Spring, summer

Where: Many parts of western Europe but not British Isles

Cicada orni, common in many wooded gardens in southern Europe, is one of the biggest and noisiest of the European cicadas. Its stout beak has no trouble in piercing the bark of trees to obtain the sap. Up to 4 cm long, it can be recognised by the conspicuous black spots on its front wings.

Noisy cicadas

Many parts of southern Europe resound to the shrill calls of cicadas during summer. Living in wooded areas, these large bugs are a problem only to gardeners with specimen trees and shrubs. Young cicadas spend several years in the soil, plugging their beaks into the roots and sucking out sap, and large colonies can weaken plants. When mature, the nymphs climb the trees and shrubs and moult into the adult stage – pale green at first and greyish-brown when their skins and wings have hardened. They continue to take sap from the plants, but serious damage is unusual and the worst thing about them may be the continuous, piercing noise emitted by the males. Of several species living in southern Europe *Cicada orni* is most likely to be seen in gardens.

Cicada orni

Looks: Adult pale green to greyish brown

Food: Various roots

When: Spring, summer

Where: Southern Europe

APHIDS

Aphids, familiar to every gardener as 'greenfly' and 'blackfly', are among the most abundant of our garden pests. Few plants escape the attentions of at least one of the 500 or so species living in the British Isles. These small, soft, pear-shaped insects are true bugs **(see p. 95)** and all are equipped with needle-like beaks with which they pierce their plant hosts and suck out the sap. Some species feed on a wide range of host plants, but most are more fussy and stick to a single species or just a few related ones. Many have complex life histories, involving both winged and wingless generations. Most species spend their whole lives on one host species, but some, including the Black Bean Aphid and several other garden pests, require two separate plant species to complete their life cycles.

Where aphids attack

Young leaves and tender young stems are the usual targets for aphids, many of which feed continuously throughout their lives. The insect plugs its beak into the host's phloem tissue, which carries food around the plant, and relies largely on the pressure in the phloem tubes to force the sap through its beak and into its mouth, although it can use its own muscles to pump up the sap if the pressure in the plant should fall for any reason. Some aphids get their food from the host's roots and some even attack the host's flowers.

The sap ingested by the aphids is very rich in sugar, but it does not contain much in the way of amino acids that the aphids need for their own growth. In order to get enough amino acids, therefore, the insects have to take in far more sugar than is good for them and they must get rid of the excess. They do this by passing it out of the rear end as drop-lets of sticky honeydew, although the sugar passed out is not quite the same as that taken in at the front. The honeydew coats the plants and anything underneath them, as anyone who has parked a car under a lime tree or a sycamore knows only too well. Bees, wasps and some butterflies all enjoy the syrupy feast, and ants are so fond of it that several species treat the aphids like cows, guarding them carefully and stroking them gently to induce them to give up their 'milk'. Some ants carry aphids into their underground nests, where the aphids plug into roots, and some even build 'cowsheds' to house the

Female aphids can pump out up to 10 youngsters each day and the babies can reproduce when only ten days old. In fact, they already have their own babies developing inside them when they are born. Aphid babies always emerge rear-end first and the process is easy to watch in the garden during the summer. Most of our aphids are only 2-3 mm long and individuals rarely live for more than a few weeks.

aphids above ground **(see p. 283)**. Any honeydew remaining on the leaves is rapidly colonised by various fungi, which form a black coating on the foliage in the summer. This is especially noticeable on lime and oak trees. Even the honeydew that falls to the ground is not wasted: the sugar stimulates bacterial activity, which in turn leads to the production of plant-nourishing nitrates – so the aphids can be said to repay some of the damage they do when they remove the sap!

Females in charge

For much of the summer, almost all the aphids that we see on our plants are females. They go in for virgin birth, technically known as parthenogenesis or asexual reproduction, and each adult can produce as many as ten babies in a single day. The youngsters can give birth themselves when only ten days old, so it is no wonder that the populations build up so quickly. Most of the early summer aphids are wingless but, as their numbers build up and the colonies become crowded, winged females begin to appear and they fly off to colonise fresh plants and produce more generations of wingless individuals. Some species, including the Shallot Aphid, have abandoned sexual reproduction completely and go on producing parthenogenetic females throughout the year. In other species, however, males and sexual females appear towards the end of the summer and, after mating, the females lay tough-shelled eggs that survive the winter and hatch in the following spring. These overwintering eggs are usually quite large – almost as large as the females themselves in some species – and the females rarely lay more than five or six such eggs. Depending on the species, eggs may be laid on the summer host or on a different host species. The Black Bean Aphid, for example, normally lays its overwintering eggs on spindle twigs **(see p. 118)**. But even those aphid species that normally lay eggs in the autumn can continue with virgin birth throughout the year if the weather remains mild.

An individual aphid does not need a lot of food, but when hundreds of aphids plunge their beaks into a plant and continuously drink its sap, it is inevitable that the plant will suffer. Small plants may become stunted and drop some of their leaves, and they may even die, but more often the leaves of an infested plant become crinkled as a result of damage to veins and other tissues, and the aphids are then largely concealed in the folds and pockets. Affected leaves may also become discoloured as a result of the aphids' toxic saliva, and infested flower buds often fail to open. Even large trees can be damaged by aphids: early leaf-fall is a common symptom, leading to slowing of growth.

Although direct feeding damage by aphids can be a problem, the insects actually do more damage by transmitting disease-causing viruses. The viruses are picked up when the aphids feed and are spread when flying aphids move away and plunge their beaks into new plants. Potato leaf roll, transmitted by various aphids and other sap-sucking insects, is one of several destructive potato diseases. It causes the leaves to thicken and roll up, with severe reduction in photosynthesis and food distribution and reduction in tuber size. Other well-known aphid-borne virus diseases include raspberry mosaic, which causes the leaves to develop yellow patches, and tomato fern-leaf disease, in which the leaflets become very narrow and incapable of efficient photosynthesis.

Aphid predators

Luckily for the gardener, aphids have many natural enemies that help to keep the pests under control. Warblers, tits and many other birds seek out aphid colonies during the summer, and the tits also do a good job of finding and eating the overwintering eggs on trees and bushes. But the best-known enemies of the aphids, of course, are the ladybirds, several

The ladybirds are among our most important allies in the war against aphids. Here, a Two-spot Ladybird (*Adalia bipunctata*) is munching its way through a colony of Black Bean Aphids.

species of which live in our gardens and wage continuous war on the aphids. Larvae **(see p. 14)** and adults are equally voracious and can munch their way through as many as 50 aphids every day. Lacewings and their larvae also feed on aphids, as do the larvae of many hoverfly species. It is worth planting a variety of flowers close to crops susceptible to aphids in order to attract hoverflies. Having refuelled on pollen and nectar from the flowers, the flies are quite likely to lay their eggs among the troublesome aphid colonies. It is now possible to buy ladybirds and green lacewings for release into your garden, and you can also buy or make 'houses' in which the insects can spend the winter **(see p. 14)**.

But the predatory insects don't have it all their own way. Although the aphids do not look as if they could put up much of a fight, they do kick out quite vigorously with their long back legs when ladybirds or other predators appear on the scene. When one member of a colony is attacked, its thrashing movements are detected by its neighbours, and they also start kicking. The aphids can also repel boarders with waxy secretions from their cornicles – the tubular outgrowths, also called siphunculi, at the rear of the body. Daubed onto the face of the attacker, the wax quickly solidifies and immobilises the jaws. In addition, the cornicles release odours known as alarm pheromones that cause neighbouring aphids to move away: they often fall to the ground, where they are well out of harm's way.

Aphids are frequently parasitised by species of *Aphidius*, which are minute relatives of the wasps. The parasite places a single egg in each aphid, and the resulting wasp grub feeds inside the aphid until fully grown. It then pupates inside the aphid skin and a new adult wasp emerges through a circular hole in the top. You can obtain *Aphidius* from suppliers to combat aphid infestations in the greenhouse.

Other aphid controls

Although the natural predators and parasites are very helpful, we sometimes need to step up the control measures. A wide range of insecticides can be used to combat the aphids, including a few systemic products that are absorbed into the plant tissues and kill the insects when they ingest the sap. Systemic insecticides are fine for protecting roses and other ornamental plants and have the advantage that they reach aphids hidden in contorted leaves, but they are not usually recommended for vegetable crops. Contact insecticides based on pyrethrins or pyrethroids are very effective but, whatever contact insecticide is used, care must be taken to spray only the aphid colonies: spray drifting onto flowers may kill bees and other harmless and potentially useful insects. Applying insecticides at dusk, when most of the bees have gone home, will also minimise the risk of harming useful insects.

Soapy water is a traditional and quite effective weapon against aphids, working by destroying their waxy coats and causing them to dry out. Insecticidal soaps, based on a mixture of fatty acids and compounds of sodium or potassium, work in the same way and they are very safe, but you can often rid your plants of aphids with a quick squirt of plain water from the hose. Fingers also do the job, for the soft-bodied aphids are very easily squashed – and no other insects are harmed.

Various aromatic herbs are known to repel aphids, and a bit of companion planting **(see p. 32)** is always a good idea. You can also use a spray made from stinging nettles: soak 200 gm of young nettles in a bucket of water for a few days. Then use the water undiluted to spray your aphid-infested plants. It's very effective – and perhaps rather odd because nettles themselves support lots of aphids! Rhubarb leaves can be used instead of nettles, but they must be boiled to extract the oxalic acid. Use 500 gm of leaves to a litre of water, but don't use your best pans for this. Some people recommend adding a bit of washing up liquid or soap powder. Ring-fencing with plants to decoy the aphids away from the crops is another way of combating the pests.

TOP TIP

Lavender growing with roses can keep down the populations of Rose Aphids without hurting the bees, while savory – both winter and summer varieties – is said to protect beans and other crops from blackfly. Sage and thyme are worth planting at the ends of vegetable rows. Garlic is also good, and if you don't want to grow it you can treat the aphids to a shower of water to which you have added a few crushed garlic cloves. They won't like it at all!

BLACK BEAN APHID
Aphis fabae

Commonly known as 'blackfly', this is one of the most familiar of our garden aphids. It is most often seen on broad beans and runner beans, but it can use a wide range of other wild and garden plants, notably spinach, poppies and fever-few. There are several other similar species, but only *A. fabae* infests beans. Its life cycle is fairly typical of those aphids that alternate between woody and herbaceous host plants. The insect passes the winter in the egg stage on spindle bushes or, less often, on viburnum and mock orange. The eggs hatch in the spring and colonies quickly build up on the twigs and young shoots and leaves **(see p. 114)**. All are wingless at first, but, as with most other aphids, winged forms develop when the colonies become crowded and they fly off to colonise more shrubs or, towards the end of spring, to invade their summer hosts.

Colonies on the summer hosts are all wingless at first, but winged individuals soon appear and quickly spread to other plants. At the end of summer the insects fly back to the winter hosts, where wingless, egg-laying females are produced. These mate with winged males arriving from the summer hosts and lay their eggs to begin the cycle again. Infesta-tions on the summer hosts tend to congregate on the tender shoot tips and young leaves, where they are easily destroyed by squashing. It is a good plan to remove the shoot-tips from broad bean plants once the pods have started to swell. This will reduce the problem, but not eliminate it, for the aphids will probably turn their attention to the young pods. Pyrethrin-based contact sprays can be used at this stage, but not while the flowers are open and still attracting bees. Leafy elder twigs stuck among the broad bean plants are said to keep blackfly at bay, although the elder itself supports another very similar aphid called **Aphis sambuci**. This is sometimes so abundant that the young elder shoots appear quite black.

TOP TIP

Leafy elder twigs placed among your broad beans are a natural way to keep blackfly at bay.

Black Bean Aphid

Looks: Tiny black insects

Food: Broad beans, runner beans, spinach

When: Spring, summer

Where: Britain and Continental Europe

CABBAGE APHID
Brevicoryne brassicae

This aphid infests cabbages and other brassicas, including swedes, radishes and oil-seed rape. The latter is being grown in increasing amounts on farmland and is a major host for the aphid during the winter. The adult insects are between 1.5 and 3 mm long and are greyish–green with a coating of pale grey waxy powder. Winged individuals have a number of black bars on the top of the abdomen. Populations are at their greatest in July and August, at which time one can find extensive 'carpets' of aphids on and under the leaves. At other times the insects may be more scattered. Many populations continue to feed and breed during the winter months, but in cooler regions the species lays eggs and passes the winter in this stage. Heavy infestations can severely weaken the plants simply by removing large quantities of sap, and small plants often wilt and die under the onslaught. The aphids also transmit several viruses that can further weaken the plants. Small clusters of aphids can be squashed, but badly infested leaves are best removed and destroyed. Widespread infestations can be controlled by spraying with insecticidal soaps or organic pyrethrin-based compounds. Stumps of broccoli and sprouts should be removed and destroyed as soon as the crop has been harvested, in order to eliminate any eggs or active aphids.

Mealy grey Cabbage Aphids sometimes completely cover brassica leaves in the summer months, causing them to become pale and crinkled.

TOP TIP

Try adding crushed garlic cloves to a watering can and spray aphids with it to discourage them.

Cabbage Aphid

Looks: Greyish green with waxy powder coating

Food: Cabbages and other brassicas, oil-seed rape

When: Most of the year

Where: Britain and Continental Europe

An adult Pea Aphid with a couple of nymphs. Notice the long pair of cornicles at the rear of the adult.

Pea Aphid

Looks: Pale green or pink with long legs and cornicles

Food: Peas and other legumes

When: Spring, summer

Where: Britain and Continental Europe

PEA APHID
Acyrthosiphon pisum

Infesting peas and many other wild and cultivated legumes, this aphid is between 2.5 and 4.5 mm long, it is pale green or pink with relatively long legs and long cornicles. The complete life cycle takes place on leguminous plants, where the aphids overwinter as eggs or active forms. Populations normally peak in midsummer. Direct damage to peas is rarely serious, although heavy infestations can cause stunting and yellowing of the pods and a reduction in yield. More serious are the numerous viruses, such as pea leaf-roll virus and pea mosaic virus, transmitted by the aphid. Treating the young plants with organic pyrethrin-based sprays will keep the aphids under control.

LUPIN APHID
Macrosiphum albifrons

Although a relatively new pest in the British Isles, this aphid has spread rapidly since its introduction from North America round about 1980 and it is now widely distributed. It is a plump, greyish-green insect up to 5 mm long and very conspicuous when clustering on the leaves and flower spikes of our garden lupins. The species reproduces entirely by parthenogenesis or virgin birth and spends the winter on the lupin buds at or just below ground level. Our native ladybirds and other predators have not yet added this aphid to their menus, but perhaps the recently arrived Harlequin Ladybird **(see p. 162)** will have some effect on it. Various systemic insecticides can be used to control the pest, as can insecticidal soaps and contact insecticides based on natural or synthetic pyrethrins, but squashing them with the fingers is as effective as anything else!

TOP TIP

The simplest way to deal with Lupin Aphids is to squash them with your fingers.

Lupin Aphid

Looks: Plump, greyish green, to 5 mm long

Food: Lupins

When: Spring, summer

Where: American insect now present in Europe

Lupin Aphids are among the largest aphids in our gardens.

The Cypress Aphid causes brown patches to develop on *leylandii* hedges, but it is not the only insect to attack these hedges. Cypress bark beetles of the genus *Phloeosinus* attack the trunks and branches, burrowing just under the bark like the elm bark beetles (see p. 181) and causing whole branches or even complete trees to turn brown and die. But these areas lack the black mould associated with the Cypress Aphid. Look for the beetles' tunnels on the trunks. At least three species of *Phloeosinus* occur on the continent, and two have recently been discovered in southern England. Plants weakened by drought seem to be particularly susceptible.

Cypress Aphid

Looks: Light brown with grey or red tinge

Food: *Leylandii* trees

When: Present most of the year

Where: Britain and Continental Europe

CYPRESS APHID
Cinara cupressi

This aphid is responsible for most of the ugly brown patches that are becoming increasingly common on *leylandii* hedges. Affected hedges may take years to recover and some never do, but with *leylandii* being at the top of many people's hate-lists, the neighbours may consider the aphid to be an ally rather than a pest! The insect is about 4 mm long and is light brown, often with a grey or light red tinge, and it is very hard to spot on the twigs. First indications of its presence are yellowing patches of foliage in the summer, and then the leaves gradually turn brown and die. Drought and 'sunburn' can cause similar damage, but this is not accompanied by the sooty fungal growth that is always associated with aphid damage. The Cypress Aphid is one of those species that need only a single host species to complete their life cycles. Eggs laid in the autumn survive the winter and produce a new generation of aphids in the spring, but in areas with mild winters the aphids can remain active and reproduce asexually throughout the year. As well as infesting *leylandii* trees and hedges, the aphid attacks the related Lawson's Cypress and some other conifers. Spraying with a pyrethroid-based contact or systemic insecticide as soon as you notice any yellowing of the foliage is the only practical way to control this aphid.

The well-named Rosy Apple Aphid causes severe distortion of both twigs and leaves.

ROSY APPLE APHID
Dysaphis plantaginea

This aphid infests young apple twigs and foliage in the spring, living in dense clusters that lead to serious distortion of the twigs and yellowing and premature death of the leaves. Later in the year the bark of the affected twigs develops deep cracks, which may allow disease-causing organisms to enter. The aphid also attacks the apple flowers, leading to stunted and deformed fruits. Wingless individuals are usually pinkish-grey with a dusting of white wax, while the winged forms are dark green. Both forms are 2–3 mm long, with long, dark cornicles. During the summer the winged aphids migrate to plantains, where they live unobtrusively at the bases of the leaf rosettes until the autumn. Then they fly back to the apple trees, where the overwintering eggs are laid in bark crevices or at the bases of the buds. A very similar aphid, **Dysaphis devecta**, attacks apple leaves, causing the margins to roll down and become red.

Rosy Apple Aphid

Looks: Pinkish grey with white waxy covering; winged forms dark green

Food: Apple twigs and foliage as well as bark

When: Spring, summer

Where: Britain and Continental Europe

PEAR-BEDSTRAW APHID
Dysaphis pyri

The commonest aphid that attacks pear trees, this species resembles the Rosy Apple Aphid in size and colour and behaves in much the same way, causing severe distortion of the leaves and young shoots. It spends the summer months living on bedstraws and goosegrass, where dense colonies can develop before the insects fly back to the pear trees in the autumn.

Pear-bedstraw Aphid

Looks: PInkish grey

Food: Pear trees

When: Spring, summer

Where: Britain and Continental Europe

CURRANT-SOWTHISTLE APHID
Hyperomyzus lactucae

This is the commonest aphid on blackcurrant bushes. It also attacks red and white currants, although it is less common on these plants. A fairly slender green aphid, it causes severe crinkling and yellowing of the leaves and may also stunt the growth of the young shoots in spring and early summer. The aphids then fly to sowthistles, where they breed in the flower-heads for the rest of the summer. Aphids returning to the currant bushes in the autumn lay their eggs at the base of the buds. Removal of infested leaf clusters is the best way to deal with the pest. The **Gooseberry-sowthistle Aphid** (*Hyperomyzus pallidus*) is almost identical, but infests gooseberry bushes in the spring.

Currant-sowthistle Aphid

Looks: Slender green aphid

Food: Black, white and red currants

When: Spring, summer

Where: Britain and Continental Europe

WOOLLY APHID
Eriosoma lanigerum

This is another apple pest although, unlike the Rosy Apple Aphid, it also attacks pears and other rosaceous trees, such as cotoneaster, firethorn and *Sorbus* species. The insect is 1–2 mm long and basically purplish-brown, but it is normally clothed with the strands of white wax that give it its common name. It is also known as American blight because it was originally introduced to Europe from America in the 18th century. Populations start to build up in the spring and the first thing that the gardener notices is normally a woolly cluster on young shoots or on the bark of older branches, especially where the tree has been wounded. The pest is especially common around pruning cuts and the bases of the slender water shoots that spring from them. Infested twigs become cracked and the wounds serve as entry points for canker and other diseases. Males and eggs are very rare in this species and reproduction is almost entirely by virgin birth. In the autumn the aphids tuck themselves into bark crevices, where they can feed through the winter. No other host species is required: winged individuals may fly to fresh host trees, but the whole life cycle can be completed on the apples. Squash the insects as soon as you spot the fluffy white clumps in the spring, or cut off and burn the affected twigs. Pyrethroid-based sprays are helpful, but the waxy coverings protect the insects from sprays to some extent, and better results are obtained by dipping a paint brush into the insecticide and giving the clusters a good soaking. Soapy water

TOP TIP

Plant nasturtiums around apple trees and let the plants climb into the branches where the scent of the leaves may repel the aphids.

and insecticidal soaps also work quite well, or you can simply wash the insects away by squirting the clusters with a jet of water from the hose. A more interesting way to combat the pests is to plant nasturtiums around the trees and let the plants climb into the branches. The pungent scent of the leaves is believed to repel the aphids. Don't worry if the nasturtium leaves are eaten by 'cabbage white' caterpillars – the damaged leaves give out even more odour, and if the caterpillars are eating the nasturtiums, they are leaving your cabbages alone! When you are planning to plant new apple trees, try to find out on which rootstocks they have been grown, for some stocks are fairly resistant to Woolly Aphids.

Woolly Aphid

Looks: Small, purplish brown insect clothed with strands of white wax

Food: Apples, pears, cotoneaster, *Sorbus* species

When: Spring, summer

Where: Britain and Continental Europe

Woolly Aphids attack many members of the rose family, but are most often seen on apple trees. The species gets its name because each purplish brown aphid is clothed with fluffy white wax. Adult aphids pass the winter in wounds and bark crevices, and it is from such spots that the woolly clusters appear in the spring.

These crumpled cherry leaves have been attacked by the Cherry Blackfly, which has long black cornicles. Much of the black coloration on the leaves is due to the fungi that colonise the aphids' copious output of honeydew.

TOP TIP

Apply a winter wash to fruiting and ornamental cherry trees to kill Cherry Blackfly eggs.

Cherry Blackfly

Looks: Shiny and black

Food: Fruiting and ornamental cherry trees

When: Spring, summer

Where: Britain and Continental Europe

CHERRY BLACKFLY
Myzus cerasi

This aphid attacks both fruiting and ornamental cherries including Bird Cherry, although some Japanese varieties appear to be less susceptible to attack by this pest. The shiny black aphids hatch from their eggs when the buds begin to open and multiply rapidly on the undersides of the leaves. The latter become strongly curled and form protective 'nests' around the aphids. As spring turns into summer the affected leaves turn black as a result of the black fungi growing on the aphids' honeydew, causing the trees to look rather unsightly for the rest of the summer, although the infestation does not appear to do any long-term harm. Some of the aphids may remain on the cherry trees throughout the summer and autumn, but most winged individuals, which start to appear in midsummer, fly to their summer hosts, which are mainly bedstraws and speedwells. A later generation returns to the cherries where eggs are laid in the autumn. Because the aphids are well-protected in their 'nests', spraying with contact insecticides is of limited value, although a pyrethroid-based spray is worth using soon after bud-break where cherries are regularly infested. A systemic insecticide can also be used on ornamental cherries, and a winter wash (see p. 42) can be applied to both fruiting and ornamental varieties to kill the eggs.

LARGE RASPBERRY APHID
Amphorophora idaei

This large, shiny yellowish-green aphid has very long legs and antennae. It passes the winter in the egg stage on the lower parts of the canes and wingless females leaving the eggs in spring start to feed on the flower and leaf buds. Winged aphids appear in the summer and move to the main stems, where mating and egg-laying eventually take place. The aphid is a major carrier of viruses that weaken the plants and seriously reduce the fruit crop. Spraying with pyrethroid-based insecticides in the spring gives a fair degree of control, as does treatment of the canes with a winter wash (see p. 42) to kill the eggs. Some raspberry varieties are resistant to the aphid, and these are obviously the ones to plant. Autumn-fruiting varieties, which are cut to the ground after fruiting, are less likely to be affected than summer-fruiting ones.

Large Raspberry Aphid

Looks: Shiny and yellowish green

Food: Raspberries

When: Spring, summer

Where: Britain and Continental Europe

SMALL RASPBERRY APHID
Aphis idaei

Forming dense colonies on the leaves and shoot-tips of raspberries in the spring, this pest often causes severe distortion of the upper parts of the canes. Spring insects are greyish-green and wingless, and dusted with waxy powder. Later generations, with or without wings, are yellowish-green and tend to spread themselves around instead of living in colonies. The insects pass the winter in the egg stage at the base of the buds. The aphids carry a virus that causes the leaves to become very yellow, especially along the veins, and is responsible for a marked reduction in fruit yield. Infestations can be controlled with pyrethroid-based treatments in the spring.

Small Raspberry Aphid

Looks: Greyish green in spring; yellow green later

Food: Raspberries

When: Spring, summer

Where: Britain and Continental Europe

The Currant Blister Aphid (BELOW) feeds on the undersides of currant leaves in spring and early summer. Later generations live on hedge woundwort, so if you are worried by aphids on your currants, make sure there is no hedge woundwort lurking in the vicinity. The bright red blisters on currant leaves (RIGHT) are galls, induced by the Currant Blister Aphid.

CURRANT BLISTER APHID
Cryptomyzus ribis

This is the aphid responsible for the crinkly red or yellowish blisters or domes that develop on the upper surfaces of currant leaves, especially those of red and white currants. Clusters of wingless, yellowish-green aphids live under the domes in spring and early summer, but then winged aphids start to appear and they fly off to spend the rest of the summer rearing further generations of winged and wingless individuals on hedge woundwort, a relative of the deadnettles. Winged aphids fly back to the currant bushes in the autumn and overwintering eggs are laid on the twigs. A winter wash can be used on the bushes to kill off the eggs, or one can use a pyrethroid-based spray when the leaves first open and the eggs begin to hatch, but infested plants do not seem to suffer much and their fruit yield is not seriously affected so, unless you are offended by the puckered leaves, there is little to be gained from such treatments.

Currant Blister Aphid

Looks: Winged or wingless, yellowish green

Food: Red and white currants

When: Spring, summer

Where: Britain and Continental Europe

HONEYSUCKLE APHID
Hyadaphis foeniculi

The Honeysuckle Aphid forms dense clusters on honey-suckle shoots and flower buds in spring and early summer and may prevent the flowers from opening properly. At this stage the insects are bluish-green with a waxy grey coating and they have long black cornicles. Most of them are wing-less, but winged individuals gradually appear and they migrate to hemlock and other members of the carrot family, such as hogweed and possibly your garden carrots. Here, the summer generations are often yellow or brown. In the autumn winged individuals fly back to the honeysuckle, where the overwin-tering eggs are laid. Pyrethroid-based sprays can be used to get rid of the aphids on the honeysuckle shoots and buds, but do not use this once the flowers have opened. Insecticidal soaps or plain soapy water can be used then, or you can resort to fingers or the hose. Honeysuckle is naturally a woodland plant and, if possible, it should be planted so that its roots are in a cool, shaded spot, even if it grows up to expose its flowers to the sun. Plants grown in this way do seem less susceptible to aphid attack.

Honeysuckle Aphid

Looks: Bluish green with waxy coating in spring

Food: Honeysuckle shoots and flowers, and also on umbellifers in summer, when the insects are often brown

When: Spring, summer

Where: Britain and Continental Europe

TOP TIP

• *When the flowers have opened, use insecticidal soap or soapy water on the aphids.*

• *Or more simply, just use your fingers or spray them off with a hose.*

The Honeysuckle Aphid deforms the flowers and shoots of honeysuckle in early summer before transferring its attention to various umbellifers including, perhaps, your garden carrots.

ROSE APHID
Macrosiphum rosae

The commonest of several aphids that infest garden roses, its black cornicles readily distinguish this species from the other aphids. The body may be pink, green, or greenish-yellow and it is about 2 mm long. Clusters of wingless aphids build up on the young shoots and leaves and on the flower buds in the spring, often leading to stunted growth and misshapen flowers. Winged individuals migrate to scabious and teasel plants in the summer, and their progeny fly back to the roses in the autumn. The aphid normally passes the winter in the egg stage, although it can remain active in mild winters. Ladybirds and lacewings are particularly helpful on roses, but in their absence systemic insecticides and contact insecticides will control this aphid.

Rose Aphid

Looks: Plnk, green or greenish yellow with black cornicles

Food: Garden roses

When: Spring, summer

Where: Britain and Continental Europe

TOP TIP

On roses, ladybirds and lacewings often provide the most effective control of aphids.

Rose Aphids clustering around a rose bud. Most of the insects seen here are nymphs, but there are a few adults, identified by their black cornicles.

Rose-grain Aphids jostling for feeding space on a grass blade. The winged individuals will fly to other feeding grounds if they get too crowded and food supplies deteriorate. The small white objects are empty skins, left behind when the young insects moult, which they do four times during their short lives.

ROSE-GRAIN APHID
Metopolophium dirhodum

Between 1.5 and 3 mm long with pale cornicles, the wing-less insects, which are quite common on roses in the spring, are normally yellowish-green with a darker green stripe along the back. Winged forms, which appear quite early in the season, are brighter green with no obvious stripe on the back. They fly to various grasses, especially wheat and other cereals, where they continue to breed and may cause the leaves to turn yellow. Heavy infestations may lead to a reduction in yield. Enormous populations can build up on the cereals in favourable years, and then the winged aphids take to the air in their millions – the only time that aphids annoy us directly. Aphids normally return to wild and cultivated roses in the autumn and eggs are laid on the twigs, although in mild winters the insects can continue to breed partheno-genetically on the grasses. Infestations on roses can be controlled in the same way as those of the Rose Aphid.

Rose-grain Aphid

Looks: Yellowish green with dark stripe on back; winged foms bright green

Food: Roses and grain crops

When: Spring, summer

Where: Britain and Continental Europe

The Peach-potato Aphid ranges from pale green to reddish brown and can carry a wide range of viral diseases, affecting many different plant species apart from potatoes.

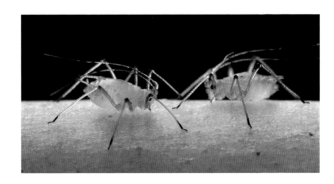

PEACH-POTATO APHID
Myzus persicae

This is a very serious pest of field and garden crops, because it has a very wide range of host plants and can transmit over 100 different disease-causing viruses. One of the most damaging is potato leaf-roll, in which the leaves become yellow and in-rolled and lose much of their photosynthetic ability, leading to a dramatic reduction in yield. The aphid is between 1 and 2.5 mm long and normally pale green, although it has pink and reddish-brown forms in the young stages. Winged forms have a black patch on the upper side of the abdomen. Eggs are laid on peach and almond twigs in the autumn and hatch in the spring. The resulting aphids and their wingless offspring feed on the peach leaves and cause them to curl up. Dense clusters may develop at this time, but winged aphids soon appear and migrate to their summer hosts which include potatoes, beans, lettuces, cabbages, chrysanthemums and a wide range of other herbaceous plants. Unlike most other aphid pests, this species does not form dense colonies on the summer hosts: the insects wander all over the plants and feed whenever they are hungry. Winged aphids go back to the host trees in the autumn, but many individuals remain on their hosts and breed asexually throughout the year. Peach trees are mostly confined to the southern counties in Britain, so most aphids have to stick to their herbaceous hosts. Many use broccoli and other brassicas at this time, but cannot survive really cold winters and the species is usually absent from Scotland and northern areas in the spring. As Peach-potato Aphids are absent from northern areas we are always advised to buy Scottish 'seed potatoes' for planting: with no aphids around when they are growing, the tubers are not likely to contain the virus.

TOP TIP

Control of the Peach-potato Aphid on herbaceous crops is best achieved by chemical means, using insecticidal soaps or sprays based on pyrethroids. Because the insects spread themselves fairly thinly, hand picking is not very efficient. Keep a close eye on any peach trees in the area and remove any infested leaves and twigs in the spring.

Peach-potato Aphid

Looks: Pale green; can be pink or reddish brown

Food: Peach, almond, potatoes, beans, lettuces, cabbages and other plants

When: Spring, summer

Where: Britain and Continental Europe

LETTUCE ROOT APHID
Pemphigus bursarius

Wilting lettuces may simply be crying out for a drink, but they could also be suffering from an attack by the Lettuce Root Aphid, colonies of which can drain sap from the plants more quickly than it can be replaced. The aphids cluster around lettuce roots in the summer and can be particularly harmful in dry weather. Large populations often kill the plants. The aphids themselves are pale and wingless at this stage of their life cycle, but winged individuals appear in the autumn and migrate to black poplar trees, especially the cultivated Lombardy poplars, where overwintering eggs are laid. These eggs hatch in the spring to produce wingless female aphids, which feed on the young leaf stalks of the poplar and bring about the formation of purse-like galls **(see p. 24)**. The aphids live in the galls and, without male assistance, produce numerous offspring in late spring and early summer. The new aphids then fly off to find another crop of lettuces. They can also use sowthistles during the summer, and in mild climates they can survive on these plants and on lettuces throughout the year. Most of our garden lettuce varieties are susceptible to the aphid, and the best way to control the pest is to avoid growing lettuces in the same patch every year and to make sure that your crops are adequately watered.

TOP TIP

Don't grow lettuces in the same place every year to avoid establishing a colony of Lettuce Root Aphids.

Lettuce-root Aphid

Looks: Pale and wingless

Food: Lettuces

When: Spring, summer

Where: Britain and Continental Europe

Wingless Lettuce Root Aphids clustering around a lettuce root in summer.

Galls of the Grape Phylloxera on vine leaves. The infestation here is so heavy that the leaves have curled up to reveal the galls on the underside. The galls open on the uppersides of the leaves to allow the aphids to escape.

GRAPE PHYLLOXERA
Daktulosphaira vitifoliae

During the second half of the 19th century, European vineyards and the wine industry were almost destroyed by this North American intruder. This minute, yellowish-green insect, not closely related to the other aphids, does little harm in its natural home because the vines there are fairly resistant to it. European vines have little resistance and the pest spread rapidly across the continent after its arrival. It feeds mainly on the roots, stunting their growth and leading to severe wilting and death of whole plants. The leaves of infected plants usually take on a strong red coloration. The pest was eventually brought under control by grafting European vines onto resistant American rootstocks, and it is no longer a serious problem in Europe. It is most noticeable in neglected or abandoned vineyards, where the vines lose vigour and become more susceptible to attack. Here the insect may also attack the leaves, causing small spherical galls on the undersides. Heavy infestations cause the leaves to curl up and, because the galls are often red, the vines take on a quite spectacular appearance. Opening up the curled leaves may well reveal hundreds of the tiny insects – almost always wingless in Europe. The Grape Phylloxera is not established in the British Isles, but it can arrive on imported vines or with fruit, and any suspected infestation must be reported to the local DEFRA office.

Grape Phylloxera

Looks: Very tiny yellowish green aphid

Food: Vines

When: Spring, summer

Where: Continental Europe: rarely imported to British Isles

WHITEFLIES

Whiteflies are tiny insects clothed with powdery white wax. Rarely more than about 2 mm long, they are often mistaken for little white moths, but they are neither moths nor true flies: they are actually bugs related to the aphids and scale insects. They have piercing beaks and suck sap from the undersides of the leaves of their host plants. There are about 30 different kinds in Europe, although several of these have been introduced from warmer parts of the world. Most of them are confined to just one host-plant or a group of closely related plants.

The most common are the Cabbage Whitefly and the Greenhouse Whitefly (see overleaf). Several other whiteflies may occur in the garden, although rarely in any number and rarely needing any sort of control measures. They include species affecting rhododendrons, azaleas and honeysuckle. The **Citrus Whitefly** (*Dialeurodes citri*), originally from Eastern Asia, damages citrus crops in southern Europe and also occurs on figs and pomegranates. The **Tobacco Whitefly** (*Bemisia tabaci*) is a serious pest in southern Europe, where, in addition to spreading viruses in the tobacco fields, it attacks a wide range of garden plants. It resembles the Greenhouse Whitefly, although the resting insect has a less triangular outline. The species occasionally reaches the British Isles in consignments of ornamental plants, and if its presence is suspected it must be reported to the local DEFRA office.

CABBAGE WHITEFLY
Aleyrodes proletella
Disturb a patch of broccoli or other leafy brassicas at more or less any time of the year and you are likely to send up clouds of Cabbage Whitefly, an abundant, but not usually serious pest of all kinds of brassicas. Although dense colonies can weaken the plants, normal populations have little effect because the individual insects are so small. Adults remain active in all but the coldest weather and there are several generations in a year. The female lays up to about 100 eggs, often in circles around her body, and the eggs produce nymphs after a few days. The nymphs, which are clothed with wax like the adults, soon plug themselves into the leaf, and then they hardly move until they turn into adults three

TOP LEFT: Cabbage Whitefly with its characteristic circle of eggs. The white patch consists of flakes of wax rubbed from the insect's body as she swivels round to lay the eggs.

TOP RIGHT: Final nymphal instars, or puparia, and a few adult whiteflies.

ABOVE: Cabbage Whitefly on the underside of a broccoli leaf, with a batch of Large White Butterfly eggs.

Cabbage Whitefly

Looks: Small, with white wings with dark spots. Nymphs are waxy

Food: Leafy brassicas

When: Most of the year

Where: Britain and Continental Europe

or four weeks later. In common with the aphids, whiteflies produce a lot of sticky honeydew **(see p. 113)**. Their wax coatings ensure that they don't get in a mess, but the leaves soon get sticky and the honeydew is commonly colonised by a black fungus **(see p. 114)**, which can actually cause more damage than the whiteflies themselves.

Ladybirds, lacewings and other predators help to keep whiteflies under control and it is rarely necessary to take any action against the Cabbage Whitefly in the garden, but if the infestation is particularly severe, the plants can be sprayed with one of the pyrethrin-type insecticides. The latter, being knock-down insecticides, must make contact with the insects and must be sprayed on the undersides of the leaves if they are to have any effect. Fatty acids **(see p. 117)** are also effective, and it is now possible to obtain organic pesticides specially formulated for use against whiteflies. Total removal and destruction of old brassica stumps after harvest cuts down the number of adult insects available to lay eggs on the next crop.

GREENHOUSE WHITEFLY
Trialeurodes vaporariorum

This species lacks dark spots on its wings but it is otherwise very similar to the Cabbage Whitefly and all the other whiteflies. It is much less fussy in its choice of host plants, however, and it attacks a wide range of indoor and greenhouse plants, including tomatoes, cucumbers, chrysanthemums and fuchsias. It can breed throughout the year and populations can build up rapidly in the warm atmosphere. Males are rare in this species and the females can lay fertile eggs without mating. Dense populations can kill small and tender plants, and honeydew falling onto the lower leaves can spoil the look of all the plants, especially when the black fungus gets going on it. Greenhouse White-flies can escape into the garden and breed there in the summer, but they will not infest brassicas because they are repelled by the mustard oils that attract various other insect pests. The same mustard oils are found in nasturtiums, and it is worth growing some of these plants among your toma-toes to give them some protection from whitefly. A native of the warmer parts of the world, the species is unlikely to survive the winter out of doors. Various pyrethroid-based sprays can be used against the Greenhouse Whitefly, and thiacloprid can be added to the pots in which flowers are grown, but such treatments will not necessarily work every-where because some populations have become resistant to many insecticides **(see p. 43)**. Fatty acids and sticky traps resembling the old-fashioned fly-papers are useful, and basil interplanted with tomatoes is said to keep the whitefly away. It is now possible to achieve a good level of biological control in the greenhouse by releasing a little parasitic wasp called *Encarsia formosa* **(see p. 38)**.

Greenhouse Whitefly

Looks: Small with pure white wings

Food: Chrysanthemums, tomatoes, cucumbers, fuchsias

When: All year

Where: Continental Europe; rare in Britain

TOP TIP

Plant basil among tomato plants to keep whitefly away in the greenhouse.

The Greenhouse Whitefly has pure white wings. It infests a wide range of plants growing in the greenhouse as well as those in the house.

SCALE INSECTS

Scale insects are all sap-feeders, belonging with the aphids, whiteflies and other true bugs in the order Hemiptera. They get their name because for most of their lives they live under horny or waxy scales that they secrete from their bodies, so they don't look like insects at all. Males are rare or absent in many species and the females lay fertile eggs without mating. Even when they do exist, the adult males are rarely seen: they live for a very short time and never feed; their sole aim is to find and mate with the females. With just two wings, they resemble minute midges. Adult females never move: they have no wings and most of them lack legs. They plug their beaks into the host plants and just keep sucking in sap at the front and pumping honeydew out at the rear like the aphids **(see p. 113)**. The sweet honeydew attracts numerous other insects, and what they don't consume tends to become blackened with fungi. The females die after egg-laying, but their tiny eggs – sometimes as many as 2,000 – remain protected under the scales and the scales themselves may remain on the plants for years. The nymphs that hatch from the eggs are called crawlers and they roam all over the host plants on their minute legs. Many are carried to new plants by the breeze, and some hitch lifts on other insects or birds that visit the plants. The young scale insects soon settle down to feed, and quickly secrete their protective scales, also known as tests. Male and female tests usually have different shapes and the male tests are also smaller.

Scale insect problems

Some scale insects exist in enormous numbers and seriously weaken their host plants by removing large amounts of sap. Some also transmit viruses. Native British scale insects do not do very much harm, but alien species can do a lot of damage, both out of doors and in greenhouses and conservatories. Fruit trees and ornamental shrubs are particularly susceptible. Control of these pests is not easy because their scales protect them from sprays, but systemic insecticides containing imidacloprid or thiacloprid can be used on ornamental plants. Complete removal of twigs or even whole branches may be necessary to deal with large infestations.

TOP TIP

• Scrub away small scale insect infestations with a toothbrush dipped in insecticidal soap. This method is advised for use on fruit trees.

• Treatment is most likely to be successful if applied when the crawlers are active.

• Watch out for ladybirds: these will destroy many of the scale insects for you for free.

• Larger infestations may require complete removal of twigs and branches.

Brown Scales, found on a wide range of trees and shrubs, can reach 5 mm in diameter and look like miniature tortoises.

BROWN SCALE
Parthenolecanium corni

This scale attacks a wide range of garden trees and shrubs, with peaches and grape vines among its favourite hosts. The shiny brown, oval scales of the adult females are up to 5 mm long and can be found on twigs and branches throughout the year, although they are often concealed in crevices and under flakes of loose bark. The insects reproduce almost entirely by parthenogenesis, with each female laying up to 2,000 eggs during the summer. Hidden under the domed scales, the eggs hatch after three or four weeks and the crawlers then make their way to the leaves. They feed under the leaves for a while before making their final move to the twigs in the autumn. They remain dormant through the winter and mature in early summer to begin the cycle again. Old scales may remain fixed to the twigs long after the insects have died – often staying put for several years.

Brown Scale

Looks: Females have shiny brown oval scales

Food: Garden trees especially peaches and grape vines

When: All year

Where: Britain and Continental Europe

A heavy infestation of Rose Scale on a garden rose. The circular scales are those of the females, up to 3 mm across, while the tubular objects in the lower part of the picture are those of the young males.

ROSE SCALE
Aulacaspis rosae

Also called scurfy scale, this pest clusters around the stems of roses, especially the older stems, and, from a distance, a colony looks like a crusty white growth. The female scales are flat white discs, up to 3 mm across, while those of the males are smaller and more or less tubular. Eggs are laid in the summer and they hatch quite quickly, allowing the crawlers to disperse and feed for a while before settling down in their permanent quarters. The species is also found on blackberry canes.

Rose Scale

Looks: Female scales are white discs; males are smaller and tubular

Food: Rose and blackberry bushes

When: All year

Where: Britain and Continental Europe

MUSSEL SCALE
Lepidosaphes ulmi

The Mussel Scale gets its name because the scales resemble tiny brown mussel shells, about 3 mm long. It is also known as the Oyster Shell Scale. It can be found on a wide range of trees and shrubs, including olives, currants and heathers, but is especially common on old apple trees that have already lost some of their strength. The scales can form thick carpets on the bark, although they may not be obvious from a distance. Old scales become clothed with lichens and then blend incredibly well with the bark. Fresh, clean specimens are best sought under flaking bark. Eggs are laid in late summer but they do not hatch until the following spring. The crawlers soon settle on the bark, lose their legs, and form their scales. Apart from the delicate males, which leave their scales in the summer, they don't move again. But males are very rare and reproduction is almost entirely partheno-genetic or non-sexual. Heavy infestations of Mussel Scale may weaken the host and lead to the death of branches or even complete old trees, but the insect does not usually do much harm and treatment is rarely of any use.

Mussel Scale

Looks: Scales look like miniature mussel shells; form thick carpets on bark

Food: Olives, currants and heathers, old apple trees

When: All year

Where: Britain and Continental Europe

Mussel Scales on young apple bark.

The Soft Scale, which normally attaches itself close to the mid-rib of a leaf, is a troublesome citrus pest, but in Britain and other parts of northern Europe it is confined largely to indoor plants.

SOFT SCALE
Coccus hesperidum

Attacking a wide range of herbaceous and woody plants, Soft Scale is a well-known pest of citrus trees in southern Europe. Figs and bay laurel are other common host plants. In Britain and other more northerly parts of Europe it is unlikely to be more than a minor nuisance in the garden, surviving only in the warmest areas or very sheltered, south-facing gardens, but it can be troublesome on indoor plants, including ferns and cacti. The mature scale is oval and about 5 mm long, with a dark brown centre and a paler margin. It is normally found close to the veins on both surfaces of the leaves. Males are extremely rare and reproduction is almost entirely asexual and viviparous, with each female producing up to 1,000 active nymphs during her lifetime. The crawlers roam around for a few days before settling down to produce their protective scales. The pest can breed continuously indoors and produce several generations in a year. Infested plants become weak and droopy and leaves may die, but it is quite easy to remove the insects by squashing them with the fingers or brushing them off with an old toothbrush.

Soft Scale

Looks: Oval with dark brown centre and pale margin; found close to veins on leaves

Food: Figs, bay laurel, citrus trees

When: All year under cover

Where: Everywhere under cover: a problem out of doors only in southern Europe

The mass of waxy threads bulging from the rear of this Woolly Vine Scale conceals hundred of eggs. All that is left of the female at this stage is the empty scale covering the egg mass.

WOOLLY VINE SCALE
Pulvinaria vitis

This scale is a pest not only of grape vines, but also of currant and gooseberry bushes and peach trees. The female scale is up to 7 mm long, dark brown, and commonly heart-shaped or triangular, and it can be found on the branches, leaves and roots. During the spring each female produces a mass of waxy white threads, amongst which she lays several hundred eggs. The waxy mass bulges from the rear end of the scale and whole branches can turn white with a heavy infestation. Brushing the scales and egg masses with horticultural oil or soapy water should keep the Woolly Vine Scale under control and reduce damage to the host plants.

Woolly Vine Scale

Looks: Heart-shaped, dark brown with bulge at rear

Food: Grape vines, currants, gooseberries, peaches

When: All year

Where: Britain (uncommon) and Continental Europe

Fig Wax Scale

Looks: Female scales are white with brown markings

Food: Fig trees

When: All year

Where: Can be a problem in southern Europe

FIG WAX SCALE
Ceroplastes rusci

A major pest of fig trees in southern Europe, the female scales are white with brown markings. Up to 5 mm across, they resemble barnacles. They clothe the young shoots and also cling to the midribs of the leaves. Heavy infestations seriously weaken the trees and may kill young shoots.

The Fig Wax Scale is quite attractive and, with its pinkish brown decoration, it resembles a tiny iced bun or even a miniature birthday cake. Its eggs remain hidden under the scales, unlike those of many other scale insects.

Horse Chestnut scales on a branch of a bay tree. The scales are rarely noticed until the fluffy white egg masses protrude from their rear ends in the spring.

HORSE CHESTNUT SCALE
Pulvinaria regalis

This insect lives on a wide range of wild and cultivated trees and shrubs, including bay, magnolia and ornamental maples. It is widely distributed in southern and central Europe but it has only recently established itself in the British Isles, where it is still found mainly in the southern counties. Its flat brown scales are about 4 mm across and can be found mainly on the trunks and branches. They are most obvious when accompanied by their white egg masses, which bulge out from underneath the scales in spring and early summer. The eggs hatch in the middle of summer and the crawlers move to the undersides of the leaves, where they secrete oval yellow scales. They return to the bark after a few weeks

and mature in the following spring. Males are unknown in this species and reproduction is entirely parthenogenetic. Even heavy infestations seem to do little harm to the host plants, although they may look unsightly on specimen plants growing in tubs. The simplest way to control the beast is to brush scales from the bark in spring before the eggs hatch.

FLUTED SCALE
Icerya purchasi

Originating in Australia, the Fluted Scale resembles the Horse Chestnut scale. The female scale is brown and oval and up to 3 mm across, but is not usually noticed until it has produced its large white egg mass, which is up to 1 cm long and conspicuously grooved. It may contain over 500 eggs. The insect infests a wide range of plants but is best known for its attacks on citrus fruits in southern Europe. In the British Isles and other northern regions it is found mainly in greenhouses and conservatories, although it can survive outside in sheltered spots and in areas with a mild climate. It is fairly easy to remove the scales by hand or with a wet sponge. Sprays have little effect on adults under their scales, but insecticidal soaps can be used against the crawlers.

WHITE PEACH SCALE
Pseudaulacaspis pentagona

This scale attacks a vast range of woody and herbaceous plants, including mulberry, buddleia, lilac, fig and magnolia as well as peach. Female scales are circular, about 2.5 mm across and dirty white with a yellowish spot near the middle. Male scales look more like tiny grains of white rice, about 1.5 mm long with a yellowish spot at the rear. The scales are sometimes so numerous that twigs and branches look as if they are covered with snow or icing. Such infestations cause severe damage to the host plant: the leaves turn yellow and often fall, twigs collapse, and whole branches may die. Even whole trees can be killed, especially young ones. Spraying with pyrethroid-based insecticides and insecticidal soaps when the crawlers are active may help to control the pest, but large infestations are best treated by removing the affected branches completely and burning them. Originally from eastern Asia, the insect has been in Europe for many years and has recently been spreading northwards. Only a few occurrences have been reported in Britain so far but, with increasing trade in ornamental shrubs – and possibly aided by global warming – the insect could well establish itself before long. As this is potentially such a damaging pest, any discovery must be reported to the local DEFRA office.

TOP TIP

• Spray with pyrethroid-based insecticides when the insects are crawling.

• Control large infestations by removing and burning affected branches.

White Peach Scale

Looks: Females circular with yellow spot at rear; males are like rice grains

Food: Many trees and shrubs, including peach, mulberry, magnolia, as well as numerous herbaceous plants

When: All year

Where: Continental Europe

White Peach Scale clothing a mulberry twig. These are all female scales, characterised by the yellowish spot near the centre. Infestations like this can easily kill the branches.

JUMPING PLANT LICE OR PSYLLIDS

Often mistaken for aphids, these well-named little bugs can be found on many different plants, where they sit and suck sap from the leaves throughout their lives. When disturbed, they leap away with the aid of their powerful back legs. In this respect they resemble the leafhoppers, but they can be distinguished from the latter by their much longer antennae. Most also have transparent front wings. The adults are usually green or brown. Their nymphs are usually green and very flat and they tend to be gregarious, often surrounding themselves with dense deposits of wax.

BAY PSYLLID
Trioza alacris

Also called the Bay Sucker, it lives on bay trees and causes the leaf margins to thicken and curl downwards to form elongate pouches in which the psyllids and their offspring live and feed. The pouches are thus true galls **(see p. 24)** and they are very conspicuous on the trees because the affected parts of the leaves become quite yellow. Eggs are laid in the galls in the spring and the new generation of psyllids matures in late summer and autumn. The stripy brown adults then pass the winter in the old galls or in leaf litter on the ground and wake to begin the cycle again in the spring. The insects do no long-term harm to the trees, but the old galls look unsightly and it is best to remove galled leaves as soon as they are seen. Systemic insecticides can be used to treat small trees, especially those growing in containers.

Bay Psyllid

Looks: Adults are striped and brown

Food: Bay trees

When: Spring, summer

Where: Britain and Continental Europe

BELOW LEFT: The Bay Psyllid is responsible for the puckering and yellowing of these bay leaves. The thickened margins curve downwards and form pouches in which the insects live and feed. The nymphs living in the galls produce loads of wax.

BELOW RIGHT: Adult Bay Psyllids feeding on the underside of a leaf. Being true bugs, they feed by plunging their needle-like beaks into the leaf tissues and sucking out the sap.

APPLE SUCKER
Psylla mali

This is a common pest of apple trees, although it rarely causes serious damage. Pale orange eggs are laid on young twigs, usually close to the flower buds, in the autumn, and they hatch when the buds start to open in the spring. The nymphs, which are green or orange, feed in or on the opening buds and this is when most of the damage is done. The flowers may not open properly, and if they do open the petals are often distorted and discoloured. Young leaves may also be distorted. New adults appear later in the spring. They are about 3 mm long and, being bluish-green, they are very difficult to spot when feeding on the undersides of the leaves. Later in the year, they become yellowish-brown and blend well with the yellowing leaves. If necessary, control of the pest can be achieved by spraying the buds before they open. Contact insecticides based on pyrethroids will kill the nymphs before they enter the buds, while systemic compounds will continue their work when the nymphs are hidden.

Apple Sucker

Looks: Nymphs are green or orange

Food: Apple trees

When: Spring, summer

Where: Britain and Continental Europe

TOP TIP

• Kill nymphs with contact insecticides before they have a chance to enter the buds.

• Systemic compounds are best for when the nymphs are hidden.

The Apple Sucker blends quite well with the underside of an apple leaf and, being only about 3 mm long, it is not often seen.

PEAR SUCKER
Psylla pyricola

Though it resembles the Apple Sucker in shape, this psyllid is usually red or brown and it has a very different life cycle. Whereas the Apple Sucker has just a single generation in a year, the Pear Sucker normally has three. The insect spends the winter in the adult stage, tucked up in bark crevices. The females lay their eggs close to the pear buds in the spring and the resulting nymphs tunnel into the buds and feed there for a few weeks, causing damage similar to that brought about by the Apple Sucker. New adults appear in late spring and immediately lay their eggs. The nymphs from these eggs feed on the undersides of the leaves and produce another generation of adults by midsummer. A third generation appears in the autumn, and these are the insects that go into hibernation. Insects of the spring and summer broods have clear, transparent wings, but the wings of the autumn brood bear numerous cloudy patches. Huge populations can develop during the year, making the Pear Sucker a much more damaging pest than its apple-dwelling relative. Sooty moulds often develop on the leaves, feeding on the copious honeydew secreted by the suckers **(see p. 114)**. Pear Suckers have become more common in many areas in recent years, but control measures are rarely needed in the garden. If you do have a problem with this pest you can spray small trees before the buds open and again in late summer after harvesting your pears. A systemic insecticide is best, but a pyrethroid-based contact insecticide will also do a good job at combating the insect.

Pear Sucker

Looks: Nymphs are red or brown; adults have clear to cloudy wings

Food: Pear trees

When: Spring, summer

Where: Britain and Continental Europe

THRIPS

Thrips are tiny winged or wingless insects, rarely more than 2 mm long, belonging to the order Thysanoptera. There are about 160 species in the British Isles and most of them are black or dark brown. Their wings, when present, are like miniature feathers, although you will need a good lens to appreciate their delicate structure. One of the commonest species is the Cereal Thrips – the name is the same in both singular and plural. This is the species that annoys us in the summer when millions of insects drift from the wheat and barley fields in which they grew up and get almost everywhere – in our hair, in our eyes and mouths, and into the smallest crevices, where they pass the winter. They are often called 'thunder flies' or 'thunder bugs' because they are most likely to fly in the humid conditions associated with thunderstorms. In the garden, thrips are most often seen in flowers, where they gather to suck fluids from pollen or to pierce the petals and suck out the sap. White spots often develop on the petals where pigmented sap has been removed. Many species attack leaves and fruits and their presence may be indicated by shiny streaks or patches, caused by the draining and subsequent collapse of the epidermal cells. If buds are attacked by large numbers of thrips the flowers may be deformed or may not open properly. Thrips can also carry viral diseases, but most species are pretty harmless and few garden plants actually suffer serious attack by these little insects. They have plenty of natural enemies, including an assortment of small predatory bugs, so control measures are rarely needed, but any of the contact insecticides suggested for aphid control **(see p. 117)** can be used against them if necessary. Systemic compounds such as thiacloprid or imidacloprid can be used on ornamental plants and it is now possible to obtain predatory mites and nematodes for biological control of thrips in greenhouses and conservatories.

A typical thrip, highly magnified. The feathery wings can be seen on the right side of the body. The insects grow to about 1.4 cm in length in some places, although the largest British thrips, in the genus *Megathrips*, are only about 7 mm long.

GLADIOLUS THRIPS
Thrips simplex

Gladiolus Thrips

Looks: Young are pale with no wings; adults are darker with wings

Food: Leaves of gladioli and many other plants

When: Spring, summer

Where: Britain and Continental Europe, especially in greenhouses

This thrips can cause severe damage to gladioli leaves and flowers, infested regions exhibiting bleached or silvery streaks. Eggs are laid in little slits, which the female thrips makes with her saw-like egg-laying apparatus, and they hatch in a couple of weeks or so. The youngsters then suck sap just like the adults. The young thrips are pale and wingless at first and they pass through several stages before turning into mature, winged adults. The insects shun strong light and on sunny days they hide between leaves and come out to feed early in the morning or late in the afternoon, although they can be found feeding at any time on dull days. Gladiolus Thrips originated in Africa and cannot survive our winter out of doors but, because we usually lift and store gladioli corms in the autumn, the insects, both adults and young, can survive on the stored plants and spread to new growth in the spring. Badly infested corms may turn brown and woody and fail to grow when replanted. The species is not confined to gladioli and attacks a wide range of other plants, especially those growing in greenhouses and conservatories, where it can go on breeding through the winter. Larvae of the Iris-fly **(see p. 263)** produce superficially similar damage, although these insects are actually inside the leaves.

ONION THRIPS
Thrips tabaci

Onion Thrips

Looks: Yellow-grey with dark blotches on body

Food: Onions, brassicas, peas, tomatoes and many greenhouse crops

When: Spring, summer

Where: Britain and Continental Europe

This yellowish-grey insect, about 1 mm long, often has dark blotches on the body. Despite its name, it attacks a wide variety of wild and cultivated plants, including brassicas, peas and tomatoes in the garden and many greenhouse plants. It also attacks grape vines on the Continent. All affected plants exhibit the characteristic pale or silvery spots and streaks on the leaves and flowers. When feeding on onions the insects tend to gather low down on the plants and tuck themselves away in the leaf sheaths, so they are not always easy to see. Affected areas become very pale and silvery and the leaves flop over. Consequently, the bulbs make little growth. Damaged areas allow the entry of various fungal diseases. The Onion Thrips also transmits a number of damaging viruses, including the spotted wilt virus of tomatoes. Males are very rare in this species and most females lay fertile eggs in the spring without mating. The eggs are placed in slits in the plant tissues and they hatch in a few days. The youngsters, which are bright yellow, mature in three or four weeks. There are usually just two generations per year in the garden, with the winter being spent in sheltered spots, often amongst plant debris on the ground – so it is wise to remove all debris after lifting your onions. The insects can breed throughout the year in greenhouses.

PEA THRIPS
Kakothrips pisivorus

This insect breeds on a variety of wild and cultivated legumes, usually in the flowers. The adult insect is shiny black and about 1.5 mm long, but the youngsters are yellow. Eggs are laid on the stamens of the pea flowers in the spring and they hatch in about a week. The adults and the young thrips feed on the flower tissues and, if numerous, may cause severe distortion of the petals and the developing pods. When the petals fall, the thrips transfer their attentions to the pods, which become noticeably silvery, although this has little effect on the peas inside the pods: the real damage is caused in the flower stage. The adult thrips remain on the pods until the middle of the summer, but the youngsters do not stay for long: when they are about two weeks old they burrow into the ground and stay there until the following spring. Then they turn into adults and emerge to mate and start the life cycle again. The pest is widely distributed in the southern half of Britain, where it attacks sweet peas as well as garden peas, but appears to be absent from Scotland.

Pea Thrips

Looks: Shiny black adult, yellow young

Food: Leguminous plants

When: Spring, summer

Where: Southern Britain and Continental Europe

WESTERN FLOWER THRIPS
Frankliniella occidentalis

A relative newcomer to the British Isles, this native of California and neighbouring parts of the USA, was first seen in Britain in the 1980s, but it is now a major pest of greenhouse plants, including chrysanthemums, cacti, peppers and cucumbers. The insect also lives in our gardens during the summer, often attacking strawberries, although it is probably unable to survive the winter out of doors in Britain. On the Continent it is a minor pest of grape vines. Eggs are generally laid in the leaves, but the hatchling thrips soon move to the flowers or developing fruits. In the flowers they destroy

Western Flower Thrips

Looks: Yellowish brown adults, orange young

Food: Greenhouse plants including cacti, peppers and cucumbers

When: Spring, summer

Where: Continental Europe and Britain, especially in greenhouses

a lot of pollen grains, although they may compensate for this by helping with pollination, but they also damage the petals and spoil the look of the flowers. Fruits also develop unwelcome blemishes and distortions. Strawberries, for example, may exhibit dry, yellow patches where the thrips have fed. Adults are yellowish-brown and 1–1.5 mm long. The young thrips are orange and they can complete their growth and turn into adult insects in under three weeks in a warm greenhouse, where they can go on breeding throughout the year. Growing up takes somewhat longer in the garden and there may be no more than two generations in a year. Males are very rare and reproduction is very largely parthenogenetic.

ROSE THRIPS
Thrips fuscipennis

Rose Thrips

Looks: Males yellowish; females dark brown

Food: Roses and other plants

When: Spring, summer

Where: Britain and Continental Europe

The Rose Thrips attacks the flowers of roses and several other plants, especially other members of the rose family. It causes the petals to develop pale spots and streaks. These blemishes may darken after a while and badly affected petals may rot away; heavy infestations can also lead to poorly formed fruits, especially strawberries and other soft fruits. Silvery streaks may also develop on the foliage and the leaves often curl up. The males are yellowish, but the females are dark brown. Breeding may go on throughout the year in areas with mild winters, but in most areas the mated females fly off to spend the winter in secluded spots, including hollow stems and crevices in walls and fences. They emerge and start laying their eggs early in the spring.

BEETLES

The beetles form the largest of all insect groups – the order Coleoptera, of which there are over 300,000 known species in the world and more than 20,000 in Europe. They include some of the smallest insects, many of them less than 0.5 mm in length, while at the other end of the scale there are beetles the size of a man's fist. Most beetles have four wings, although they might appear wingless at first sight because the front pair, known as the elytra, are tough and horny and they remain closed over the body for much of the time, acting as protective coverings for the flimsy hind wings. Only when the insects take to the air do the hind wings appear. When beetles are at rest, the elytra usually meet in a straight line down the centre of the body, and this helps to distinguish them from the bugs **(see p. 95)**, with which they are commonly confused. The beetles' biting jaws are also very different from the piercing, needle-like beaks of the bugs, and, unlike the bugs, the beetles pass through a larval stage – equivalent to the caterpillars of butterflies and moths – as they grow up. The larvae are nothing like the adults and have to pass through a pupal or chrysalis stage before reaching maturity.

Gardener's friend or foe?

Beetles include carnivores and herbivores together with numerous scavengers that feed on rotting vegetation, dung and carrion – unpleasant habits maybe, but these scavenging species play a major role in the recycling of materials and many are important residents of the garden compost heap. The carnivorous species include many of the gardener's friends, such as the aphid-eating ladybirds and most of the ground beetles, while most of the herbivores are pests in the garden. Leaf-eating species, including the dreaded Lily Beetle and the brassica-wrecking flea beetles, are among the most conspicuous of these pests, but every part of a plant, from the roots to the seeds, is likely to be attacked by some kind of beetle. Some seed-eating beetles cause immense damage in granaries and other food stores and, although they might not concern the gardener too much, they can cause alarm in the house when they emerge, often in large numbers, from cereal packets and other dried foods.

The Strawberry Beetle can often be seen scuttling over the soil at night. Exploring the garden by torchlight is an excellent way of finding out what friends and foes are at work under cover of darkness.

STRAWBERRY BEETLE
Pterostichus madidus

This is one of several quite similar beetles that, although belonging to the essentially carnivorous family of ground beetles, enjoy tucking in to our strawberries. Up to 2 cm long, the beetle is shiny black with rust-coloured legs and it nibbles both the flesh and the seeds of strawberries, usually at night. It has no hind wings and is therefore flightless, spending its whole life on or under the ground. It is common in a wide range of habitats and away from the strawberry bed both adult and larva can be useful in destroying other pests, but if you grow a lot of strawberries you may well need to keep the beetle population in check. A good way to do this is to set a few pitfall traps among the plants. You can use jam jars sunk in the ground so that their rims are level with the soil surface, but a better method is to use pairs of smooth plastic beakers, sinking one beaker in the ground and then placing the other one inside it. Beetles roaming the surface at night fall into the traps, and it is then easy to lift out the inner beaker and release the insects away from the garden without hurting any useful or harmless species. In wet weather it is a good idea to cover the traps with a piece of wood raised up on stones to allow the beetles room to fall in. If you put straw under your strawberries, you should lift it in the morning and dispose of any beetles that have settled down to rest there – and don't plant your strawberries too close to a hedge or to rough grass that might afford shelter for the beetles.

Strawberry Beetle

Looks: Shiny black, up to 2 cm with russet legs

Food: Strawberries

When: Most of the year

Where: Britain and Continental Europe

ROSE CHAFER
Cetonia aurata

A rather flat green or bronze beetle, this species has a few white streaks on the elytra. The underside is reddish-purple and very shiny. The insects fly by day, especially around hedgerows and woodland margins, but they are most often seen resting or feeding in flowers, where they nibble the pollen and stamens and also take nectar. When disturbed they may fly off with a loud buzzing noise. The larvae, resembling those of other chafers, live in rotting wood and other decaying vegetation, especially in piles of grass cuttings. Once quite a serious pest of roses, the insect is now less common and found mainly in the southern counties of Britain, although it remains widely distributed in southern and central Europe.

Rose Chafer

Looks: Fairly flat, green or bronze; shiny reddish purple underside

Food: Roses and other plants

When: Adults spring and summer: larvae all year

Where: Southern Britain; central and southern Europe

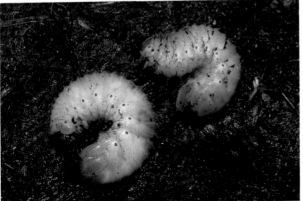

ABOVE: The adult Rose Chafer feeds mainly on pollen, taken from a wide variety of flowers and not just roses. About 2 cm long, it may nibble a few petals and stamens, but otherwise does no harm in the garden.

LEFT: Rose Chafer larvae , in common with other chafer grubs, they are most often seen in their characteristic C-shape, although they can straighten out in order to move around.

A male Cockchafer displaying its enormous, fan-shaped antennae. Cockchafer grubs resemble those of the Rose Chafer on the previous page but, with lengths up to 4 cm, they are considerably larger. They feed on the roots of many woody and herbaceous plants.

COCKCHAFER
Melolontha melolontha

Also known as the maybug, this is more of an agricultural pest than a garden pest, although it can cause damage in larger gardens. It is a hefty insect, up to 3 cm long, and it commonly causes alarm by crashing into lighted windows and car windscreens on summer evenings – mostly in May and June. The male antennae can open into broad fans, providing a large surface area to pick up the scent of the females. The adult insects nibble the leaves of many trees and shrubs, but the females prefer more open areas for egg-laying. They lay their eggs in the ground and it is the fat, white larvae that do most of the damage. They live in the soil for three or four years and destroy the roots of a wide range of plants.

Cockchafer

Looks: Up to 3 cm, chunky and brown

Food: Nibble leaves of various trees and shrubs while larvae eat roots

When: Adults spring and summer: larvae all year

Where: Britain and Continental Europe

GARDEN CHAFER
Phyllopertha horticola

This insect resembles the Cockchafer but is no more than about 1.2 cm long and it has a metallic green thorax. The elytra may also have a dark green sheen. Adults occur mainly in June and July and are generally active by day, feeding on the shoots and leaves of many herbaceous and woody plants and often causing damage in orchards by nibbling young fruits. Their larvae feed on grass roots and are particularly troublesome on grazing land, where they have been known to reach densities of a million per acre. The insects are less common on cultivated land, but can still cause a good deal of damage to parkland and large lawns.

Garden Chafer

Looks: Up to 1.2 cm with metallic green body

Food: Various herbaceous and woody plants

When: Adults summer; larvae all year

Where: Britain and Continental Europe

The Garden Chafer can be recognised by its dark green, metallic thorax. The elytra are usually brown, but sometimes take on a shiny green appearance.

The Summer Chafer differs from its relatives in being entirely brown and very hairy. Although its grubs feed mainly on grass roots, the beetle is most common in areas with plenty of trees.

SUMMER CHAFER
Amphimallon solstitialis

This beetle is easily distinguished from the two previous species by its hairiness and its entirely brown thorax and elytra. The beetles, up to 1.8 cm long, swarm around trees and shrubs and chew the leaves on summer evenings and, like Cockchafers, they often come to lighted windows. Their grubs resemble those of the Cockchafer and feed mainly on grass roots. Most common in well-wooded areas, the species occurs only in the southern half of the British Isles, but it is abundant in many parts of continental Europe.

Summer Chafer

Looks: Shiny brown body with long white hairs

Food: Grubs feed mainly on grass roots

When: Adult in spring and summer: larvae all year

Where: Southern Britain and Continental Europe

ROSE JEWEL BEETLE
Coroebus rubi

A very striking, bullet-shaped beetle, about 6 mm long with wavy lilac bands crossing its black elytra. A serious pest of roses in southern and eastern Europe, it has recently been spreading northwards and is now found in most parts of France. It is one of a number of pests that could well become established in the British Isles in the near future. Adult beetles are active in the summer months, although they are fairly sluggish and fly only in the hottest weather. The larvae burrow into the stems and branches of wild and cultivated roses, usually just under the surface, and their spiral galleries interfere with the flow of nutrients and water around the plants. Treatment with a systemic insecticide kills the insects, but the plants are readily reinfested by insects breeding in wild roses and also in brambles.

Rose Jewel Beetle

Looks: Bullet-shaped with lilac bands on elytra

Food: Roses

When: Adult in spring and summer: larvae all year

Where: Southern and central Europe, including France

Click beetles

Adult click beetles chew leaves and flowers and are particularly interested in pollen, but it is the larvae that really do the damage. These are the infamous wireworms – shiny, yellowish-brown creatures up to 2.5 cm long with three pairs of legs right at the front. They may spend as long as five years in the ground before turning into adult beetles. Although most common in grassland soils, they can destroy the roots and underground stems of many garden plants, often tunnelling into potatoes with their tough jaws and paving the way for other troublesome pests such as slugs and millipedes. Apart from destroying the adult beetles when you see them, there is not much that can be done to combat these pests, although good weed control and regular cultivation will deprive the wireworms of food and shelter. No insecticides are available for treating the soil.

COMMON CLICK BEETLE
Agriotes lineatus

This is one of several rather similar, slender species also known as 'skipjacks'. When one of these beetles is disturbed, it commonly falls to the ground where, with its legs pulled tightly in, it is easily overlooked as a piece of twig or a seed. If the beetle lands on its belly, it merely extends its legs and scurries away, but if it lands on its back it must right itself before it can make good its escape, and the click beetles have perfected a neat trick that helps them to get back on their feet. There is a very flexible joint in the thorax and the beetle is able to arch its back strongly at this junction. Muscle tension is then suddenly released and the beetle jack-knifes;

Common Click Beetle

Looks: Slender beetle, yellowish brown and slightly hairy

Food: Wireworm larvae eat the roots and seedlings of a wide range of plants

When: Adult in spring and summer: larvae all year

Where: Britain and Continental Europe

The Common Click Beetle can be distinguished from several similar-shaped beetles found in the garden by its reddish brown antennae. Thorax and elytra are all basically light brown.

its 'shoulders' are pushed hard down against the ground, and the elasticity of the insect's outer covering causes it to spring as much as 30 cm into the air. During its 'flight' it may perform several somersaults, but it is a matter of chance whether it lands the right way up: if it fails, it merely repeats the process until it succeeds. The loud click that accompanies each leap gives the beetles their common name. Up to 1 cm long, the Common Click Beetle is yellowish-brown and slightly hairy with darker stripes on the elytra. Brick-coloured antennae distinguish it from most of its relatives.

GARDEN CLICK BEETLE
Athous haemorrhoidalis
This beetle is 1–1.5 cm long and has deeply grooved but more or less uniformly brown elytra. It inhabits wild and cultivated land almost everywhere.

Garden Click Beetle

Looks: Adult has deeply grooved brown elytra

Food: Wireworm larvae destroy roots of many garden plants

When: Adult in spring and summer: larvae all year

Where: Britain and Continental Europe

RIGHT: A click beetle larva – the wireworm that destroys the subterranean parts of many garden plants. Wireworms are sometimes confused with soil-dwelling centipedes, but they have only three pairs of legs.

BELOW: The Garden Click Beetle has a darker thorax than the smaller Common Click Beetle.

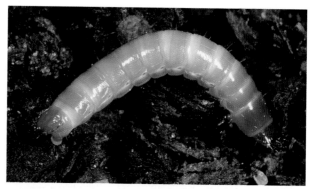

The 24-spot Ladybird is rarely a serious pest but watch out if you are a carnation-lover.

24-SPOT LADYBIRD
Subcoccinella 24-punctata

Most of our ladybirds have carnivorous habits and are only too ready to mop up aphids and other small pests in the garden, but there are a few exceptions and the **24-spot Ladybird** is one of them. It is a vegetarian and is most common in grassland, although it feeds on a wide range of plants in many habitats. The insect is basically dull red with a variable number of black spots. Some of the spots may be fused and there are rarely exactly 24 spots! The elytra are slightly hairy, unlike those of any other British ladybird, although you might need a magnifying glass to see this. In common with all other British ladybirds, the 24-spot passes the winter in the adult state – usually dormant in low-growing vegetation. Although it damages carnations in some areas, the insect is rarely a serious pest and there is no need to take any action against it. The **22-spot Ladybird** (*Psyllobora 22-punctata*) is another very spotty and very common garden vegetarian, but this black and yellow species feeds mainly on mildews and does no harm at all.

24-spot Ladybird

Looks: Dull red with variable black spots

Food: May damage carnations

When: Larvae in spring and summer: adults all year, but dormant in winter

Where: Britain and Continental Europe

22-spot Ladybird

Looks: Yellow; black spots

Food: Feeds mainly on mildews

When: Larvae in spring and summer: adults all year, but dormant in winter

Where: Britain and Continental Europe

The 22-spot Ladybird is a common garden inhabitant found on many different woody and herbaceous plants. It is often common on gooseberry and currant bushes and, although you might think it is up to mischief, it is simply mopping up mildews.

ABOVE LEFT: Three spiky Harlequin Ladybird larvae and, at the top, a pupa.

ABOVE RIGHT: One of the commonest varieties of the Harlequin Ladybird is busy tucking into an aphid. The more or less triangular white spot on the head is characteristic of this newcomer.

HARLEQUIN LADYBIRD
Harmonia axyridis

This species is a not entirely welcome recent arrival because, although it is a voracious predator of aphids, it is equally happy to devour useful insects, including the larvae of other ladybirds. Originally from Asia, the beetle is now widely distributed in North America and in many parts of Europe, and it has spread with alarming speed to most parts of Britain and to most habitats since its arrival in 2004. One reason for its rapid increase is the fact that it can produce two generations in a year, whereas most of our ladybirds have only a single generation. The insect is extremely variable: some individuals are black with either two or four red spots, while others are yellow or orange with anything up to 21 black spots. The thoracic shield, just in front of the elytra, is usually white with variable black markings. With a length of up to 8 mm, the Harlequin is slightly larger than most of our other ladybirds, but perhaps the best way to identify the beast is to turn it upside down and look for the characteristic red rim around the rear of the body. Harlequin larvae are quite easy to recognise, being rather spiny and having in their later stages five bright yellow or orange spots on each side. Time will tell if this invader really is a serious threat to out native insects. If you have just a few in your garden they can be left alone, but if the population explodes you can easily pick up the insects and destroy them. Recent observations suggest that the insect does not cope with cold winters as well as native ladybirds.

Harlequin Ladybird

Looks: Variable colour and number of spots; thoracic shield is white with black markings

Food: Predator of many useful insects including other ladybirds

When: Larvae in spring and summer: adults all year, but dormant in winter

Where: Britain and Continental Europe

RASPBERRY BEETLE
Byturus tomentosus

This beetle is responsible for the pale, dry patches that develop near base of the fruits and spoil so many of our raspberries. Blackberries, loganberries and tayberries are also affected. The adult beetle is about 4 mm long and dull brown with clubbed antennae. It overwinters in the soil, emerging in spring to feed on various flowers, being especially interested in the stamens and their pollen. When the raspberries come into flower the beetles move to them and lay their eggs in the flowers. The resulting larvae tunnel into the fruits, cutting off the food supplies to some of the drupelets and causing them to shrivel and dry up. Older larvae feed in the core of the fruit and often alarm the cook when they creep out of the harvested fruits. When fully grown, with a length of about 8 mm, the brownish grubs fall to the ground and pupate in the soil. Raspberry Beetles are common, but not usually serious pests in the garden – affected fruits (and grubs!) are quite edible. Only when crops are grown commercially is it really necessary to take steps to reduce the population. But control of this pest is not easy because numbers are regularly reinforced by beetles flying in from the surrounding countryside. Dusting or spraying with a pyrethroid-based insecticide will certainly help, but it must be done at the right time – when the petals have fallen and there is little risk to pollinating insects. Autumn-fruiting raspberries do not suffer much as they flower after most of the beetles have disappeared.

The Raspberry Beetle is a fairly nondescript minor pest of raspberries.

TOP TIP

Dust or spray with a pyrethroid-based insecticide when the petals have fallen.

Raspberry Beetle

Looks: Small, dull brown with club-shaped antennae

Food: Blackberries, loganberries, raspberries

When: Spring, summer

Where: Britain and Continental Europe

The adult Lily Beetle is certainly attractive, but it is definitely a pest and not something that any gardener will want in the flowerbeds. All kinds of liliaceous plants fall victim to this voracious species.

Lily Beetle

Looks: Vivid red beetle to 8 mm long; black legs

Food: Adults and larvae eat all parts of various species of lilies

When: Larvae in spring and summer: adults all year, but dormant in winter

Where: Britain and Continental Europe

LILY BEETLE
Lilioceris lilii

One of the most hated of present-day garden pests, not just because of the damage it does but also because of the disgusting habits of its larvae. Up to 8 mm long, the adult beetle is actually very attractive in its bright red coat, but it is certainly not welcome in the garden. It belongs, together with the next few species, to the immense group of leaf beetles and it chews holes in the leaves of lilies, crown imperials and other liliaceous species. When numerous it quickly defoliates the plants. Madonna lilies are especially susceptible to this pest, which will strip entire flowering spikes, removing flower buds as well as leaves. The insect has two or three broods in a year and can be seen from early spring until the autumn. The beetles then burrow into the soil and remain there in a dormant state until the spring, when they lay clusters of orange eggs, usually on the undersides of the leaves. The resulting grubs are orange, but they cover themselves with

This is how one usually sees the Lily Beetle grub – covered with its own excrement with just the head poking out, it is extremely well protected, for no bird is likely to investigate it! Remove the faecal umbrella if you dare and you will find the fleshy orange grub. And then squash it if you value your lilies.

their slimy black excrement and are often mistaken for small slugs or the droppings of some other creature. They are even more damaging than the adults, scraping the surface layers from the leaves, which then turn brown and shrivel. The pest is widely distributed on the Continent but until the 1980s it was quite rare in the British Isles and confined to the southern counties. The increasing popularity of garden lilies, possibly combined with climate change, has allowed it to spread rapidly in recent years and it now occurs in many parts of the country. Contact insecticides can be used against the insects, but fingers are better! The grubs are easily squashed where you find them – a messy job perhaps, but you get your reward when your lilies come into flower. Alternatively, you can remove the infested leaves and tread on them. The adult beetles are not quite so easy to destroy because they tend to drop to the ground when disturbed and their black undersides make them difficult to spot if they fall onto their backs. Regular destruction of the egg batches is the best method of all.

The very similar **Lilioceris merdigera** is common on the Continent where, in addition to attacking various lilies, it can cause serious damage to onions and leeks. It can be distinguished from the Lily Beetle by its reddish-brown legs.

TOP TIP

The easiest way to deal with Lily Beetles is to squash the grubs with your fingers.

Lilioceris merdigera

Looks: Vivid red beetle to 8 mm long. Red-brown legs

Food: Onions and leeks

When: Spring, summer

Where: Britain and Continental Europe

The Asparagus Beetle is another colourful insect, but it and its larvae can quickly defoliate your asparagus plants if you don't keep it under control.

ASPARAGUS BEETLE
Crioceris asparagi

An attractive little beetle – as long as you don't grow asparagus, for both adult and larva feed on the leaves and stems, and the insect is a serious pest in some parts of Europe. The adult beetles are 5–8 mm long, with a brownish thorax and rust-coloured edges to the elytra. The latter are basically black with three more or less rectangular cream patches on each, although the latter vary in size and may be separated by no more than thin black lines. Adults hibernate in soil or leaf litter and wake to lay their black eggs on the asparagus spears and foliage in the spring. The resulting soft-bodied larvae are grey with black spots and up to 1 cm long when fully grown. They pupate in the soil and there are two generations in a year. Spraying with a pyrethroid-based insecticide will control the pest in large asparagus beds, but fingers are better if you have just a few plants – although the adults are pretty fidgety and often drop to the ground as soon as they detect any disturbance. Destroy old stems and other plant debris to remove potential hibernating sites.

Asparagus Beetle

Looks: Slim beetle with black, brown and cream markings; larvae are grey with black spots

Food: Asparagus

When: Larvae in spring and summer: adults all year, but dormant in winter

Where: Britain and Continental Europe

The Spotted Asparagus Beetle is a serious asparagus pest on the continent, but not yet resident in Britain. Squash the adults if you can catch them but, in common with the previous species, it tends to drop to the ground as soon as it is disturbed.

SPOTTED ASPARAGUS BEETLE
Crioceris duodecimpunctata

Slightly larger than the previous species, this beetle has orange or red elytra, each bearing six black spots. It is a troublesome pest on the Continent, although it is not resident in the British Isles. The adults behave just like those of the Asparagus Beetle, but the larvae live inside the fruits and do little or no harm to the crop.

Spotted Asparagus Beetle

Looks: Orange or red elytra with six spots on each side

Food: Asparagus plants

When: Larvae in summer (but hidden in fruits): adults all year but dormant in winter

Where: Continental Europe

The Colorado Beetle is the most infamous of potato pests. Its name indicates its North American origin, and it would probably have stayed there doing no harm if potatoes had not been introduced to its home territory from South America. The beetle quickly transferred its attention to the new food source and has since followed potato cultivation to most parts of the world.

A Colorado Beetle larva (INSET). These fleshy grubs should be destroyed as soon as they are seen, or they will reduce your potato plants to smelly bare stems in a very short time.

Colorado Beetle

Looks: Black and yellow stripes; yellow thorax

Food: Potatoes

When: Larvae in spring and summer: adults all year, but dormant in winter

Where: Rare in Britain, common in Europe

COLORADO BEETLE
Leptinotarsa decemlineata

Mention of the Colorado Beetle strikes fear into potato growers, for this is one of the most serious of our potato pests. Originally from North America, where it fed harmlessly on wild plants, it has now followed potato crops to most parts of Europe and to many other parts of the world. Up to 1.2 cm long, the adult beetle is easily recognised by its black and yellow stripes. It feasts on the potato leaves and a heavy infestation can quickly reduce the plants to bare stems, usually liberally spattered with the insects' black droppings. The fleshy pink larvae are equally damaging. The insects are less commonly found on tomatoes and nightshades. Adult beetles burrow into the soil in the autumn and pass the winter there in a dormant state, waking to lay their eggs on new potato crops in the spring. A new generation of adults appears in a couple of months and a second generation may appear in late summer in warm areas. Pyrethroid-based insecticides give fairly good control of the beetle when applied to the infested foliage, and thorough winter digging also helps by disturbing the hibernating beetles and exposing them to predators. Although extremely common on the Continent, the pest is rarely seen in the British Isles, where strict inspection routines have prevented the beetle from establishing itself. Occasional specimens arrive on imported produce and any suspected occurrence must be reported immediately to the local DEFRA Office.

ROSEMARY BEETLE
Chrysolina americana

Despite its scientific name, the Rosemary Beetle does not come from America. This rather beautiful, if troublesome, insect is a native of southern Europe and has been spreading northwards in recent decades, arriving in the British Isles in the 1980s. Up to 1 cm long with metallic green and purple stripes on its elytra, it is not likely to be confused with any other beetle in the garden. Both adults and their dingy grey larvae browse on rosemary leaves and flowers, and they also nibble the bark of young shoots, causing the upper parts to die back. Lavender and thyme may also be attacked. The insects are usually present throughout the year, although damage is most serious in spring and autumn. Careful hand removal is the most efficient control.

The Rosemary Beetle, easily identified by its green and purple stripes, is a pest of thyme and lavender as well as rosemary.

Chrysolina fastuosa

A beautiful iridescent beetle, this insect is up to 6 mm long and sometimes entirely green, though it often has violet or coppery patches on the elytra. Adults and larvae feed mainly on deadnettles and their relatives, but the insect is occasionally a nuisance to beetroot growers in the summer and can also be found on sugar beet and, less often, on spinach. Damage is rarely severe and hand-picking of the beetles will suffice in the garden. Although it is widely distributed and quite common on the Continent, the insect occurs only locally in the British Isles.

Chrysolina fastuosa is one of our most colourful leaf beetles. Although uncommon in the British Isles, it can be a nuisance for beetroot and spinach growers.

Rosemary Beetle

Looks: Up to 1 cm with green and purple metallic stripes

Food: Leaves, flowers, and shoots of rosemary and other scented labiates

When: All year

Where: Much of Europe, including Britain

Chrysolina fastuosa

Looks: Iridescent beetle, usually green but with violet or copper patches

Food: Beetroot, sugar beet, spinach

When: All year

Where: Much of Europe, but of local occurrence in Britain

Flea beetles

Brassica seedlings commonly develop small, pale-rimmed pits almost as soon as they stick their heads above the ground in the spring. The culprits are various flea beetles, so named because they leap about with the aid of their broad and muscular back legs.

Phyllotreta nemorum

This is one of the commonest flea beetles with a broad yellow stripe on each elytron and, although only about 3 mm long, it is frequently called the Large Striped Flea Beetle – to distinguish it from its smaller cousin the Small Striped Flea Beetle! It is also called the Turnip Flea, although this name is also given to several other closely related species. The adult beetles hibernate in the soil and in plant debris and wake just in time to attack the germinating seedlings. Eggs are then laid in the soil and the resulting larvae tunnel into the roots or leaves of the developing plants. Although turnips and radishes are their main targets, the beetles attack all kinds of brassicas and many related plants, including wall-flowers. Dusting the seedlings and the surrounding soil with a pyrethroid-based insecticide provides good protection. Keeping the seed-bed free from debris also helps to reduce the flea beetle population in the spring, although the adult insects can fly in from neighbouring gardens and from fields where rape is grown. Covering the rows with horticultural fleece gives extra protection to the seedlings, or you can try an ingenious method of catching the insects when they jump. All you need is a piece of cardboard coated with grease or glue, and you simply drag it over the tips of the plants: the beetles sense the disturbance, leap into the air – and become stuck on the card! A clump of mint planted in the cabbage patch is also reputed to deter flea beetles.

Phyllotreta nemorum

Looks: Broad yellow stripe on each black elytron

Food: Germinating seedlings of turnips, radishes and brassicas

When: Adults all year, but dormant in winter

Where: Britain and Continental Europe

Phyllotreta nemorum, one of several tiny beetles commonly called turnip fleas, nibbles the leaves of a wide range of brassicas and is especially damaging to seedlings, as illustrated here. They take chunks out of the leaf margins and chew conspicuous pits and holes all over the surface.

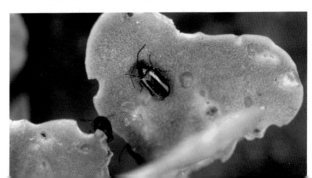

CABBAGE STEM FLEA BEETLE
Psyllioides chrysocephala

This pest has golden brown legs and the elytra, which are either bluish-black or occasionally golden brown, are strongly curved on the outer edge. Adults feed on the leaves and flowers of mature brassicas for much of the year, while the larvae tunnel inside the stems and mid-ribs.

Cabbage Stem Flea Beetle

Looks: Golden brown legs; elytra are bluish black or brown

Food: Mature brasssicas

When: Much of year

Where: Britain and Continental Europe

The Cabbage Stem Flea Beetle is found on brassicas at most times of the year.

Phyllotreta nigripes

This beetle is also bluish-black, but has black legs and the elytra, like those of *P. nemorum*, are more or less parallel-sided. The adults behave like those of *P. nemorum*, but the larvae feed mainly on the roots.

POTATO FLEA BEETLE
Psylliodes affinis

Found almost everywhere on potatoes and tomatoes, the rusty-brown adults nibble small holes in the leaves and the larvae feed on the roots, but rarely do much damage and control is not usually needed. The species is also common on woody nightshade, a wild relative of the potato.

Potato Flea Beetle

Looks: Rusty brown

Food: Potatoes and tomatoes

When: Larvae in spring and summer: adults all year, but dormant in winter

Where: Britain and Continental Europe

The Potato Flea Beetle is less than 3 mm long and rarely noticed.

Adoxus obscurus

This beetle is sometimes a pest of vines in southern Europe, although it attacks plenty of other plants, including willow-herbs and wild and cultivated evening primroses. The adult beetle, about 5 mm in length, is usually shiny black, although some specimens are rusty brown with pale hairs. It can be found chewing leaves and flowers and also fruits throughout the summer months. The larvae feed on the roots of various plants, overwintering in the soil and pupating in the spring. Although widely distributed on the Continent, the beetle does not occur in the British Isles.

Adoxus obscurus

Looks: Shiny black, up to 5 mm; some rusty brown

Food: Vines and other plants including evening primrose

When: Adult in summer: larvae much of the year but dormant in winter

Where: Widely distributed in Europe, but not in Britain

VIBURNUM LEAF BEETLE
Pyrrhalta viburni

Anyone growing guelder roses or other viburnums is likely to find at least some of the leaves reduced to lacy skeletons in late spring and summer. Whole bushes are commonly defoliated. The culprit here is the Viburnum Leaf Beetle. Its spotty, creamy white larvae begin the onslaught as soon as they hatch from their eggs in the spring, and the adults take over later in the summer, removing all the soft leaf tissue and leaving only the tough veins. The adult beetle is a rather downy brown creature, about 6 mm long and carrying slender antennae almost as long as its body. It lays its eggs in small hollows on the young twigs and the eggs remain there until they hatch in the spring. Mature larvae pupate in the soil and new adults start to appear in June. Regular inspection of the bushes in the spring should reveal any incipient problems, and if only a few leaves are affected they can be removed and destroyed, along with the offending insects. Large-scale infestations should be treated with contact insecticides as soon as the damage is noticed.

TOP TIP

Combat initial infestations by removing and destroying the leaves and any insects that remain on them.

Viburnum Leaf Beetle

Looks: Greenish-yellow larvae; adult is brown with downy hairs

Food: Viburnums

When: Larvae in spring: adults in summer and autumn

Where: Britain and Continental Europe

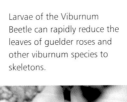

Larvae of the Viburnum Beetle can rapidly reduce the leaves of guelder roses and other viburnum species to skeletons.

Look for the two black spots right at the tip of the abdomen to distinguish the Pea Beetle from several similar species. It is often seen basking on walls in the spring.

PEA BEETLE
Bruchus pisorum

One of several similar beetles affecting leguminous crops. All have truncated elytra, which leave the tip of the abdomen exposed, and the Pea Beetle can be recognised by the two large black spots at the rear of the abdomen. The adult, about 5 mm long, can often be seen basking on walls in the spring sunshine. Females lay their eggs on the young pea pods as the flowers begin to fade, and the resulting larvae then tunnel into the pods and enter the developing seeds – just one larva to each seed. The larvae feed inside the peas and pupate there when fully grown, although few ever get to that stage in the garden because we usually step in and harvest the peas long before the larvae are ready to pupate. Only those in peas destined for the next year's seed packets or those that fall to the ground reach maturity. They pass the winter in the seeds and emerge to begin the cycle again in the spring. The insect is much more common in field crops than in gardens because many field crops are harvested later and many of the ripe peas fall to the ground.

Pea Beetle

Looks: Brown with two large black spots at rear of abdomen

Food: Leguminous crops

When: Larvae in spring and summer: adults much of the year but dormant in winter

Where: Britain and Continental Europe

The Broad Bean Beetle is very similar to the Pea Beetle, but much less common in the British Isles.

Broad Bean Beetle

Looks: Dark brown body and red front legs

Food: Broad beans

When: Larvae in spring and summer: adults most of the year but dormant in winter

Where: Britain and Continental Europe

BROAD BEAN BEETLE
Bruchus rufimanus

Very similar to the Pea Beetle, the Broad Bean Beetle is usually paler and it lacks the black spots at the tip of the abdomen. It also has entirely red front legs. The insect's life history is very like that of the Pea Beetle, although there may be more than one grub in each bean. As with the Pea Beetle, the life cycle is likely to be completed only in those beans that are saved and dried for sowing in the following year. The presence of the beetles does not seem to affect germination unduly, but many broad beans are sown early in the year and if the beetles then emerge before the seeds germinate their exit holes can allow fungi and bacteria to enter and this can lead to decay and death of the seed. Apart from ensuring that no old seed pods are left lying around in the garden, there is no effective way of controlling these beetles, so it is fortunate that they are not serious pests.

PEA WEEVIL
Sitona lineatus

This little beetle nibbles the leaf margins of peas and broad beans, and also clovers and other wild leguminous plants, leaving them with wavy edges resembling the perforations on the edges of postage stamps. This does not do much harm to mature plants, although it can certainly weaken seedlings, but it is the larvae that are the real pests. They feed on the roots in the spring and are particularly fond of the root nodules – the bacteria-filled swellings that provide the plants with valuable nitrates. Again, it is the young plants that suffer most. The adult beetle, about 5 mm long with a blunt snout and conspicuously striped elytra, appears in the summer and, after feeding on a range of leguminous plants, hibernates in turf and leaf litter. It lays its eggs in the soil in the spring. It is not possible to control the larvae in the soil, but covering the seed rows with horticultural fleece will deny access to many of the adult beetles and, by keeping the soil a little warmer, it will encourage growth and allow the seedlings to 'get away' before too much damage can be caused. Dusting young plants with a contact insecticide in the spring as soon as any leaf damage is noticed will also reduce the amount of egg-laying by the adult beetles.

Pea Weevil

Looks: Light brown, striped elytra

Food: Peas, broad beans and other legumes

When: Larvae in spring and summer: adults all year, but dormant in winter

Where: Britain and Continental Europe

BELOW RIGHT: The Pea Weevil has larger eyes and a much shorter snout than most other weevils.

BELOW LEFT: Damage to clover leaves caused by the Pea Weevil. Similar damage can be seen on peas and other leguminous plants from spring to autumn, and in the early stages the perforations tend to be much more regular.

NUT WEEVIL
Curculio nucum

This insect grows up in hazel nuts and its fat white grubs often wriggle out when we open the nuts to eat the kernels. Left to its own devices, each grub remains in its nut until the latter falls in the autumn, and then eventually chews a neat round exit hole in the shell. It pupates in the soil and the adult weevil emerges in the spring to feed on pollen and nectar from various flowers. This beetle has one of the longest snouts in the weevil family and its jaws are right at the tip. The female uses her jaws to bore into the young nuts in the summer before laying an egg in each one. Although not a serious pest, the weevil can ruin a high proportion of nuts on some trees – and there is not really anything that can be done to control it. **Curculio elephas**, found mainly in southern Europe, has an even longer and somewhat straighter snout and is a pest of sweet chestnuts. It also attacks acorns.

Nut Weevil

Looks: Brown with very long, curved snout

Food: Hazel nuts

When: Adult in spring and summer; larvae in late summer and autumn

Where: Britain and Continental Europe

The Nut Weevil, here using its extremely long, slightly curved snout to probe a hazel bud, is up to 9 mm long. Although the adult weevil feeds mainly on pollen and nectar, it frequently attacks buds and chews holes in leaves.

APPLE BLOSSOM WEEVIL
Anthonomus pomorum

Apple buds that turn brown and do not open are sometimes simply the victims of late frosts, but could equally well have been attacked by this little black or brown beetle. Up to 6 mm long, it lays its eggs in the flower buds, and the resulting larvae feed there, protected by a dome of unopened petals. There is usually just one off-white larva in each bud, and it pupates there when fully grown. Adult weevils emerge in midsummer and nibble the leaves for a while before going into a long hibernation in leaf litter or under loose bark. The insect attacks pear trees as well as apples, although it is rarely abundant enough to need controlling. If it is a problem spray your trees with a pyrethroid-based insecticide just before the buds open.

The Apple Blossom Weevil is a minor pest of apples and pears.

Apple Blossom Weevil

Looks: Small black or brown weevil

Food: Apple buds

When: Adult much of the year, but active only in spring and summer: larvae in spring and summer

Where: Britain and Continental Europe

APPLE BUD WEEVIL
Anthonomus piri

Closely related to the Apple Blossom Weevil, this weevil lays its eggs in the buds in the autumn, when the buds are at a much earlier stage of development – and they don't develop any further because the weevil grubs hollow them out. Affected buds never open and badly affected branches remain bare when those around them are turning green. This weevil attacks only apples in the British Isles, where it is a rare insect, but on the Continent it is a common pest of pears as well.

Apple Bud Weevil

Looks: Small black or brown weevil

Food: Buds of apple and pear trees

When: Adult in summer and autumn: larvae in buds from autumn to spring

Where: Only apples in Britain; pears in Europe

TURNIP GALL WEEVIL
Ceutorhynchus pleurostigma

The larvae attack the roots of turnips and swedes, as well as those of the cabbage tribe. The adult weevils, essentially black and only about 3 mm long, lay their eggs on the roots of their host plants in spring and early summer and the resulting grubs tunnel into the roots. Their feeding activity stimulates the roots to swell up around them, forming more or less spherical galls **(see p. 24)**. The grubs continue to feed in the galls until late in the winter, when they make their way out and pupate in the surrounding soil. Damage to cabbages and other leafy brassicas is slight, but the roots of turnips and swedes can become stunted and unusable if heavily infested. Chemical control of the pest is not feasible and the best way to keep its numbers down is to destroy all brassica roots as soon as the crops have been harvested. Galls caused by this weevil are easily distinguished from the swellings caused by club-root fungus because the latter are solid and those induced by the weevil are hollow.

Turnip Gall Weevil

Looks: Black, up to 3 mm

Food: Roots of turnips and swedes as well as cabbages

When: Adult in spring and early summer: larvae in roots from summer until late winter

Where: Britain and Continental Europe

HOLLYHOCK WEEVIL
Rhopalapion longirostre

This is a small black weevil with an extremely long snout. The adults pass the winter in plant debris or in the hollyhock seeds and wake to attack the buds in the spring. They feed mainly on the buds at this time and the females use their long snouts to drill deep into the buds before laying their eggs there. The buds can still open, and the weevil larvae live and feed in the developing seeds. They also pupate in the seeds and new adults emerge in late summer, although some may remain in the seeds until the following spring. Those weevils that are active in late summer feed mainly on the petals, which then tend to become rather ragged. The species is a native of central and eastern Europe, but has been spreading in recent years and had reached southern England by 2006. Removal of the hollyhock seed pods as soon as the petals have fallen will reduce the weevil population, and spraying with a contact insecticide when the buds begin to swell in the spring will kill off many of the feeding adults.

Hollyhock Weevil

Looks: Small and black with long snout

Food: Hollyhock plants

When: Larvae in buds and flowers in spring and summer: adults much of the year but dormant in winter

Where: Central and eastern Europe; southern England

Rhynchites bacchus, sometimes called the Peach Weevil, damages the flowers and fruits of a wide range of rosaceous trees.

Rhynchites bacchus

An attractive beetle up to about 6 mm long, with a deep purple iridescence and rather hairy elytra, this species lives on various rosaceous trees, and although often called the Peach Weevil, it is more likely to damage apples, plums and apricots. It also attacks cherries. The adult beetles feed on buds, flowers and fruits throughout the summer. Eggs are laid in the ripening fruits during the summer, and the females then nibble through the fruit stalks, causing the fruits to fall. The eggs hatch in about a week and the larvae feed in the decaying fruits. When fully grown, with a length of about 1 cm, they make their way into the surrounding soil and pupate. New adults emerge in late summer and autumn and chew the buds and young shoots for a while before seeking overwintering sites under loose bark or among fallen leaves and other debris. Collecting and destroying fallen fruits and leaves is the best way to combat this pest. The beetle occurs in many parts of Europe, but it has not been found in the British Isles for many years.

Rhynchites cupreus

Equally colourful although usually somewhat redder than *R. bacchus* and with a distinct coppery sheen, this species is a little smaller than *R. bacchus* and has a shorter snout. The two species have very similar life histories. Unripe plums and cherries are the main targets of *R. cupreus*, but it is not a serious pest. It is a rare insect in many parts of Europe, especially in the British Isles, where it is more likely to be found on rowan trees than on our cultivated fruit trees.

Rhynchites bacchus

Looks: Iridescent hairy purple beetle, up to 6 mm

Food: Apples, plums, apricots, cherries

When: Adults most of the year, but dormant in winter: larvae, concealed in fruits, in summer

Where: Continental Europe; rare in Britain

Rhynchites cupreus

Looks: Reddish with coppery sheen

Food: Plums and cherries

When: Adults most of the year, but dormant in winter: larvae, concealed in fruits, in summer

Where: Rare in much of Europe

The adult Vine Weevil (RIGHT), one of several quite similar insects found in the garden and the open countryside, nibbles the leaves of various shrubs, but it is the larva (LEFT) that does most of the damage in the garden. It is also a serious pest of pot plants in the greenhouse and the home.

TOP TIP

For indoor vines, the parasitic nematode worm, Steinernema kraussei, *which attacks the grubs, is an excellent form of biological control.*

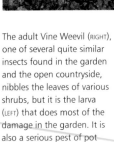

Vine Weevil

Looks: Largely black, up to 1 cm with golden scales on elytra

Food: Grape vines, polyanthus, strawberries

When: Spring and summer out of doors: all year under cover

Where: Britain and Continental Europe

VINE WEEVIL
Otiorhynchus sulcatus

This is one of several very similar destructive weevils, named for its liking for the roots of grape vines although it attacks many other shrubs and herbaceous plants, with polyanthus and strawberries among its favourite targets in the garden. The insect is particularly damaging to pot plants, both indoors and in the garden. The adult weevils are rather slug-gish, flightless creatures up to 1 cm long and largely black with small patches of golden, hair-like scales on the strongly domed elytra. They feed mainly on the leaves of various shrubs. Males are extremely rare, and absent altogether from some populations, and the females normally lay fertile eggs in the soil without mating. The fat, legless white grubs have brown heads and are far more damaging than the adult beetles. They munch their way through roots and rhizomes, and rapidly cause wilting and death of the affected plants. When fully grown, they pupate in the soil, and those living out of doors usually remain in the pupal stage throughout the winter. New adults then emerge in the spring. Indoors or under glass, however, adults and larvae can be found throughout the year.

Effective control of Vine Weevils can now be achieved by either chemical or biological means. Ornamental pot plants can be protected by mixing a suitable insecticide with the potting compost. Imidacloprid, a relatively new synthetic insecticide related to nicotine, is particularly good in this respect: granules added to the compost can protect plants for several months **(but see p. 41)**. The related thiacloprid sprayed onto the plants will be absorbed by the leaves and transported to the roots to do its work on the grubs. Biolog-ical control is centred on one or two species of parasitic nematode worms **(see p. 38)**, including *Steinernema kraussei,* which tunnel into the grubs and kill them. Although these worms do a really good job for indoor plants, they are less successful out in the garden because they need constant warmth. They can also be washed down to lower levels, away from their intended targets. If you don't want to mess about with chemicals or with microscopic worms, you can protect your pot plants to some extent by putting sticky bands around the pots to trap the wandering weevils before they reach the plants. The adults are active mainly by night, so it is always worth having a look at your plants then and destroying any weevils that you find, and always be on the look-out for grubs when re-potting your plants.

ELM BARK BEETLE
Scolytus scolytus

This beetle is the notorious carrier of Dutch elm disease[1], which has killed millions of elm trees in Europe over the past few decades. The disease is caused by a fungus that came originally from central Asia and started to spread around Europe early in the 20th century, although current outbreaks are due to a more virulent strain accidentally imported from Canada in the 1960s. As only elms are affected by the disease, you are unlikely to be bothered by it unless you have an elm hedge. The first signs of trouble are wilting and yellowing of the leaves, which gradually shrivel and die: shoots and branches follow, and the whole tree eventually dies. Adult females are attracted to trees already weakened by the disease and they make small holes in the bark. The scent of their droppings attracts males – and more females – and the insects pair up and mate just inside the holes. Each pair then sets to work to tunnel through the bark to reach the nutritious cambium layer just below it. The female does most of the drilling, while the male removes the debris. When she has reached the cambium region between the bark and the true wood, the female chews out a short vertical gallery and lays her eggs at intervals on each side. When the eggs hatch, the larvae tunnel away from the main gallery in a more or less horizontal direction, producing the character-istic patterns that can be seen on fallen bark and the denuded

Elm Bark Beetle

Looks: Shiny black thorax and brown elytra

Food: Elm trees

When: Adult in spring and summer: larvae all year

Where: Britain and Continental Europe

---

1 The name is somewhat unfortunate: the disease did not originate in the Netherlands, but acquired its common name because Dutch scientists carried out much of the early research on the problem.

The Elm Bark Beetle is about 5 mm long and it can be distinguished from most of its relatives by its shiny black thorax.

trunks. The larval tunnels get wider as they get further from the main gallery. The larvae eventually pupate at the ends of their tunnels and the emerging adults chew small round exit holes in the bark. Because additional females are attracted to the scent of the first arrival, elms often have numerous gallery systems, and a heavy infestation can kill a tree by completely separating the bark from the underlying wood, although affected trees are already condemned to death by the fungus.

The adult beetles feed mainly on the young elm shoots, and this is how the fungus gets into new trees, because beetles emerging from infected trees nearly always carry fungus spores on their bodies. Spores entering the damaged shoots start to grow and the fungus then spreads back down the shoots and branches, gradually blocking the tubes carrying food and water around the tree and causing the familiar symptoms.

Control of the bark beetles and the disease is almost impossible. Some success has been achieved by injecting trees with a fungicide, but this is very expensive and worthwhile only for valuable specimen trees. Some elm cultivars are less susceptible than our native elms, although wych elm seems to have some degree of resistance to the disease. If you have an elm hedge, the best way to keep the disease at bay is to trim regularly and keep the hedge down to about 2 metres in height. The adult beetles prefer to feed at higher levels, and even if they do nibble your hedge, regular clipping will remove any infected shoots before the fungus can spread to the main branches.

Several other trees are attacked by other bark beetles, with each species producing its own characteristic tunnel pattern

TOP TIP

• *Keeping an elm hedge trimmed to 2 m or less helps to control Elm Bark Beetles as they prefer to feed at higher levels.*

• *Clip regularly to remove infected branches.*

Galleries of the Elm Bark Beetle on a trunk from which the bark has already fallen. The same patterns can be seen on the bark itself, although these are always a little deeper because the grubs actually feed on the nutritious inner bark.

under the bark. Apples and other fruit trees, for example, play host to the **Fruit Bark Beetle** (*Scolytus rugulosus*), whose tunnel patterns are very similar to those of the Elm Bark Beetle. It normally chooses small trees, and although it does not carry anything like Dutch elm disease, a small number of beetles can kill a whole tree simply by loosening the bark. See also page 122 for the Cypress Bark Beetle.

BUTTERFLIES AND MOTHS

Butterflies and moths all belong to the order Lepidoptera and their wings are clothed with tiny overlapping scales that give the wings their colourful patterns. The scales are easily rubbed off, however, and the wings of older adult insects often have 'bald' patches. Butterflies all fly in the daytime, while most moths are nocturnal, although there are quite a few day-flying species. The adult insects feed mainly on nectar, which they suck from the flowers through a slender, hollow tube called the proboscis. This is coiled under the head when not in use and extended by blood pressure and muscular action when the insect starts to feed. Some adult moths do not feed at all and don't even have a proboscis. The adult insects do no harm and they add to the enjoyment of our gardens as they flit from flower to flower. Many gardeners actually grow buddleias and other nectar-rich plants specifically to attract butterflies. The insects may also help to pollinate the flowers as they feed. It is the young stages – the caterpillars – that do the damage. They have chewing mouths and most of them feed on leaves. Some feed inside flowers and fruits and a few feed inside stems, including tree trunks and branches. Several species can be a nuisance in the garden, although few are sufficiently numerous to qualify as pests and need any sort of control. All species pass through a chrysalis or pupal stage before becoming adults.

Troublesome butterflies

The only butterflies that cause serious problems in British gardens are the **Large White** (*Pieris brassicae*) and the **Small White** (*Pieris rapae*), both commonly referred to as 'cabbage whites' because their caterpillars feed mainly on cabbages and other brassicas. They also attack garden nasturtiums, which contain similar-tasting mustard oils.

TOP TIP

Control Large Whites in a small garden by regularly inspecting brassicas and squashing eggs and caterpillars.

LARGE WHITE
Pieris brassicae

Easily the largest of our white butterflies, the Large White has a front wing up to 3.5 cm long, with an extensive black tip on the upper side. The female also has two large black spots on the upper side near the middle of the front wing. It flies from April to September and lays its skittle-shaped, yellow eggs in batches on the brassica leaves. The resulting caterpillars are black and yellow and they feed gregariously for much of their lives, quickly reducing our cabbage leaves to skeletons. When nearing full size, they go their separate ways and look for somewhere to turn into pupae. These are cream or greenish-grey with black spots and are often seen on fence posts or the walls of the garden shed. The insects pass the winter in the pupal stage. The Large White is fairly easy to control in a small garden by squashing the eggs and caterpillars, although this is a smelly business and you need to inspect your plants every day in the summer. Don't let the caterpillars get too big.

Large White

Looks: Wings 3.5cm with large black tip; female has spots on wing

Food: Brassicas

When: Adult spring to autumn: caterpillar summer and autumn

Where: Britain and Continental Europe

LEFT: The Large White Butterfly, seen here feeding on buddleia, is easily recognised by its size and extensive black wing-tips. Attractive though it may be in such a situation, it is a major pest in the cabbage patch and its bright yellow egg batches (INSET) should be destroyed on sight.

BELOW LEFT: The gregarious caterpillars of the Large White grow to 4 cm in length and rely on their bold pattern (warning coloration) for protection. Anyone who has squashed them will know that they smell (and presumably taste) awful. Caterpillars of the Small White, however, live singly and rely mainly on camouflage for protection. There is one caterpillar in the centre of the picture.

ABOVE: A mating pair of Small White butterflies: the male on the left is identified by the single black spot on each front wing. Notice also the relatively small black wing-tip patch.

INSET: The velvety green Small White caterpillar is quite hard to spot when resting along the mid-rib of a cabbage leaf. It grows to a length of about 2.5 cm.

Small White

Looks: Front wing to 2.5 cm with greyish wing-tip

Food: Brassicas

When: Adult and caterpillar spring to autumn

Where: Britain and Continental Europe

SMALL WHITE
Pieris rapae

The front wing of the Small White is rarely more than 2.5 cm long and often much less, with a much smaller and greyer wing-tip than the Large White. The female has two black spots on the upper side of the front wing, but the male has only a single spot or none at all. The butterfly is on the wing from spring until well into the autumn and it lays its yellowish-green eggs singly. They are not easy to see on the cabbage leaves, and the plain green caterpillars are equally well camouflaged. Winter is passed as a green or pale brown chrysalis, attached to upright supports just like that of the Large White. The Green-veined White is also very common in gardens, but it rarely takes any notice of our brassicas and usually lays its eggs on their wild relatives. It is easily distinguished from the Small White by the green stripes under the hind wings. It is less easy to destroy the eggs and caterpillars of the Small White by squashing because they are more difficult to find. You can spray or dust the young crops with a pyrethroid-based insecticide, or you can cover your crops with horticultural fleece to keep the egg-laying butterflies away. Or, you can lure butterflies away from cabbages by spraying neighbouring plants with cabbage water (see p. 34).

Helpful parasites

Luckily for us, the cabbage whites, in common with all other butterflies and moths, have numerous enemies to keep their numbers down. One of these is a tiny parasitic wasp called Cotesia glomeratus. It lays its eggs inside the caterpillars of the cabbage whites and its grubs gradually eat the caterpillars from the inside. Infected caterpillars become lethargic but do not die until they are nearly full-grown. The parasitic grubs then emerge and pupate in small cocoons around the shrivelled caterpillar skins. You may well find clusters of cocoons on fences and shed walls in the autumn, and if you leave them alone the next generation of adults will continue their good work. Pteromalus puparum targets the chrysalis rather than the caterpillar, laying its eggs in fresh chrysalids of both Large and Small Whites before their skins have hardened. Numerous grubs grow up inside a single chrysalis and pupate inside it. The resulting adults emerge through tiny holes. And then, of course, there are the minute egg parasites that actually grow up inside the butterflies' eggs – but that's another story.

LEFT: *Pteromalus* adults emerging from a chrysalis. RIGHT: Cocoons of *Cotesia* surrounding a recently dead Small White caterpillar.

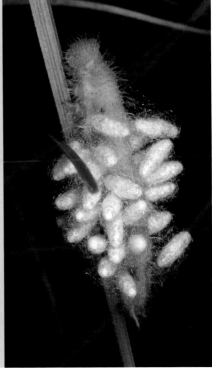

Black-veined White

Looks: Strongly marked black or brown veins on wings with dark outline

Food: Roses, apples, pears, plums, peaches

When: Adult in spring and summer: caterpillar summer to spring, but dormant in winter

Where: Continental Europe

BLACK-VEINED WHITE
Aporia crataegi

Continental Europe has one or two other harmful butterfly species, the best known of which is probably the Black-veined White, named for the prominent black or brown veins on its white wings. It flies in late spring and early summer and lays its eggs in batches on the leaves of various members of the rose family. Blackthorn and hawthorn are the main food-plants in the wild, but cultivated roses are readily attacked and the insect causes serious damage to orchard trees, including apples, pears, plums and peaches. The eggs hatch in the summer and the young caterpillars feed communally in a silken web for a few weeks. The half-grown caterpillars hibernate in the web and emerge to complete their growth in the spring, when they usually feed singly or in small groups. They are recognised by their black and orange backs and pale grey undersides.

RIGHT: A caterpillar of the Black-veined white munching its way through plum leaves. It grows to a length of about 3.5 cm.

BELOW: A mating pair of Black-veined Whites, extinct in the British Isles but still a considerable pest of rosaceous trees and shrubs on the Continent.

ABOVE: The Geranium Bronze butterfly, a recent arrival in southern Europe, is named for the coppery sheen on its upperside. INSET: The bristly caterpillar of the Geranium Bronze actually looks more like a chrysalis. It blends well with the geranium foliage.

GERANIUM BRONZE
Cacyreus marshalli

This is a South African butterfly that has recently established itself in southern Europe, probably having arrived with imported plants. Its caterpillars feed on pelargoniums and cause damage in nurseries and wherever else the plants are grown in quantity. The caterpillars are green and bristly, with rosy pink spots on the back and sides, and are very difficult to see on the host plants. They chew the flower buds and leaves and tunnel inside the stems. The adult butterfly has a beautiful bronze or coppery sheen on its upperside and a prominent 'tail' on each hindwing. Occasional specimens have been found in southern England but the species may not be able to survive the winter out of doors in the British Isles. Suspected occurrences of this insect in Britain should be reported to the local DEFRA office.

Geranium Bronze

Looks: Bronze or copper sheen to wings; caterpillars green with bristles

Food: Pelargoniums

When: Spring, summer

Where: Continental Europe, mainly in the south; occasionally imported into Britain

Problem moths

Hundreds of different kinds of moths visit our gardens to sip nectar from the flowers. Most of them treat it simply as a filling station and move on once they have re-fuelled. Nectar is nectar and, as long as they can reach it with their tubular tongues or probosci, they don't mind which flower it comes from. But caterpillars are different: most species have definite preferences for food-plants and will often starve rather than eat the wrong kind of leaves. The adult moths usually ensure the well-being of their offspring by selecting the right food-plants on which to lay their eggs, so not all moths will settle down and breed in the garden, and of those that do take up residence relatively few do any serious harm. If you are bothered by a lot of caterpillars you can remove them by hand – wearing gloves to deal with hairy ones – and then release them on similar plants in the wild.

The adults of many moth species, both residents and casual visitors, are attracted to lighted windows and other lights at night, and this gives you, the gardener, a good opportunity to have a look at them and appreciate their delicate and often beautiful patterns – patterns that generally afford superb camouflage when the insects are at rest on tree trunks or amongst the vegetation during daylight hours.

GHOST SWIFT
Hepialus humuli

This moth is named for the ghost-like courtship flight of the male. The uppersides of his wings are pure white, in contrast to the greyish-brown undersides, and when he hovers up and down at dusk, almost like a yo-yo, all you see are intermittent flashes of white. This is what attracts the dull yellow female. The moths are on the wing from June to August and, after mating, the female simply scatters her eggs over the ground. The caterpillars burrow into the ground to feed on roots of almost any kind, either nibbling them from the outside or tunnelling right inside them. They are dirty white with a brown head and dark brown or black patches along the sides, and they can reach 4 cm in length. No root vegetable is safe from this pest and it also attacks bulbs and rhizomes and the roots of trees and shrubs. It is patchily distributed, however and, although it is believed to reach densities of over 10,000 per hectare in some places,

Ghost Swift

Looks: Upperside of male wing is white; undersides grey; female dull yellow

Food: Roots and bulbs of all kinds

When: Adult summer; caterpillar all year

Where: Britain and Continental Europe

Male (bottom) and female
Ghost Swift moths at rest.
Their front wings are up to
3.5 cm long.

TOP TIP

*Hoe the soil around
your vegetables
regularly to disturb
caterpillars and pupae.
Destroy any that you
unearth.*

it is absent from many gardens. The caterpillars feed
throughout the winter and many individuals take two years
to complete their growth. They pupate in the soil when
fully grown, the pupae being long and slender and rather
spiny. Regular hoeing will disturb the caterpillars and pupae
and you can squash any that you uncover.

Common Swift

Looks: Rusty brown wings with occasional white patches

Food: Roots of all kinds

When: Adult summer: caterpillar most of the year

Where: Britain and Continental Europe

TOP TIP

Hoe regularly to disturb the caterpillars and their pupae.

COMMON SWIFT
Hepialus lupulinus

This is a very common garden resident that flies at dusk during the summer, usually keeping low over the vegetation. The pale markings on the wings vary in extent and density and are sometimes lacking altogether, especially in the female. Eggs are simply scattered over the ground and the caterpillars feed on all kinds of roots, sometimes boring right into larger roots and stem bases. Peonies and phlox and other plants with extensive rootstocks may harbour several caterpillars without suffering too much, but smaller plants, such as lettuces, can be killed when a single caterpillar chews through the base of the stem. Common Swift caterpillars are smaller and slimmer than those of the Ghost Swift and have a 'cleaner' appearance. They feed through the winter and pupate in the soil but, unlike those of the Ghost Swift, they complete their growth in one year. Regular hoeing around your plants is the best way to keep the pest in check.

Adult and larva of the Common Swift Moth. The adult's front wings are up to 2 cm long and the caterpillar rarely exceeds 3.5 cm in length.

The Goat Moth looks very much like a piece of bark, and is not easy to spot on a tree trunk. Its front wings reach about 4 cm in length.

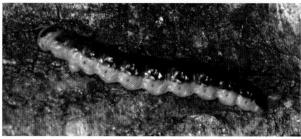

A Goat Moth caterpillar, having left its tree-trunk hole to look for a pupation site. If it has been breeding in your trees you will certainly smell it!

GOAT MOTH
Cossus cossus

This species gets its name for the strong goat-like smell of its shiny pink and brown caterpillar. Although the caterpillar spends its life tunnelling deep in the trunks of various deciduous trees, it ejects large quantities of droppings or frass from its tunnels and these can be smelt from quite a distance. Cherry trees are the most likely targets in the garden, although plums and apples are also attacked. The caterpillars may take three years to grow up and when they are fully mature, with a length of about 6.5 cm, they leave their burrows to pupate in debris at the base of the tree. Adult moths are on the wing in June and July, but are rarely seen because they are so well camouflaged when resting on the tree trunks by day. When, as often happens, several caterpillars live in a single tree, the tree can be seriously damaged. The burrows can be sealed with putty or woodfiller to entomb the caterpillars, but if many holes are present such treatment is probably too late to save the tree. Luckily, the Goat Moth is not a common insect and few gardeners or orchard owners are likely to meet it.

TOP TIP

If you spot any burrows in a tree, seal them with putty to trap the caterpillars within the tree.

Goat Moth

Looks: Pale, camouflaged against tree bark; pink and brown caterpillars

Food: Cherries, plums, apples

When: Adult summer: caterpillar (concealed in tree trunks) all year

Where: Britain and Continental Europe

LEOPARD MOTH
Zeuzera pyrina

Easily recognised by its spotty, thinly scaled wings, the Leopard Moth flies throughout the summer and its caterpillars live in the branches of various trees and shrubs, including apples and other rosaceous trees and also blackcurrants. In southern Europe it can be a pest of grape vines and olives and a serious nuisance to citrus growers. The caterpillar, which is dirty white with black 'warts', takes two or three years to grow up, and then pupates under the bark. Young trees are particularly susceptible to damage by this species but it is very difficult to spot an infested tree because, although the caterpillars push their droppings out of their tunnels, they do not smell and are not easy to see on the bark. If you do find any holes you can stop them up as described above for Goat Moth burrows. The insect does not occur in the northern half of Britain, although it is widely distributed on the continent.

The Leopard Moth is much more of a pest on the Continent than it is in the British Isles. Its front wings are up to 3.5 cm in length.

Leopard Moth

Looks: Spotted wings, thinly scaled and partly translucent

Food: Blackcurrants, apples; citrus fruits in southern Europe

When: Adult summer: caterpillar all year in branches of trees and shrubs

Where: Southern Britain and Continental Europe

HORNET MOTH
Sesia apiformis

This is one of a group of moths known as clearwings. Their wings are largely transparent because most of their scales fall off during their first flight. This species gets its name for its remarkable resemblance to a Hornet **(see p. 271)**. This mimicry is exhibited both at rest and in flight, when it even makes a noise like a Hornet, and this affords the insect excellent protection from birds. In common with all British clearwing moths, it flies only in the sunshine, but it is not likely to occur in any but the largest gardens with mature trees. Its caterpillars live in poplar trunks, usually quite low down, and are occasionally numerous enough to kill the trees by eating the living tissues just under the bark. Their presence may be indicated by accumulations of brown droppings in bark crevices. In common with most other clearwing caterpillars, they are creamy white with a brown head. The adult moths emerge in June and July, when they can sometimes be seen sitting on the trunks to dry their wings. Their empty pupal cases can also be seen protruding from their exit holes. The moth is absent from the northern half of Britain. The Lunar Hornet Moth is quite similar but lacks the yellow patches on the 'shoulders'. It breeds mainly in willows, including the pussy willow that is often grown in gardens.

Hornet Moth

Looks: Yellow and black striped body with yellow 'shoulder pads': virtually clear wings

Food: Poplar trees

When: Adult summer: caterpillar all year in tree trunks

Where: Britain and Continental Europe

The Hornet Moth, freshly emerged from its chrysalis and still having a fair coating of scales on its wings. Most of these scales will fall off during its first flight, and then the moth will look even more like a hornet – but it is perfectly harmless! Its front wings are about 2 cm long.

A Red-belted Clearwing Moth, displaying its characteristic abdominal pattern. Its front wings are only 10 mm long.

RED-BELTED CLEARWING
Synanthedon myopaeformis

Also known as the Apple Clearwing, this species is named for the narrow red belt about half way along its abdomen. It flies in the summer and lays its eggs on the bark of various rosaceous trees, especially apples and pears. Its caterpillars live in the trunks and branches and may cause die-back of the smaller branches. Clusters of brown droppings on the bark may indicate its presence and removal of the affected branches is the best way to combat the problem. The species is absent from Ireland and the northern half of Britain. The Large Red-belted Clearwing, which breeds in birch trees, is similar, but has a red patch at the base of each front wing.

Red-belted Clearwing

Looks: Narrow red belt on black abdomen; wings virtually clear

Food: Rosaceous trees, especially apples and pairs

When: Adult in summer: caterpillar in tree trunks for much of the year

Where: Britain and Continental Europe

CURRANT CLEARWING
Synanthedon tipuliformis

This moth could be mistaken for a fly when resting on or flying around currant and gooseberry bushes in the summer sunshine. The male abdomen carries four narrow yellow bands, but the female has only three. The caterpillar feeds inside the branches of currant and gooseberry bushes and often pushes out piles of brown frass. It causes severe wilting of the leaves, and death of the affected branches often follows. As with the Red-belted Clearwing, removal of the branches is the best treatment. Because the eggs are laid singly, and the little caterpillars tunnel straight into the stems as soon as they hatch, there is little chance of success with insecticidal treatment.

Currant Clearwing

Looks: Male has four bands on abdomen; female has three

Food: Currant and gooseberry bushes

When: Adult late spring and summer: caterpillar in branches most of the year

Where: Britain and Continental Europe

A female Currant Clearwing Moth sunning itself on a leaf and clearly displaying its transparent wing membranes. Its front wings are 8–10 mm long.

The Raspberry Clearwing moth, with a wing length of about 10 mm, is a newcomer to the British Isles.

RASPBERRY CLEARWING
Pennisetia hylaeiformis

With somewhat cloudier front wings than most other clear-wing moths and an abdomen with three or four conspicuous cream bands, this species flies in the summer months and lays its eggs in the soil around the bases of raspberry canes and, less commonly, around blackberry bushes. The resulting larvae tunnel into the roots and spend the winter there before moving up into the bases of the canes, where their activity induces the development of rather knobbly galls. The leaves of infested canes wilt and the flower buds often fail to open. Mature caterpillars, about 2 cm long, pupate in the galls and new adults emerge in the summer. Systemic insecticides applied to the soil or the new young canes after harvest may be of some use in areas where the pest is known to occur, but once the leaves have started to wilt, the only remedy is to cut the canes down to ground level – below any galls that might appear. Although the insect is widely distributed on the continent, it is known only from a small area of eastern England, where it was discovered only in 2007.

Raspberry Clearwing

Looks: Cloudy front wings and four cream bands on abdomen

Food: Raspberries and blackberries

When: Adult late spring and summer; caterpillar much of the year (concealed in stems)

Where: Britain and Continental Europe

LACKEY MOTH
Malacosoma neustria

The colour ranges from straw-coloured to brick red, with two lines crossing the front wing and often enclosing a darker area. The outer margins of the front wings are spotted with brown and white. The moth flies in July and August and lays cylindrical masses of eggs around the twigs of its food-plants. The eggs do not hatch until the spring and the caterpillars feed in spring and early summer on a wide range of trees and shrubs, especially members of the rose family. Hawthorn hedges are regularly attacked, as are plum and apple trees. The caterpillars are largely blue with red stripes along the back and two large black spots on the head and reach a length of about 5.5 cm. They feed communally in silken webs for the first few weeks, often defoliating whole branches. In sunny weather they can be seen basking on the outside of their webs. They disperse shortly before pupating in yellowish cocoons in bark crevices or among dead leaves. The insect is rarely found north of Yorkshire.

Lackey Moth

Looks: Straw to brick red with two dark lines on front wing

Food: Hawthorn, plum and apple

When: Adult in summer: caterpillar in spring and early summer

Where: Britain and Continental Europe

The male Lackey Moth, seen here, has a wing length of about 1.5 cm, but females are a little larger. The caterpillars spend most of their lives communally in large silken tents draped over the foliage (inset).

ABOVE: The Garden Carpet Moth has a wing length of about 1.5 cm and always rests with its wings swept back to give it a triangular outline.

RIGHT: The caterpillar of the Garden Carpet Moth exploring a cabbage leaf. It can be found from spring until late autumn. Winter is passed in the chrysalis stage, wrapped in a silken cocoon in the soil.

Garden Carpet Moth

Looks: Black 'cloak' below head and square patch in centre of wings

Food: Brassicas, including garden wallflowers

When: Adult and caterpillar spring to autumn

Where: Britain and Continental Europe

GARDEN CARPET
Xanthoroe fluctuata

The Garden Carpet can be distinguished from several rather similar moths by the black cloak-like patch on the 'shoulders' and the more or less square dark patch near the middle of each front wing. With two or three broods each year, the moth is on the wing from early spring until well into the autumn. Its caterpillar, up to 2.5 cm long, is green, grey or brown with darker patches on the back. It is one of the looper caterpillars, which move by stretching forward and then arching the body into a loop as they bring the rear end forward (see opposite). There are no legs on the middle part of the body. It feeds on most wild and cultivated members of the cabbage family, including garden wallflowers. Nasturtiums may also be attacked.

LEFT: The adult Magpie Moth, with front wings reaching 2.5 cm in length, is a very attractive insect but, like many other brightly coloured species, it has a disagreeable taste. Even spiders will not eat it.

BELOW: The caterpillar exhibits warning colours like those of the adult. Here, it is displaying the typical looper position. It is about to stretch the front end forward, almost as if measuring the leaf.

MAGPIE MOTH
Abraxas grossulariata

This distinctive moth is not likely to be mistaken for anything else. Its bold black and white pattern, including a yellow line across each front wing, warns of its bitter taste and birds avoid it. Even spiders cut it from their webs if they catch it. The moth is on the wing in the summer. The caterpillars, which are loopers (see the previous species), resemble the adults in colour and feed on numerous deciduous shrubs. Gooseberry and currant bushes are favourite targets in the garden, although the species is less of a problem today than it was a few years ago. The caterpillars feed for a short while in late summer and then, while still quite small, they go into hibernation under loose bark or in debris under the bushes. They complete their growth in the spring and this is when they can defoliate the branches. When fully grown, with a length of about 4 cm, they spin flimsy cocoons in which they turn into black and yellow pupae. The caterpillars are easy to remove by hand in the spring, but young ones can be killed with a contact spray or dust in the autumn – especially if your gooseberry bushes are particularly prickly. The larvae of the Common Gooseberry Sawfly (see p. 296) are sometimes confused with Magpie Moth caterpillars but they are less colourful and have far more legs.

Magpie Moth

Looks: Cream wings with black spots and wavy yellow line outlined with black spots

Food: Gooseberry, currants and other shrubs

When: Adult in summer: caterpillar summer to spring, but dormant in winter

Where: Britain and Continental Europe

The resting caterpillar of the Peppered Moth is easily mistaken for a twig.

Peppered Moth

Looks: Exists in speckled and almost black forms

Food: Roses, raspberries; various herbaceous plants

When: Adult in summer: caterpillar in late summer and autumn

Where: Britain and Continental Europe

PEPPERED MOTH
Biston betularia

This moth has two main forms and they are so different that they could easily be taken for two separate species. One is essentially white with a liberal peppering of black dots, while the other is almost completely black. This black or melanic form was virtually unknown until the middle of the 19th century, but then it increased rapidly in the industrial regions of north-west England and by 1895 it made up about 98 per cent of the Peppered Moth population around Manchester. What had happened was that the melanic form had been given a tremendous advantage by the air pollution associated with the industrial revolution. Sooty deposits blackened trees and walls and also killed off the lichens, and any normal (speckled) Peppered Moths that settled there were quickly spotted and eaten by birds, but the melanic moths escaped detection and survived to breed. This is the traditional explanation, although the full story is a little more complicated because melanic moths also became common in many rural areas. Several factors were undoubtedly involved in the spread of the melanic form, including increased tolerance to low-level atmospheric pollution by the larvae. With the introduction of legislation to reduce air pollution since the 1950s, the proportion of normal Peppered Moths began to increase again, but melanic moths are still common in many rural areas. The moths are on the wing throughout the summer. Their twig-like looper caterpillars are green or brown with a deeply notched head. Up to 6 cm long when fully grown, they feed on many woody and herbaceous plants, including garden roses and raspberries, in late summer and autumn and pupate in the ground, but are rarely numerous enough to do any harm.

Normal (top) and melanic Peppered Moths at rest on lichen-covered bark. The normal moth is well camouflaged, but the melanic one is very obvious.

WINTER MOTH
Operophtera brumata

The males of this species fly in the depths of winter and can often be seen on window panes at night. They vary from light grey to blackish-brown. The females have only tiny stumps for wings and are quite unable to fly. They look more like spiders than moths and they sit in the trees waiting for the males to arrive and mate with them. Apples and pears are the main targets for this pest in the garden, although it attacks many other deciduous trees. Eggs are laid on the bark and they hatch just as the buds are beginning to open. The little caterpillars then make their way to the young leaves, joining them together with silk to form small shelters and then settling down to feed. They chew little holes in the leaves, but the damage is not usually noticeable until the leaves expand. The caterpillars may attack the flowers and developing fruits as well. Damaged fruits may fall early, while those that remain on the trees usually exhibit sunken brown scabs. Although deformed, such apples are still perfectly edible. The caterpillars are some shade of green and they are of the looper type **(see page 201)**. They mature in June, when they are about 2 cm long, and they drop to the ground to pupate. New females emerge and climb the trees in the winter. Mature trees are not usually harmed by Winter Moths and, although fruit yields may be slightly reduced, treatment is rarely necessary. The easiest way to control the pest is to fit grease bands to the trunk to trap the females before they can get up into the branches. Small trees can be sprayed with a pyrethroid-based insecticide when the buds start to open, but this is not worth doing unless you have experienced trouble in previous years and in any event it must be done before the flowers open to minimise the risk to pollinating insects.

TOP TIP

Fit greasebands to the trunk of any susceptible trees to trap female moths before they can reach the branches of the tree.

Winter Moth

Looks: Light grey to blackish brown; females are flightless

Food: Apples, pears, and many other deciduous trees and shrubs

When: Adult in winter months: caterpillar in spring and early summer

Where: Britain and Continental Europe

The male Winter Moth has front wings about 1.5 cm long.

The male Mottled Umber moth varies a good deal in colour but the front wings, up to 2.5 cm long, are nearly always crossed by a dark, wavy band. Look also for the dotted margins, although several related moths have these.

Mottled Umber

Looks: Variable ranging from dirty white to brick red with wavy band on front wing; female wingless

Food: Caterpillars feed on deciduous trees

When: Adult in autumn and winter: caterpillar in spring

Where: Britain and Continental Europe

BELOW LEFT: The wingless, spidery female of the Mottled Umber moth.

BELOW RIGHT: The Mottled Umber caterpillar feeds on a wide range of trees and shrubs and commonly rests with its head raised, as shown here.

MOTTLED UMBER
Erannis defoliaria

This is another moth with a virtually wingless, spider-like female. The male is a very variable creature, with wings ranging from dirty white to brick red, but there is usually a dark wavy band crossing the front wing. It flies from late autumn until early spring and is abundant in parks and gardens, where almost any deciduous tree or shrub is fair game for the caterpillars. These are of the looper type **(see p. 201)**, up to 3 cm long and usually pale brown with a black stripe and rust-coloured patches on each side. As indicated by the scientific name, they can completely defoliate branches when numerous. They are fully grown by June, when they drop to the ground to pupate. Grease bands can be used to trap the new females as they climb fruit trees in autumn and winter, but hand-picking of the caterpillars is a better way of controlling the species on shrubs: look for nibbled leaves and droppings to lead you to the well-camouflaged caterpillars.

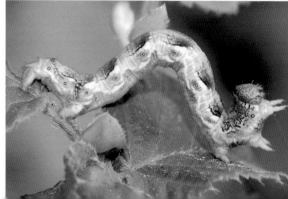

ABOVE: The Death's-head Hawkmoth is one of Europe's largest moths. A rare visitor to the British Isles, it is more likely to worry bee-keepers than gardeners.

RIGHT: The caterpillar of the Death's-head Hawkmoth is usually yellow or green, with blue or purple stripes. There is also a dark brown form with a white head. The normal diet of this magnificent caterpillar is potato leaves but it is found on tomatoes and also on wild nightshades. The horn on its rear end is more curved than that of other hawkmoth larvae and more 'warty'.

DEATH'S-HEAD HAWKMOTH
Acherontia atropos

Named for the skull-like pattern on its thorax, this is one of Europe's largest moths, with wings spanning up to 13.5 cm and an unusually thick body. The moth flies from late spring until the autumn. If handled, it can squeak by forcing air out through its short tongue. It does not visit flowers, but it often steals honey from bee hives. Although only a rare visitor to the British Isles, the species is widely distributed on the continent. Its caterpillar, up to 12.5 cm in length, is as thick as a man's finger and usually yellow or green with bluish or purple diagonal stripes. In common with most other hawkmoth caterpillars, it has a prominent horn at the rear. It feeds mainly on potato leaves and, because of its size, just a few caterpillars can do considerable damage. Winter is passed in the pupal stage deep in the soil, but the species cannot survive the winter in the British Isles or elsewhere in the northern half of Europe.

Death's Head Hawkmoth

Looks: Up to 13.5 cm wingspan; thick striped body with death's head on thorax

Food: Potato leaves

When: Adult spring to autumn: caterpillar summer

Where: Continental Europe: a rare visitor to Britain and northern Europe

Privet Hawkmoth

Looks: Wingspan 10 cm or more; purple and white striped abdomen; looks like broken twig at rest

What: Honeysuckle, privet, lilac

When: Adult in summer: caterpillar summer and autumn

Where: Britain and Continental Europe

PRIVET HAWKMOTH
Sphinx ligustri

Britain's largest resident moth, the Privet Hawkmoth has a wingspan of over 10 cm, although when at rest it pulls its wings tightly into the sides of its body and then is easily mistaken for a broken twig. It flies in June and July, feeding from honeysuckle and other tubular flowers and laying its eggs on privet hedges and lilac bushes. The caterpillar reaches a length of about 10 cm and can look quite scary when it raises its front end, although it is quite harmless. It is surprisingly difficult to spot among the leaves because the purple and white stripes break up its outline and help it to merge with its surroundings. Luckily for our hedges, the caterpillars are usually well scattered, for a group of them would rapidly defoliate a stretch of hedgerow. It pupates in the soil and, like most of our hawkmoths, it spends the winter in the pupal stage. Caterpillars are very occasionally found on currant bushes.

LEFT: A Privet Hawkmoth caterpillar in typical resting pose.

BELOW: The adult moth displaying its pink-striped hindwings and abdomen.

CONVOLVULUS HAWKMOTH
Agrius convolvuli

Superficially like the Privet Hawkmoth, this moth is much greyer and without pink bands on the hind wings. It also lacks the conspicuously black thorax seen in the Privet Hawkmoth. On the wing throughout the summer, the moth has a very long tongue and feeds from all sorts of tubular flowers, mainly at dusk. The caterpillar, up to 10 cm long, is brown or green with pale diagonal stripes and, like most hawkmoth caterpillars, it has a curved horn at the rear. It feeds mainly on convolvulus plants and can damage morning glories in the garden. It is also a minor pest of grape vines. The species is resident in the Mediterranean area, but migrates northwards in the spring and reaches most parts of central Europe during the summer, although it is only a rare visitor to the British Isles.

Convolvulus Hawkmoth

Looks: Resembles Privet Hawkmoth but is greyer; caterpillar is green with diagonal white stripes

Food: Convolvulous plants; morning glories

When: Adult and caterpillar in summer and autumn

Where: Mainly resident in Mediterranean; rare visitor to British Isles

The Convolvulus Hawkmoth, a rare visitor to the British Isles, is a minor pest of grape vines and also morning glory plants. It resembles the Privet Hawkmoth (see opposite page), but is much greyer.

ELEPHANT HAWKMOTH
Deilephila elpenor

This unmistakable moth, feeds at a variety of tubular flowers from May to July. It gets its name for its caterpillar, which has an extensible snout with a fanciful resemblance to an elephant's trunk. Up to 9 cm long, the caterpillar is even more scary than that of the Privet Hawkmoth because, when alarmed, it withdraws its snout into the front end of the body, causing that region to swell up and display its eye-like spots. At the same time, the caterpillar may wave its front end to and fro and this display is more than enough to frighten small birds that might be tempted to have a go at it. This species feeds mainly on willowherbs, but can be a pest of grape vines in southern Europe. Occasional specimens also occur on garden fuchsias and, being quite large, they can remove a fair number of leaves.

Elephant Hawkmoth

Looks: Pink and gold wings; caterpillar, up to 9 cm has snout that resembles elephant's 'trunk'

Food: Mainly willowherbs, but also vines and fuchsias

When: Spring, summer

Where: Britain and Continental Europe

BELOW: The Elephant Hawkmoth is another minor pest of grape vines on the Continent, and its caterpillar (TOP LEFT) can also damage fuchsias.

BELOW LEFT: When alarmed, the Elephant Hawkmoth caterpillar adopts a somewhat frightening pose by pulling its head and thorax into the front of the abdomen so that the eye-spots swell up.

BUFF-TIP
Phalera bucephala

This moth is named for the pale brown patch at the tip of each front wing. The thorax is also clothed with pale brown hairs, and when the moth is at rest with its wings pulled tightly round its body it is easily mistaken for a broken twig. It is on the wing for much of the summer and the female lays her egg batches on a wide variety of hedgerow shrubs and fruit trees as well as on amenity trees of urban parks and roadsides. The hairy black and yellow caterpillars live gregariously for much of their lives and can quickly defoliate small trees. Their bold markings advertise their unpleasant taste and ensure that most birds and other predators leave them alone. When fully grown, with a length of about 6 cm, they pupate in the soil.

Buff-tip

Looks: Thorax has pale brown hairs; pale brown patch at tip of each wing; can look like broken twig when at rest

Food: Caterpillars feed on a wide range of trees and shrubs

When: Adult in summer: caterpillar summer and autumn

Where: Britain and Continental Europe

ABOVE: The adult Buff-tip moth bears a remarkable similarity to a broken twig when at rest – usually on the ground. Its front wings can be up to 3.5 cm long.

INSET: The Buff-tip caterpillar relies on warning coloration to deter potential enemies.

PALE TUSSOCK
Calliteara pudibunda

On the wing in spring and early summer, this moth is rarely noticed because its mottled grey wings blend beautifully with lichen-covered fences and tree trunks in the day-time. Its caterpillar, however, is one of our most conspicuous species. Up to 4.5 cm long, it is bright green or yellow and very hairy, with a slender red tuft at the rear and four prominent white or yellowish tufts resembling tiny shaving brushes near the front. It is wise not to handle either the adult or the caterpillar with bare hands because the hairs can cause severe skin irritation. The caterpillar feeds on a wide range of deciduous trees and shrubs, including hops, during the summer. It was once common in the hop fields of southern England, where it was known as the 'hop dog'. In the garden, it is most likely to be found on cherries and plums. Winter is spent as a chrysalis in a flimsy cocoon on or under the food-plant. Although widely distributed in the southern half of Britain and in Ireland, the moth does not reach Scotland.

Pale Tussock

Looks: Adult well camouflaged with mottled grey wings; caterpillar bright green or yellow and very hairy

Food: Deciduous trees and shrubs, hops

When: Adult in spring and early summer; caterpillar in summer

Where: Southern Britain and Continental Europe

ABOVE RIGHT: The caterpillar of the Pale Tussock is an unmistakable creature, ranging from pale green to deep yellow or orange, but always with white tufts on the back. It is wise not to handle this caterpillar.

RIGHT: The adult Pale Tussock moth, seen here in its typical resting pose, is very hard to spot on lichen-covered bark. Its wing length ranges from about 2 to 3 cm. It is one of many species that lack a functional proboscis and do not feed in the adult state.

ABOVE: The adult male Vapourer moth flies by day, especially along hedgerows. It has a wing length up to 1.7 cm.

LEFT: The unmistakable caterpillar of the Vapourer Moth.

VAPOURER
Orgyia antiqua

The male flies by day and is on the wing throughout the summer and autumn, often flying rapidly along hedgerows as it searches for the wingless female. The caterpillar, up to 2.5 cm long, is easily recognised by the four pale 'shaving brushes' on its back and the two horn-like tufts of dark hair at the front. The hairs can cause a rash if the caterpillar is handled. It can be found feeding on almost any deciduous tree or shrub in spring and summer, although hedgerows are its favourite haunts. When fully grown it spins a cocoon on the vegetation. The adult females, which are little more than bags of eggs, rarely move far, usually mating and laying their eggs on their empty cocoons. The caterpillars tend to stay together for the early part of their lives and may defoliate small branches or stretches of hedgerow before separating. There are usually two broods in a year, with eggs laid in the autumn not hatching until the spring.

Vapourer

Looks: Adult male has golden brown wings with two white spots; caterpillar grey with red spots and cream 'brushes' on back

Food: Most deciduous shrubs

When: Adult spring to autumn: caterpillar in spring and summer

Where: Britain and Continental Europe

Yellow-tail

Looks: White wings; yellow tuft on rear of abdomen

Food: Raspberries, plums, hawthorn, blackthorn

When: Adult mainly in summer: caterpillar summer to spring, but dormant in the winter

Where: Britain and Continental Europe

The male Yellow-tail in its typical resting pose. Its wing length ranges from about 1.5 to 2.5 cm.

YELLOW-TAIL
Euproctis similis

Also known as the Gold-tail, this common moth has plain silky white wings, although the male usually has a small black smudge near the rear of the front wing. There is a tuft of golden yellow hair on the rear of the abdomen in both sexes. The moth flies mainly in July and August and eggs are laid on a wide range of deciduous trees and shrubs. Raspberries and *Prunus* species are commonly attacked in the garden, while hawthorn and blackthorn are major targets in the wild. The eggs are covered with hairs from the female's abdominal tuft. The caterpillars hibernate when still very small and complete their growth in the spring. Up to 4 cm long, they are black with red and white spots and long hairs that can cause an unpleasant rash if they are handled. Mature caterpillars pupate in cocoons which are spun between the leaves and which incorporate many of the larval hairs. Although common in the southern half of Britain the moth is absent from most of Scotland and Ireland.

TOP: When disturbed, the Yellow-tail moth often rolls over and pretends to be dead. The abdominal hair tuft is exposed when the insect 'plays possum' like this and may give it extra protection.

BOTTOM: The caterpillar of the Yellow-tail moth is unlikely to be confused with that of any other species. Few hawthorn hedges in England manage to escape the attentions of this species.

ABOVE: The Brown-tail moth, seen here playing possum and exposing its large brown abdominal hair tuft, has a wing length up to 2 cm.

RIGHT: The caterpillar of the Brown-tail moth spends much of its early life in a silken nest with hundreds of its brethren. Hundreds of such nests can be seen in hedgerows in some areas, and few species of deciduous trees and shrubs seem immune to attack.

Brown-tail

Looks: White with brown tuft at end of abdomen

Food: Garden hedges, fruit trees

When: Adult in summer; caterpillar much of the year, but dormant in winter

Where: Southern Britain and Continental Europe

BROWN-TAIL
Euproctis chrysorrhoea

Closely resembling the Yellow-tail, this moth bears a tuft of brown hairs on its abdomen instead of yellow. The moth flies in July and August. Although widely distributed on the continent, it was until recently confined largely to coastal areas in the south and east of England, but it has been spreading inland in recent years and is now common in many areas. Its gregarious caterpillars, which live in silken nests, can cause severe damage to garden hedges and fruit trees. Up to 4.5 cm long when mature, they are dark brown or black with red spots on the back and white spots along the sides. The hairs of this species are extremely irritant and have been known to cause skin rashes even when blown around in the air.

ABOVE LEFT: A female Gypsy Moth with her egg batch, which is covered with hairs from her abdominal tuft. Her wings are up to 3.5 cm in length, but she rarely uses them for flight.

ABOVE: The male Gypsy Moth, showing the large, feathery antennae with which it tracks down the flightless females. The wings are 2–2.5 cm in length.

LEFT: The Gypsy Moth caterpillar reaches lengths of about 5 cm and feeds on a wide range of deciduous trees and shrubs. It can usually be recognised by the rows of red spots inside black circles, and also by the two more or less vertical black bars on its face.

GYPSY MOTH
Lymantria dispar

The Gypsy Moth is a serious pest of deciduous trees on the continent, where its gregarious caterpillars defoliate many forest species in the spring, as well as damaging garden, orchard and roadside trees. Plums and other *Prunus* species seem particularly attractive to this pest. The hairy caterpillars are largely black with red spots, but the head is pale with two conspicuous black streaks. Mature caterpillars pupate in flimsy cocoons on the tree trunks and produce adults in the summer. Male moths have dull brown wings crossed by darker wavy lines and they fly in the daytime as well as at night. The females, somewhat larger than the males, are creamy white with darker cross lines. Those of the European race rarely fly and usually stay close to their cocoons. Eggs are laid in batches in the summer, but they do not hatch until the spring, when many of the young caterpillars are scattered by the wind. The Gypsy Moth was once common in Britain, but the resident population died out early in the 20th century and all we have now are the occasional males that make their way across the channel. There is, however, a new threat on the horizon: an Asiatic race whose females fly well has already established itself in Europe and may well colonise the British Isles before long.

Gypsy Moth

Looks: Males dull brown wings; females creamy white. Caterpillars hairy with red spots and thin horizontal yellow bands

Food: Feeds on various decidous trees

When: Adult in summer: caterpillar in spring

Where: Continental Europe

FALL WEB-WORM
Hyphantria cunea

This American moth arrived in Europe in the middle of the 20th century and has since become widely distributed on the continent, although it does not occur in the British Isles. The adult is usually pure white, although it may have a few black spots, and it flies in spring and summer. Its caterpillars range from yellow to chestnut brown, with black spots and tufts of long whiter hairs. They feed communally in large webs on a wide range of deciduous trees and are serious forest pests. In the garden, they attack apples and most other rosaceous trees as well as grape vines and mulberries, and their webs can completely cover small trees. They are most numerous in the autumn, hence the name.

Fall Web-worm

Looks: Pure white with or without black spots; caterpillar yellow to chestnut brown

Food: Various deciduous forest trees

When: Adult in spring and summer: caterpillar in autumn

Where: North America, Continental Europe

ABOVE: The adult Fall Web-worm moth is usually pure white, but the spotted form seen here is easily confused with the White Ermine moth. The latter normally has a fairly well-marked curved line of black dots running across the centre of the front wing. The White Ermine also has at least one black spot in the centre of the hind wing, whereas the hind wings of the Fall Web-worm are pure white.

LEFT: Caterpillars of the Fall Web-worm basking on their communal web.

HEART-AND-DART MOTH
Agrotis exclamationis

Named for the two prominent dark marks on its front wing, this moth can be distinguished from several superficially similar species by its conspicuous black collar. It is on the wing in summer and early autumn and when at rest its wings are laid flat over the body. The dull brown and grey caterpillar, up to 4 cm long, is one of the large group known as 'cutworms' **(see panel on p. 220)**. It rests in the soil by day and wakes to wreck seedlings and other tender, low-growing plants at night. Young larvae feed mainly on leaves at ground level, while older ones tend to remain underground and feed almost entirely on roots. Fully grown caterpillars become dormant in the autumn and pupate in the spring.

Heart-and-dart Moth

Looks: Heart and dart shaped marks on wings. Cutworm caterpillar dull brown and grey

Food: Seedlings, roots, young leaves

When: Adult late spring to autumn: caterpillar summer and autumn

Where: Britain and Continental Europe

The Heart-and-Dart Moth pictured here clearly shows the markings that give it its name. The front wings are up to 20 mm long.

TURNIP MOTH
Agrotis segetum

The Turnip Moth has mottled brown front wings, often with a conspicuous oval and a dark 'dart' near the middle, but it is most easily identified by its very white hind wings, which have dark veins in the female. It flies through the summer and autumn and is most abundant in cultivated areas. Its caterpillar is greyish–brown with black dots all over it and usually a purple or greenish tinge on the upper surface, and it reaches a length of about 4.5 cm. Classed as a cutworm **(see panel on p. 220)**, it spends most of its time in the soil and feeds mainly on roots, although young caterpillars frequently feed on young leaves. The insect is a serious pest of carrots and beetroot as well as turnips and other brassicas. Although fully grown in the autumn, it does not pupate until the spring.

Turnip Moth

Looks: Mottled brown front wings and white hind wings; grey-brown cutworm caterpillar with purple or green tinge

Food: Carrots, beetroot, turnips and other brassicas

When: Adult late spring to autumn: caterpillar most of the year

Where: Britain and Continental Europe

The front wings of the Turnip Moth range from pale grey to deep brown and are about 2 cm long.

LARGE YELLOW UNDERWING
Noctua pronuba

The light or dark brown front wings are often heavily marked in the male, and it is well camouflaged when resting in or under the vegetation. But it is easily disturbed, and then it takes off on a short, erratic flight during which it flashes its bright yellow hind wings. It quickly drops back into the vegetation and 'disappears', leaving any bird that had been chasing it searching unsuccessfully for a yellow insect. The moth is on the wing in the summer and autumn and is the commonest large moth in many gardens. Its caterpillar, up to 5 cm long, is usually some shade of brown with two rows of short, dark bars along the back. It hides in the soil by day and feeds at night on almost any low-growing wild or cultivated plant, often cutting through the stems of tender plants in typical cutworm fashion **(see panel on p. 220)**. It becomes dormant in the soil in the autumn and completes its growth in the spring.

The forewings of the Large Yellow Underwing are 2–2.5 cm long and range from light to dark brown, but there is always a small black spot near the tip. The wings are laid flat over the body when the moth is at rest.

Large Yellow Underwing

Looks: Light or dark brown wings; bright yellow hind wings; cutworm caterpillar brown

Food: Most low-growing deciduous plants

When: Adult mid-summer to late autumn: caterpillar summer to spring, but dormant in coldest months

Where: Britain and Continental Europe

The row of dark bars on each side of the back, combined with the lack of white along the back, distinguishes the caterpillar of the Large Yellow Underwing from those of a few other superficially similar species. The caterpillar is usually brown, but green individuals are not uncommon.

The curse of the cutworms

Cutworms are the caterpillars of various moths in the family Noctuidae and they can be very destructive in the garden. Most species are grey or brown and, apart from a few bristles, they are hairless. The caterpillars get their name because they commonly nibble through the stems of seedlings and other small plants at about ground level. They attack a wide range of wild and cultivated plants and seem particularly fond of lettuces and young brassicas in the garden, although ornamental plants are by no means ignored. Most of the damage is caused at night and whole rows of young plants can be felled in a single night, with slugs often being blamed for the damage. During daylight hours the caterpillars usually hide in the soil, where they also bore into potato tubers and various root-crops. No insecticidal treatment is recommended for the control of cutworms, but parasitic nematode worms are now available to keep the pests in check. Good 'house-keeping' will also keep their numbers down. Hoe regularly around your crops to disturb the cutworms and bring them to the surface where birds will quickly find and eat them. Keep the garden free of weeds whenever you have no crops in the ground, as this will starve the caterpillars. Inspect your plants by torchlight at night and pick off any cutworms that you find. Frequent watering can also help because most cutworms dislike wet soils and will usually come to the surface after heavy rain or watering – and then you can collect and destroy them. Other soil-dwelling pests that could be confused with cutworms include the grubs of chafer beetles (see p. 155) and crane-flies (see p. 250), but the former have only three pairs of legs and crane-fly larvae (leatherjackets) have no legs at all.

DOT MOTH
Melanchra persicariae

Readily identified by the large, white, kidney-shaped spot on each glossy black front wing, this moth flies in the summer and, while not a major pest, its caterpillar feeds on many woody and herbaceous plants in the garden. These include dahlias, Michaelmas daisies and various other composites as well as strawberries and blackcurrant bushes. The caterpillar, which is largely nocturnal, reaches 4 cm in length and varies from dark green to purplish-brown. It has prominent V-shaped marks on the back and a hump on the rear end that gives it a noticeably angular appearance. The species overwinters as a pupa in the soil.

Dot Moth

Looks: White kidney shaped spot on black front wing; caterpillar dark green to purplish brown

Food: Various including dahlias, strawberries, blackcurrants

When: Adult all summer: caterpillar summer to autumn

Where: Britain and Continental Europe

LEFT: The Dot Moth caterpillar is readily identified by its markings and the angular hump at the rear.

BELOW: The adult Dot Moth at rest. Its front wings are about 2 cm long.

The Cabbage Moth varies a good deal in size, with front wings ranging from about 1.5 to 2.2 cm, but the white-edged kidney-shaped mark is usually clearly visible.

CABBAGE MOTH
Mamestra brassicae

A rather sombre, greyish-brown moth, this species usually bears a white-edged kidney-shaped mark near the middle of each front wing. Specimens can be found throughout the year, although the moth flies mainly in the summer months. True to its name, the caterpillar is a cabbage pest, often boring right into the heart and rendering the whole cabbage inedible with its foul-smelling droppings. It also attacks lettuces and many other low-growing plants and is occasionally found on currant bushes and strawberries. Up to 5 cm long, it varies from brown to dirty green, with two rows of black spots or dashes along the back and a dark band close to the rear end. Rarely specimens are bright green or flesh-coloured. The species overwinters as a pupa in the soil.

Cabbage Moth

Looks: Greyish brown; white-edged kidney-shaped mark in middle of wing. Caterpillar brown to green with black spots on back

Food: Cabbages

When: Adult mainly summer and autumn, but can be found all year; caterpillar mainly late summer and autumn

Where: Britain and Continental Europe

LEFT: The adult Clouded Drab Moth at rest. Its front wings are about 2 cm long.

BELOW LEFT: The boldly marked caterpillar of the Clouded Drab attacks raspberries and hops as well as damaging our apples and pears.

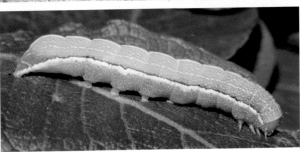

CLOUDED DRAB MOTH
Orthosia incerta

The Clouded Drab is an occasional pest of apples and pears. The adult is a rather nondescript insect, with front wings ranging from dull grey to purplish-brown. A fairly distinct white line crosses each wing towards the tip and has a sharp kink at each end. The moth flies in the spring and usually lays its eggs in bark crevices. The young caterpillars make their way into the bursting buds, where they feed on the developing flowers and leaves for a while before moving to older, more exposed leaves. After about a month some of the caterpillars turn their attention to the young fruits, and this is when they become a nuisance. They take chunks out of the fruit and may burrow in as far as the core. Destroying a few young leaves and flowers causes no real harm – it can be looked on as natural thinning of the fruit – but holes and corky scars in the mature fruit make it unappetising and certainly useless for the market. The caterpillars are up to 4 cm long and some shade of green with a broad white stripe on each side and white spots all over them. When fully grown, they leave the fruits or foliage and pupate in the soil. The insect is more of a pest in gardens than in orchards, which are usually sprayed on a regular basis.

Clouded Drab Moth

Looks: Dull grey to purple brown; caterpillar bright green with white band on side

Food: Apples and pears

When: Adult in spring; caterpillar spring to summer

Where: Britain and Continental Europe

ABOVE: The well-named Bright-line Brown-eye moth is easily recognised by the jagged white line near the wing-tips and the brown 'eye' near the middle. The front wings range from 1.5 to 2 cm in length.

RIGHT: The caterpillar of the Bright-line Brown-eye has a bright yellow line on each side of the body, but it usually has a much darker line above it than shown here.

BRIGHT-LINE BROWN-EYE
Lacanobia oleracea

Named for the distinctive markings on its front wings, this moth is abundant in many habitats in the summer. Its caterpillar, green with black and white spots and a black and yellow line on each side, eats a wide variety of wild and cultivated plants. It is not a serious pest, but it does like tomatoes and is sometimes called the Tomato Moth. Clusters of young larvae may cause extensive pale blotches on the leaves by nibbling away at the lower surface, while larger individuals are occasionally found boring into the fruit. Tomatoes grown in the greenhouse seem particularly prone to attack. Pyrethrin-based sprays can be used to control the insect, but regular inspection and removal of the young larvae will prevent serious damage.

Bright-line Brown-eye

Looks: Eye markings on brown front wings; caterpillar green with black and yellow line on sides

Food: Tomatoes and other cultivated plants

When: Adult late spring to autumn: caterpillar summer to autumn

Where: Britain and Continental Europe

MULLEIN MOTH
Shargacucullia verbasci

The moth flies in the spring but is rarely seen because, when at rest with its brown and straw-coloured wings pulled tightly back along the sides of the body, it is easily mistaken for a piece of bark or a broken twig. Its caterpillar, however, is a very conspicuous creature, going in for warning coloration rather than camouflage. Up to 6 cm long, it is white or cream with black and yellow spots and streaks and it sits openly on the leaves and flower spikes of mulleins, often reducing the spikes to mushy black stumps. It also feeds, less commonly, on buddleia leaves. Winter is spent as a pupa in a thick felt-like cocoon in the soil, and some individuals spend two or three years in this stage. Because the caterpillars are so conspicuous, they are easy to collect and destroy without the need for any insecticide.

Mullein Moth

Looks: Wings brown and straw-coloured; caterpillar cream with yellow and black spots

Food: Mulleins, buddleia

When: Adult in spring: caterpillar late spring and summer

Where: Britain and Continental Europe

TOP TIP
Pick off the vividly coloured caterpillars and squash them if you see them.

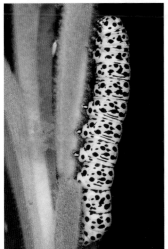

ABOVE: The adult Mullein Moth goes in for protective resemblance – it looks like a piece of bark or a broken twig and birds take no notice of it. Its front wings are up to 2.5 cm long.

LEFT: The Mullein Moth caterpillar, protected by excellent warning coloration, is a major enemy of any gardeners who grow mulleins.

The Angle Shades is easily recognised by the way in which it folds its wings at rest. The front wings are up to 2.5 cm long.

ANGLE SHADES
Phlogophora meticulosa

Unlikely to be mistaken for any other moth, the Angle Shades *could* be mistaken for a dead leaf when resting with its wings wrinkled in its characteristic pose. The V-shaped mark on the front wing is initially green and pink, but normally dull brown in older specimens. Although most common in the summer, the moth can be found throughout the year. The caterpillar is usually bright green, with a broken white line along the back and another white line on each side. It feeds on a wide range of woody and herbaceous plants, including many cultivated crops, and is active in all months of the year. It attacks chrysanthemums in the autumn, nibbling the developing flowers and preventing them from opening properly.

Angle Shades

Looks: V-shaped mark on front wing; bright green caterpillar

Food: Numerous woody and herbaceous plants, including many crops

When: Adult and caterpillar all year

Where: Britain and Continental Europe

The Angle Shades caterpillar has a white stripe on each side, a broken white line in the centre of its back and a slightly angular rear end. Up to 4.5 cm long, it can be found feeding throughout the year.

SILVER-Y
Autographa gamma

Named for the conspicuous silver mark on each front wing, this moth flies throughout the summer and autumn and feeds by day as well as by night – usually hovering in front of flowers while probing them with its long tongue. Its caterpillar, up to 2.5 cm long, comes in various shades of green and rests in a characteristic attitude with the front part of the abdomen raised into an arch. There are only three pairs of fleshy legs on the rear half of the body, whereas most caterpillars apart from the loopers **(see p. 201)** have five pairs. The caterpillar feeds on almost any herbaceous plant and often damages peas and beans in the garden. Although both adults and caterpillars have been seen in the winter months, the species does not normally survive the winter in Britain or in other northern regions and the population is replenished by immigration from southern Europe.

Silver-Y

Looks: Clear silver mark on each wing; green caterpillar with only three pairs of fleshy legs at the rear

Food: Most herbaceous plants

When: Adult and caterpillar all year in southern Europe, but mainly summer and autumn in Britain and other northern areas

Where: Britain and Continental Europe

ABOVE: The Silver-Y caterpillar in typical resting pose.

LEFT: The aptly named Silver-Y moth flies by day as well as by night and visits a wide range of flowers. It varies a good deal in size, with front wings ranging from about 1.2 to 2 cm in length.

ABOVE: The Golden Plusia's golden front wings, about 2 cm long, make it unlikely that the moth will be mistaken for any other species.

RIGHT: The caterpillar of the Golden Plusia tapers strongly towards the front and this distinguishes it from many other caterpillars with similar colours.

GOLDEN PLUSIA

Polychrisia moneta

Easily identified by the silvery figure-of-eight on each of its golden front wings, the Golden Plusia flies throughout the summer and is rarely found away from parks and gardens, where its caterpillars feed almost entirely on delphinium leaves and flower buds. Young caterpillars are grey with black dots and they live communally in silken webs for a while. Some mature quickly and pupate to produce a second generation of adults in the autumn, while others burrow into the soil for the winter. They start to feed again in the spring and become bright green with a white line on each side. Each caterpillar chews through the veins at the base of a delphinium leaf, which then collapses around it to form a shelter. Mature caterpillars are 3.5–4 cm long, tapering strongly towards the front and, like the related Silver-Y, with only three pairs of fleshy legs on the abdomen. Pupation takes place in a flimsy yellow cocoon spun under a leaf. The pupa is half green and half brown and is easily seen through the cocoon. The species is uncommon in the northern half of the British Isles.

Delphinium leaves showing damage caused by Golden Plusia caterpillars.

Golden Plusia

Looks: Silvery figure-of-eight on front wing; caterpillar bright green with white lines on sides

Food: Delphinium leaves and flower buds

When: Adult in summer and autumn: caterpillar late summer to spring, but dormant in winter

Where: Britain and Continental Europe

The adult Codling Moth at rest.

CODLING MOTH
Cydia pomonella

The Codling Moth is easily recognised by its silvery grey front wings with a brown and gold patch at the tip. It is a serious pest of apples. It occasionally attacks pears and other members of the rose family as well. The moth, which has a wingspan of only about 2 cm, flies during the summer months and lays its eggs on the swelling fruits or the surrounding leaves. Young caterpillars leaving the eggs immediately set about tunnelling into the fruit, but their presence is often undetected because they tend to enter through the shrivelled remains of the flower. They are cream at first but they gradually become a delicate shade of pink. They feed on the flesh and seeds of the fruit for several weeks and then chew their way out and make for the trunk or major branches, where they spend the winter under loose bark. They pupate in the spring and new adults emerge just as the fruits start to swell. In the warmer parts of Europe the insects develop more quickly and a second generation of adult moths may be on the wing in the autumn. This pest can reduce the apple crop considerably, but controlling it is not easy. The traditional method was to fix bands of sacking or corrugated cardboard around the trunks and branches to provide pupation sites for the descending caterpillars, and then destroy them. Although it might reduce the following year's population in an orchard if all the trees are banded, it is unlikely to provide much improvement in ordinary gardens because there will always be plenty of moths emerging from the wild or from untreated trees in neighbouring gardens.

TOP TIP

Spraying small trees with pyrethroid-based insecticides may help as long as the timing is accurate – it must be done as soon as the flowers fade to catch the young caterpillars before they can get into the fruits. A second treatment two or three weeks later will increase the chances of success.

Codling Moth

Looks: Small moth with silvery wings with brown/gold patch at tip; caterpillars cream to pink

Food: Apples, pears and roses

When: Adult spring to autumn: caterpillar summer to spring but dormant in winter

Where: Britain and Continental Europe

LEFT: The adult Pea Moth.

BELOW LEFT: An opened pea pod showing a Pea Moth caterpillar and damage to the developing peas.

PEA MOTH
Cydia nigricana

A sombre greyish-brown moth, distinguished from most of its relatives by the black and white bars along the front edge of its wings. With a wingspan of 1.5 cm, it flies in the summer months and lays its eggs on pea plants. The caterpillars, which are pale yellow with dark heads, tunnel into the pea pods and feed on the developing seeds, often hollowing them out completely and leaving the skins full of brown frass. A single caterpillar may destroy all the peas in a pod, although it usually affects only two or three peas. When mature, with a length of about 6 mm, the caterpillars leave the pods and descend to the soil, where they pass the winter without feeding before turning into pupae in the spring. The adult moths are most active in June and July, so one way to avoid serious damage is to adjust your sowing time to avoid having flowers at this time. Alternatively, cover the crop with horticultural fleece for a while: peas are self-pollinating, so the lack of insects will do no harm. Pyrethroid-based insecticides can be used on the peas, but they must be applied before the caterpillars get into the pods, so timing is critical: spray one week or so after the flowers open and again two weeks later. Although garden peas are the main targets of the Pea Moth, it also damages the seeds of sweet peas.

TOP TIP

If applying pyrethroid-based insecticides, spray a week after the flowers have opened and again a couple of weeks later to prevent the caterpillars from entering the pea pods.

Pea Moth

Looks: Tiny greyish brown: wingspan to 1.5 cm; caterpillars pale yellow with dark heads

Food: Peas

When: Adult in early summer: caterpillar summer to spring but dormant in winter

Where: Britain and Continental Europe

The Fruit-tree Tortrix is not easy to spot when resting on tree trunks. the sharply pointed wing-tips distinguish this moth from several similarly coloured species.

FRUIT-TREE TORTRIX
Archips podana

A common, but rarely serious pest of apples and related fruits, including cherries and plums, the Fruit-tree Tortrix flies during the summer months, by day as well as by night, and at rest it looks just like a dead piece of leaf. It has a wingspan of 2–2.5 cm, with the female a little larger and paler than the male. Eggs are laid on the leaves and the slender green caterpillars, which reach lengths of 2.5 cm, feed on leaves, flowers and ripening fruits, usually hiding in little shelters made by joining leaves together with silk. A caterpillar may also fix a leaf to a fruit and nibble away underneath it. Damage is confined to the surface layers of the fruit and usually consists of small craters. Injuries to young fruits usually heal over with corky scars – unsightly, but not seriously harming the fruit – but older fruits do not heal so well and fungi often enter the wounds and cause the fruit to rot. Winter is passed in the caterpillar stage, still on the trees – either in bark crevices or in clusters of dead leaves fixed to the twigs. Pupation takes place in late spring after feeding up on the buds. The insect is rarely common enough for you to have to wage any sort of war against it, but a winter wash applied to the tree trunks will get rid of the hibernating caterpillars. The **Rose Tortrix** (*Archips rosana*) is a very similar moth found on a wide variety of fruit trees and bushes. It lays batches of eggs on the bark during the summer but the eggs do not hatch until the spring and the caterpillars feed on the buds and young fruits.

Fruit-tree Tortrix

Looks: Small, mottled moth resembling fragment of dead leaf; female paler; slender green caterpillars

Food: Apples, cherries, plums

When: Adult in summer months: caterpillar summer to spring but dormant in winter

Where: Britain and Continental Europe

The Cherry-bark Tortrix at rest on a leaf surface.

CHERRY-BARK TORTRIX
Enarmonia formosana

This moth is a fairly common pest of rosaceous trees in most parts of Europe, attacking apples and pears as well as cherries and other *Prunus* species, including apricots and almonds. The adult has a wingspan of no more than 1.8 cm, but it is a pretty little moth with silvery and gold markings on a dark background. It is nevertheless difficult to spot when resting on the bark. It flies in the sunshine throughout the summer months and lays its eggs singly or in small groups on the bark. The caterpillars tunnel into the bark and their presence is commonly revealed by oozing gum mixed with frass and strands of silk. They mature in the following spring and pupate in their tunnels. The pupae are quite mobile and work their way to the surface so that the adult moths can escape, leaving the pupal cases sticking out from the bark. This tortrix prefers mature trees, especially those that have been damaged in some way. Apple trees are commonly attacked on the undersides of the branches, while cherries are more often attacked near the base of the trunk. Heavy infestations can lead to severe cracking of the bark and possibly the death of the whole tree. It is difficult to get at the burrowing caterpillars, but drenching the branches with an insecticidal oil in the spring may have some effect on the pest.

TOP TIP

Insecticidal oil applied to the branches of tree may help to control the caterpillars before they have a chance to invade the whole tree.

Cherry-bark Tortrix

Looks: Small, with silvery and gold markings on dark background

Food: Rosaceous trees including apricots and almonds

When: Adult in summer: caterpillar summer to spring, concealed in trunks and branches

Where: Britain and Continental Europe

The Carnation Tortrix moth at rest. The roughly triangular outline is typical of most tortrix moths. Its caterpillar attacks a wide range of plants and can cause a lot of damage in the greenhouse.

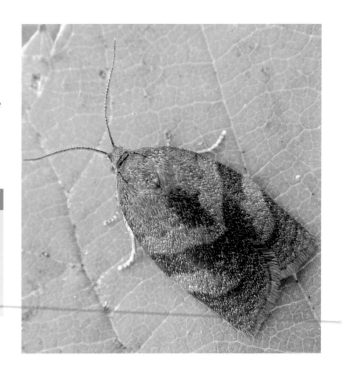

CARNATION TORTRIX
Cacoecimorpha pronubana

Superficially like the Fruit-tree Tortrix, it lacks the drawn-out pointed wing-tips and its hind wings are bright orange instead of grey. Despite its name, it attacks a wide range of plants, especially indoor and greenhouse species, and can be a serious pest of strawberries. It also damages privet and laurel hedges and several other evergreen shrubs in the garden. The adults are nocturnal and are on the wing for much of the summer. The caterpillars are green or yellow and reach lengths of about 2 cm, often creating retreats for themselves by drawing the leaves together and joining them with silk, although many individuals bore right into the flower buds and ruin the flowers. Maturing strawberry fruits are damaged when the caterpillars tunnel into them near the base. Under glass, the caterpillars remain active through-out the winter months, but those living out of doors become dormant for the winter. Contact insecticides are not a lot of good against the caterpillars because they are usually hidden in their retreats, and the best way to control them is to pull open the retreats and squash the caterpillars that wriggle out, usually moving backwards at high speed.

Carnation Tortrix

Looks: Bright orange hind wings; caterpillars green or yellow to 2cm

Food: Many herbaceous and woody plants, especially in greenhouses

When: Adult in summer: caterpillar summer to spring but dormant out of doors in winter

Where: Britain and Continental Europe

The Strawberry Tortrix moth can be distinguished from most of its garden relatives by the dark triangle at the front of each front wing.

STRAWBERRY TORTRIX
Acleris comariana

The front wings are greyish but are often heavily marked with rust-coloured stripes or patches and are sometimes almost completely brown. There is usually a large dark triangle on the front edge. The wingspan is about 2 cm. The moth is on the wing from late spring until well into the autumn and its pale green caterpillars are minor pests of strawberries. They feed mainly on the young leaves, which they join together with silken threads to make little tents. They also nibble the flowers, but appear to take little interest in the fruit. When fully grown, with a length of 1.5 cm, they fall to the ground and pupate in flimsy cocoons spun among the leaf litter. Winter is spent in the pupal stage. The insect is rarely common enough to warrant control measures in small gardens, but it is always worth keeping an eye open for its tents. Pick them off and destroy them, making sure that the caterpillars do not wriggle out and disappear among the rest of the foliage. Spraying before flowering with a pyrethroid-based insecticide may help to control large infestations, although many of the caterpillars survive such treatment because they are safely tucked up in their tents.

Strawberry Tortrix

Looks: Front wings greyish with rusty patches; sometimes brown. Pale green caterpillars

Food: Strawberries

When: Adult and caterpillar spring to autumn

Where: Britain and Continental Europe

This apple leaf carries a complete mine of the Apple Leaf Miner. Starting as a very narrow tunnel near the centre, the mine makes its way back along the mid-rib and then moves to the leaf margin before returning to the centre. The mine gradually gets wider to accommodate the growing caterpillar, and the line of brown frass (droppings) in the centre of the mine also gets wider. The pale section at the end of the mine is empty, showing that the caterpillar has already left to pupate.

APPLE LEAF MINER
Lyonetia clerkella

Apple Leaf Miner

Looks: Silky white front wings with dark patch at tip; tiny green caterpillars

Food: Apples, plums, cherries

When: Adult all year, but dormant in winter: caterpillar spring to autumn

Where: Britain and Continental Europe

A common, but not a serious pest of apples, plums and cherries, the adult moth has silky white front wings, spanning about 9 mm and having a dark patch at the tip. It hibernates in out-buildings and among dry debris and wakes to lay its eggs in the undersides of young apple leaves in the spring. The tiny green caterpillars then excavate narrow, winding mines in the leaf tissues. When mature, with a length of about 8 mm, they leave their mines and pupate on the leaf surface surrounded by silken tents. There are usually three generations in a year. Leaves with several mines may die, but the insect is unlikely to do the trees any serious harm.

LILAC LEAF MINER
Caloptilia syringella

This beautiful little moth has golden brown front wings spanning no more than about 1.2 cm, often crossed by white or silvery bars. The hind wings are like minute feathers. The moth is on the wing from April to July and in the garden it lays its eggs mainly on leaves of lilac trees and privet hedges. In the wild it also uses ash leaves. The pale, more or less translucent caterpillars are virtually legless in their early stages and they tunnel into the leaves to feed. Unsightly brown patches – blotch mines – develop on the surface over their feeding areas, with several caterpillars under each blotch. The caterpillars feed inside the leaves for a few weeks and then chew their way out and move to the tip of a leaf which they roll into a tubular retreat in which they carry on feeding gregariously until fully grown. Winter is passed in the pupal state, in a cocoon spun under a leaf or in the leaf litter below the food-plants. Although the mines and rolled leaves are unsightly when numerous, they do no serious harm to the host plants and the best treatment is to remove and destroy affected leaves.

Lilac Leaf Miner

Looks: Tiny: wings golden brown with white or silver bars and spanning up to 1.2 cm. Pale, translucent caterpillars

Food: Lilac, privet

When: Adult spring and early summer: caterpillar summer, but mines visible until leaf fall

Where: Britain and Continental Europe

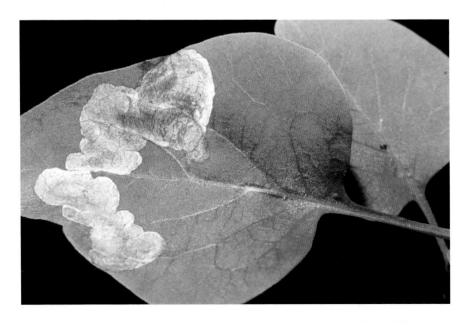

A lilac leaf exhibiting a large blotch mine caused by the Lilac Leaf Miner.

Horse Chestnut Leaf Miner

Looks: Tiny, light brown wings span about 8mm: caterpillars live inside leaves

Food: Horse chestnut trees

When: Adult and caterpillar spring to autumn

Where: Originated in Macedonia, present southern British Isles since 2000

HORSE CHESTNUT LEAF MINER
Cameraria ohridella

Although horse chestnut trees are too large for most private gardens, huge numbers have been planted in municipal gardens and town parks, where they are admired for their elegant shape and their beautiful flower spikes. But these splendid trees are now under attack by the Horse Chestnut Leaf Miner, a tiny moth with a front wing only about 4 mm long and caterpillars small enough to live inside the leaves. The caterpillars munch their way through the nutritious inner tissues of the leaves, leaving galleries or mines whose positions are marked by brown blotches on the leaf surface. Some trees are so heavily infested that they appear completely brown by mid-summer. Unable to make food in the affected leaves, these trees clearly cannot grow properly, and young trees may become seriously stunted. Badly affected trees often drop their leaves well before autumn. The moth is a newcomer to the British Isles, having arrived only in 2000 or 2001 after a remarkably rapid spread across Europe since its initial discovery in Macedonia in 1985. First noticed in the London area in 2002, it is now well established all over southern England and is still spreading rapidly, thanks to the ease with which the moth is blown by the wind and carried in vehicles. The insect can produce two or three generations in a year, so numbers can build up at an alarming rate. The caterpillars pupate in the leaves, with those pupae formed late in the year remaining in the fallen leaves until the spring. No effective treatment is yet available and it is to be hoped that a natural enemy will appear before too long.

BELOW LEFT: Part of a horse chestnut leaf bearing numerous mines. Many leaves are completely destroyed by the tunnelling caterpillars.

BELOW RIGHT: The adult Horse Chestnut Leaf Miner, freshly emerged from its chrysalis inside the leaf.

RASPBERRY MOTH
Lampronia rubiella

A pretty little moth with wings spanning no more than 1.2 cm, it has purplish-brown front wings with cream or pale yellow spots, including two more or less triangular spots on the rear edge. It is on the wing in May and June, when the females lay their eggs in raspberry and loganberry flowers. The young caterpillars are more or less colourless and they feed for a while in the central plugs or cores of the developing fruits, without doing any serious harm to the edible bits of the fruits. They then leave to spend the autumn and winter resting in the soil or leaf litter. After hibernation they climb the canes again, bore into new buds, and then usually tunnel into the young shoots, which frequently wither and die. Fully grown caterpillars are bright red and they normally pupate in the shoots, although some may pupate on the leaves or on the outside of the canes. Insecticidal treatment is not suitable, but prompt removal of withered shoots in the summer and regular hoeing around the plants in the winter will keep the pest's population down. Autumn-fruiting raspberries suffer less than summer-fruiting varieties because their flowers rarely open before the moths have finished laying their eggs.

Raspberry Moth

Looks: Up o 1.2 cm; front wings purple brown with creamy spots; caterpillars colourless

Food: Raspberries, loganberries

When: Adult late spring and summer: caterpillar summer to spring but dormant in winter

Where: Britain and Continental Europe

TOP TIP

Remove affected shoots in summer and hoe regularly around the plants in autumn. This is the best way to keep Raspberry Moth numbers down.

The dainty Raspberry Moth has muted coloration in contrast with its caterpillars which are a vivid red.

ABOVE LEFT: The silken shelter of a now-departed larva of the Fig-tree Skeletoniser Moth. Affected leaves often curl up at the tips, as pictured here.

ABOVE RIGHT: The adult Apple-leaf Skeletoniser Moth.

FIG-TREE SKELETONISER MOTH
Choreutis nemorana

The wings of this small brown, day-flying insect span up to 2 cm and are heavily dusted with grey scales. The adults hibernate, often in sheds and other out-buildings, and wake to lay their eggs on the fig leaves in the spring. The resulting larvae, green with black spots, spin silken shelters for themselves, usually close to one of the main leaf veins. There may be one or two under each shelter and they feed by scraping the surface tissues from the leaf. Up to 2 cm long when mature, they pupate in cocoons spun on the foliage. New adults appear in the summer and begin the cycle again. More adults appear in the autumn and these are the ones that go into hibernation. The insect is found all over southern Europe, but does not seem to affect the fruit yield of the fig trees. Squash the caterpillars if you don't like to see their webs on the leaves. The **Apple Leaf Skeletoniser Moth** (*Choreutis pariana*) is a very similar insect found on apples, pears and cherries in many parts of Europe.

Fig-tree Skeletoniser Moth

Looks: Small, brown with grey scales; wings spanning up to 2 cm. Caterpillars green with black spots

Food: Fig trees

When: Adult all year, but dormant in winter; caterpillar spring to autumn

Where: Southern Europe

ORCHARD ERMINE
Yponomeuta padella

The Orchard Ermine is one of several very similar small moths with wings generally spanning between 2 and 2.5 cm. The front wings are greyish-white and the fringes on the outer edges are distinctly grey. The moth flies in July and August and, in the garden, it usually lays its eggs in batches on plum and cherry twigs although hawthorn and black-thorn hedges are equally acceptable. Each batch of eggs is covered with a sticky yellow fluid that hardens into a protective shield. Most of the eggs hatch in late summer, but the tiny caterpillars do not move from their cover until the spring, when they start to feed on the opening leaves. They stay together throughout their lives, covering the twigs and branches with a silken web under which they feed. They are greyish with numerous black dots and are about 2 cm long when mature. They pupate in small cocoons in the webs. Heavy infestations of the larvae can cause severe damage to trees, so look for the small webs when the leaves open in the spring and remove the affected twigs immediately.

Orchard Ermine

Looks: Wings span 2-2.5 cm; front wings greyish white, grey outer edges. Very small greyish caterpillars

Food: Plum, cherry, blackthorn, hawthorn

When: Adult in summer: caterpillar summer to spring but dormant in winter

Where: Britain and Continental Europe

APPLE ERMINE
Yponomeuta malinellus

Confined to apple trees, the Apple Ermine has slightly 'cleaner' front wings than the Orchard Ermine but the two species are otherwise very difficult to separate when found away from their food-plants. Young larvae mine the apple leaves, but then live externally in webs just like those of the Orchard Ermine. Pheromone lures are available for trapping the adult males of these two pests.

Apple Ermine

Looks: Wings, greyish white with grey fringes, span up to 2.5 cm

Food: Apple leaves

When: Adult in summer: caterpillar summer to spring but dormant in winter

Where: Britain and Continental Europe

LEFT: The adult Apple Ermine is one of several very similar species found in and around the garden. The spot pattern and fringe colour vary slightly, but the moths are otherwise difficult to distinguish. RIGHT: A cluster of Apple Ermine larvae in their shelter under an apple leaf.

This tent of silk, completely covering a spindle bush, is the work of thousands of tiny Spindle Ermine caterpillars, some of which can be seen sunning themselves on the outside.

SPINDLE ERMINE
Yponomeuta cagnagella
Another very common species, whose larvae smother spindle bushes with their webs and rapidly defoliate them. Both wild and cultivated spindles are attacked. The adult moth differs from the above species in having white fringes.

BIRD-CHERRY ERMINE
Yponomeuta evonymella
This moth also has white fringes, but it has five or six rows of black spots whereas the three previous species have only three or four rows on each wing. The species is confined mainly to bird cherry trees and is more common in northern areas where the wild bird cherry is native. Bird cherries grown in gardens are usually cultivated hybrids. The moth sometimes attacks cultivated cherries, especially on the continent, and is occasionally found on plums.

Bird-cherry Ermine

Looks: Front wings, with white fringes and 5 or 6 rows of black spots, span 2-2.5 cm

Food: Bird cherry trees, occasionally plums

When: Adult in summer: caterpillar summer to spring but dormant in winter

Where: Britain and Europe

The adult Garden Pebble Moth in typical resting attitude. INSET: The caterpillar of the Garden Pebble is a common pest of brassicas and especially damaging to young plants.

GARDEN PEBBLE MOTH
Evergestis forficalis

The moth has a wingspan of about 3 cm and can be distinguished from several other similarly coloured moths by the brown streak running from the wing-tip to about half way along the rear edge of the front wing. Look also for the two small, dark ovals near the centre of the wing. The moth is on the wing throughout the summer and is particularly common in gardens and on other cultivated land. Its yellowish-green caterpillars feed on cabbages and other brassicas, usually on the undersides of the leaves although they often wreck cabbages by tunnelling right into them. Caterpillars maturing in the autumn burrow into the soil, where they remain dormant until they turn into pupae in the spring. Handpicking of the caterpillars is the best way of controlling them: spraying has little effect because the insects are fairly well protected under the leaves.

Garden Pebble Moth

Looks: To 3 cm; brown streak on wing; two oval spots near centre; caterpillars yellow-green

Food: Cabbages and other brassicas

When: Adult late spring to autumn: caterpillar much of the year but dormant in winter

Where: Britain and Continental Europe

RIGHT: The male Diamond-back Moth in its resting position has a row of pale diamond-shaped patches along the top. The front wings are from about 6 to 8 mm long.

BELOW RIGHT: Diamond-back Moth larvae on a young brassica leaf. The insects often feed under flimsy webs.

TOP TIP

Inspect cabbages and other brassicas regularly and squash caterpillars as you see them.

DIAMOND-BACK MOTH
Plutella xylostella

This little moth is named for the row of white diamond-shaped patches revealed when the male rests with its wings folded over the body. The female has dull grey front wings and no diamonds. Although the moth is often abundant, the adults are not often seen unless they come to lighted windows at night. The caterpillar, about 1 cm long when mature, is green with darker markings and a brown head and it feeds on various brassicas. Two or three often feed together under a flimsy silken web, commonly attacking the young leaf clusters around the growing points of the food-plants.

The insect breeds throughout the year in southern Europe, but in Britain and other cooler regions it spends the winter in the pupal stage, usually under a web on the food-plant. Adults often migrate in huge numbers and when this happens the resulting caterpillars can cause enormous damage. Regular inspection of brassicas and squashing the caterpillars with your fingers will keep most cabbage patches free of the pest. Contact insecticides are not very efficient because the caterpillars are usually well hidden.

Diamond-back Moth

Looks: Row of diamond-shaped patches when male resting; caterpillar 1 cm, green with darker marks

Food: Cabbages, other brassicas

When: All year in southern Europe. Elsewhere adult spring to late autumn: caterpillar summer and autumn

Where: Most of southern Europe

MINT MOTH
Pyrausta aurata

Also known as the Small Purple-and-Gold Moth, this is one of several rather similar moths that feed on mint, marjoram and other labiates. Adults commonly bask on the leaves in the summer and dart away rapidly when disturbed – often returning to the same perch after a short while. There is usually just a single gold spot on each front wing, although there may be a smaller one on the front margin. Related species have two or more golden spots. Young caterpillars feed on the undersides of the leaves, but later move to the shoot-tips and flowerheads where each spins itself a protective web. At this stage the caterpillars are dull green with yellow-ringed black spots. Winter is passed in the caterpillar stage in cocoons spun amongst the shrivelled flowerheads and leaves. The insect is not a serious pest, but can certainly spoil young mint leaves destined for the kitchen.

Mint Moth

Looks: Single gold spot on purplish front wing; caterpillars dull green with pale-ringed spots

Food: Mints

When: Adult late spring and summer: caterpillar much of the year but dormant in winter

Where: Britain and Continental Europe

The adult Mint Moth is commonly seen flitting around mint and marjoram plants in the summer. Its front wings are up to 8 mm long.

The Mint Moth caterpillar, seen here with its flimsy web, has yellow-ringed black spots all along the body and a light brown head.

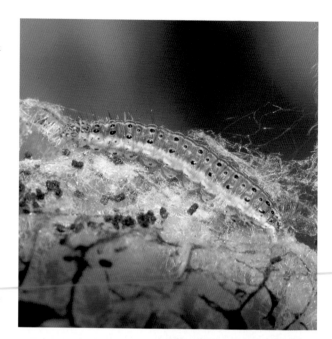

Mint leaves showing damage typical of the Mint Moth caterpillar.

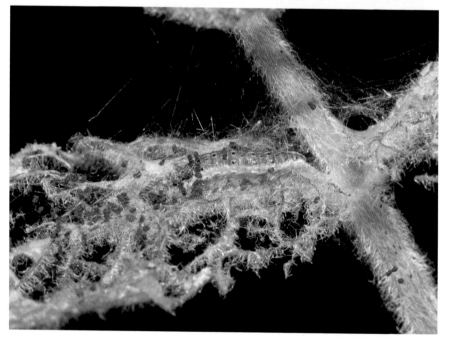

MIDGES, MOZZIES AND OTHER FLIES

True flies feed on liquids of one sort or another, including blood and nectar, and the adult insects do no direct harm to our crops. Many of them, including the often colourful hoverflies, actually benefit the garden by playing a major role in pollination. Others home in on the gardener rather than the garden plants: mosquitoes and a few other flies are always ready to plug into our bodies and sample our blood, while many flies drive us mad by continually circling around us and trying to land for a taste of sweat as we work in the garden. One traditional way of deterring these annoying insects is to wear a hat decorated with sage sprigs, but most gardeners probably prefer to be less conspicuous and use a modern insect repellent.

TOP TIP

Concentrated lavender oil is excellent for repelling mosquitoes and other biting flies in the open air. If you are annoyed by these pests in the garden, plant some lemon balm around your favourite spot. The midges do not like the citron smell.

Just two wings

True flies, which include house-flies, bluebottles, crane-flies, mosquitoes, and many much smaller insects, all belong to the order Diptera, a name meaning 'two-winged'. Most other insects have two pairs of wings, but among the flies the hind wings have evolved into tiny pin-like structures that act like gyroscopes to keep the insects steady in flight. Known as halteres, these balancing organs are easily seen in the crane-flies (see p.248). Mosquitoes and other blood-sucking flies have sharp, piercing jaws that act like hypodermic needles to draw blood from their victims. Most other flies have spongy tips to their jaws and use them to mop up liquids, although many flies do not feed at all in the adult state.

Although adult flies are rarely more than a nuisance, the same cannot be said about their younger stages, for the grubs or larvae of many species are common garden pests, chewing their way through roots and fruits and, to a lesser extent, the stems and leaves of a wide variety of plants.

While not a garden pest, the mosquito can certainly be a nuisance in the garden: the females often attack the gardener, hoping to pierce the skin with what is often quite a long beak and to get a meal of blood.

A female Marsh Crane-fly, clearly showing the pointed tip of the abdomen which she digs into the soil to lay her eggs. Male crane-flies have clubbed tips to their abdomens. One haltere can be seen just behind the left wing of this insect

Crane-flies and leatherjackets

Crane-flies are slender-bodied flies with long, spidery legs that are responsible for the insects' common name of 'daddy-long-legs'. The legs break off very easily, but as long as the insect does not lose more than two or three legs it can get on with its life perfectly well. Crane-flies may lap up small amounts of nectar or dew, although they do not feed much and their adult lives are concerned almost entirely with mating and egg-laying. There are hundreds of different kinds of crane-flies in Europe, three of which are particularly common and damaging in the garden.

COMMON CRANE-FLY
Tipula oleracea

A silvery grey insect about 2.5 cm long, with typical long, spindly legs, this species can be seen flying low over lawns and other vegetation in all but the coldest months of the year, although it is most obvious in the spring.

Common Crane-fly

Looks: Silver-grey; body to 2.5 cm; long spindly legs; grubs are greyish brown with tough skins

Food: Roots of many plants, including grasses

When: Most of year

Where: Britain and Continental Europe

MARSH CRANE-FLY
Tipula paludosa

Very similar to the Common Crane-fly, its body is somewhat browner and it is most common in the autumn. Both
species are attracted by lights and often enter houses at night
– and then dance frantically up and down as they search for
an escape. Although the adult flies are quite harmless, their
grubs certainly are not. They are the infamous 'leatherjackets'
– unattractive grey grubs up to about 4 cm long that live in
the soil and attack the roots of many different plants **(see p.
250)**. Grass roots are their favourite foods, however, and
they are most likely to be found under the lawn or in the
orchard. Yellowish patches on the lawn in the summer may
show where the insects have been destroying the roots and
killing the grass.

Marsh Crane-fly

Looks: Adult slender,
brownish with long legs;
grubs have leathery skins

Food: Grass roots and
many other plants

When: Most of the year

Where: Britain and
Continental Europe

SPOTTED CRANE-FLY
Nephrotoma appendiculata

Named for the variable black and yellow pattern on its abdomen, the Spotted Crane-fly is usually a little smaller than
the last two species and, unlike them, it rests with its wings
folded flat over its body. It can be found in the garden
throughout the summer, usually resting on the vegetation
by day. Its larva resembles those of the Common and Marsh
Crane-flies, although it is a littler smaller, and it is more likely
to live in the vegetable patch or the flower bed than under

A mating pair of Spotted
Crane-flies: the female with
her egg-filled body is the
larger insect on the left.

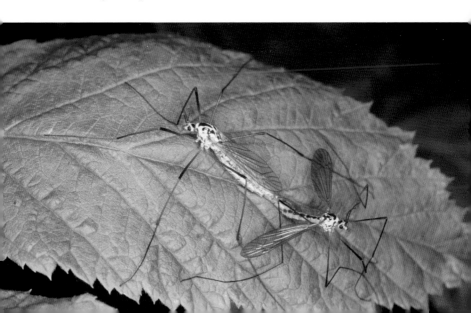

A typical leatherjacket, tough-skinned and legless; it often appears to be headless because the head is commonly pulled back into the thorax when the insects are disturbed. Leatherjackets can be found in the soil at any time of the year. Leatherjackets pupate in the soil and the pupae wriggle to the surface so that the adult flies can escape.

Spotted Crane-fly

Looks: Black and yellow pattern on abdomen; long thin legs; greyish grubs

Food: Potatoes and other root crops; strawberries

When: Adult throughout the summer

Where: Britain and Continental Europe

the lawn. It often damages potatoes and various root crops, and frequently comes to the surface to nibble through the stems of young plants. Strawberries seem to be especially attractive to this species. Damage tends to be most severe in the spring, when many of the plants are small and the leatherjackets are approaching maturity.

Controlling leatherjackets

Several methods can be used to control leatherjackets in the garden, although the populations fluctuate a great deal from year to year and it is not always necessary to do anything about them. If the lawn develops yellow patches in the summer it is worth giving the patches a good soak in the evening and then covering them with old sacking or polythene. Unhappy with the waterlogged conditions, the leatherjackets will make their way to the surface and can be destroyed when the covering is lifted in the morning. This method can also be used to reduce the leatherjacket population among flowers and vegetables. Regular hoeing also helps, by disturbing the pests and possibly exposing them to birds and other predators. Biological control of leatherjackets is now possible with the aid of a parasitic nematode worm called *Steinernema feltiae*. Watered into the infested areas in warm weather, these tiny worms seek out and destroy the leatherjackets without harming any other soil-living creatures.

These swollen and contorted violet leaves have been attacked and galled by the tiny midge *Dasineura odoratae*.

Problem midges

Dasineura odoratae

This tiny midge causes cultivated violet leaves to become thick and furry and to roll in from the edges. The midge grubs, only about 2 mm long, live and feed in the rolls. They are white at first, but gradually become orange as they mature. They turn into pupae in white cocoons inside the rolled leaves. The insect has several generations in a year, so the swollen leaves can be found at any time. Affected plants look unsightly and gradually become weaker, failing to produce good flowers, but regular removal of affected leaves will reduce the midge population and allow the plants to recover.

TOP TIP

Remove affected leaves to reduce the midge population and let the plants recover.

Dasineura odoratae

Looks: Tiny insect; white to orange 2 mm grubs

Food: Violets

When: Galls are visible all year

Where: Britain and Continental Europe

A twig of honey locust on which many of the leaflets have been converted into pouch galls by the presence of larvae of the midge *Dasineura gleditchiae*.

Dasineura gleditchiae

This is another troublesome midge, causing severe distortion of the leaves of the popular honey locust tree. A native of North America, it is now common in many parts of Europe, including much of England. The insects spend the winter in the soil as mature larvae or pupae and adults emerge to lay their eggs on the leaflets in the spring. Affected leaflets swell up and become folded to form small pouches, each of which contains several orange grubs. These first-generation grubs pupate in the pouches and a further one or two generations may be produced during the summer. Grubs produced in late summer fall with the leaves and eventually pupate in the soil. Small trees known to suffer from this pest can be sprayed with a pyrethroid-based insecticide when the leaves first open, or you can spray the soil around the trunks to kill the emerging adults. A systemic insecticide, such as imidacloprid, can be sprayed on to the soil, from where it will be taken up by the roots and give the trees further protection.

Dasineura gleditchiae

Looks: Minute yellowish flies: grubs cause leaflets to form 'pouches'

Food: Honey locust trees

When: Adults fly and grubs can be found in the galls throughout the summer

Where: Europe, much of England

Contarinia quinquenotata

Related to the preceding two species, this midge is responsible for distorting the buds of day-lilies. Female midges emerge from their subterranean pupae in late spring or early summer and lay their eggs in the flower buds. The resulting grubs cause the buds to swell, but they do not open. The petals become thick and crinkled, with jagged edges, and if the buds are broken open they reveal writhing masses of tiny white grubs. As the grubs mature, the buds turn brown and fall, and the grubs escape to pupate in the soil. This is a relatively new pest in the British Isles, having arrived from the Continent in the 1980s, but it has now spread to many parts of southern England. Insecticides are of little use against the pest because they cannot reach the grubs in the buds, and the best way to control it is to remove and burn the infested buds as soon as they are seen. This will reduce the midge population for the following year, although midges can still fly in from neighbouring gardens. Late-flowering varieties of day-lily are usually relatively free from the pest because their buds do not appear until the female midges have finished laying their eggs.

TOP TIP

Remove and destroy affected lily buds as soon as you see them to reduce the next year's midge population.

Contarinia quinquenotata

Looks: Grubs cause buds to swell and distort

Food: Day-lilies

When: Adult spring and early summer: galled buds visible in late spring and much of the summer

Where: Continental Europe; Southern England

Two day-lily buds galled by the midge *Contarinia quinquenotata*, with a normal bud on the left.

A pea pod opened to show the larvae (maggots) of the Pea Midge. Although not very pleasant for a cook to discover, the larvae do not do much harm to the actual peas as they prefer to feed on the inner lining of the pod.

TOP TIP

Regularly rotate crop plantings to keep Pea Midges under control without the use of pesticides.

Pea Midge

Looks: Up to 3.5 cm dirty yellow; grubs are white

Food: Garden peas and sweet peas

When: Adult and larva in spring and summer

Where: Britain and Continental Europe

PEA MIDGE
Contarinia pisi

This midge attacks both garden peas and sweet peas and its grubs are responsible for densely clustered, stunted shoot tips, unopened flowers and distorted young pods. The midge is no more than 3.5 mm long and, in common with many of its relatives, it is dirty yellow in colour. Adults emerge from their pupae in the soil in late spring and lay their eggs on the shoot tips or in the flower buds. The resulting white grubs feed there for about two weeks before dropping down to pupate in the soil. A second generation of adults appears in July and lays its eggs on the pods, where the grubs feed mainly on the inner lining without doing too much damage. These grubs are legless and much smaller than those of the Pea Moth **(see p. 231)**, which feed on the developing peas rather than the surrounding pod. When mature, they make their way into the soil to pupate. Crop rotation, together with complete removal of all pea debris, is the best way to keep this pest under control, for adults emerging in the spring will not then find anywhere to lay their eggs. The midge is less of a problem in gardens than in the fields, where crops are often harvested later and the insect has more of a chance to complete its life cycle.

PEAR MIDGE
Contarinia pyrivora

This very common pest of pears causes considerable damage to the crop every year. Up to 4 mm long, it flies in spring and lays its eggs in the flower buds of pear trees. The resulting grubs tunnel into the developing fruits, and the infested fruitlets swell up more quickly than unaffected ones. Each fruitlet may contain dozens of yellowish grubs. The infested fruitlets soon turn black and fall and, about a month after the eggs were laid, the grubs leave to pupate in the soil. New adults emerge in the following spring, just in time to lay eggs in the fresh buds. Affected fruitlets should be removed and destroyed as soon as they are seen – and don't forget to pick up all those that have already fallen. If you keep chickens it is worth letting them scratch around under the trees when the fruitlets are falling – they will mop up many of the grubs before they can burrow into the soil. Small garden trees can also be sprayed with insecticides based on pyrethroids, but this must be done just as the buds begin to show a bit of white. Spraying when the flowers have opened will kill bees and other pollinators and there will be no crop at all!

TOP TIP

Remove affected fruitlets from the tree and from the ground where grubs can remain.

Pear Midge

Looks: Up to 4 mm; causes developing fruit to turn black and fall

Food: Pears

When: Adult in spring: larva, in fruit, spring and early summer

Where: Britain and Continental Europe

PEAR LEAF MIDGE
Dasineura pyri

Another very tiny fly associated with pears, this one affects the leaves. It lays its eggs around the edges of the leaves and the feeding of the grubs causes the edges to swell and curl inwards. One or both edges of a leaf may be affected, and badly affected leaves lose much of their ability to photosynthesise. They often turn red and black and fall prematurely. A severe infestation can lead to a reduction in fruit yields, but the midge is rarely abundant enough to cause any real damage. Because the grubs are tucked up in the leaf rolls, spraying is ineffective. The **Apple Leaf Midge** (*Dasineura mali*) affects apple leaves in a very similar way. Both species have two or three generations a year, with grubs of the final brood overwintering in soil before pupating in the spring.

Pear Leaf Midge

Looks: Edges of leaves swell and curl inward

Food: Leaves of pear trees

When: Adult and larva spring to autumn

Where: Britain and Continental Europe

CARROT-FLY
Psila rosae

This dark, slender fly, 4–5 mm long, is on the wing, searching for our carrot crops, throughout the summer. Parsnips, parsley and celery also succumb to this pest to a lesser degree. The insects spend the winter as grubs or pupae in the soil and the adults emerge to lay their eggs in the spring. The eggs are usually laid in the soil close to the host plants and they hatch after about a week. The creamy white grubs quickly set about the finer roots, but as they get older they start to burrow in the main tap root, often leaving rust-coloured patches when they tunnel close to the skin. Fungi and bacteria can invade these damaged tissues and render the carrots even more useless. The grubs pupate after four or five weeks and new adults appear in late summer. In warmer regions there may even be three generations in a year. The foliage of affected plants frequently takes on a rusty tinge and this is often the first sign of trouble.

Crop rotation is important in controlling the insect, so that flies emerging in the spring do not find themselves surrounded by a fresh crop, but this will not prevent flies arriving from further afield. Carrots give off a very distinctive scent and the insects can detect this and home in on it from a distance of several hundred metres. The scent of fresh roots is especially strong, so it is a good plan to sow your carrots thinly so that they do not need thinning: female Carrot-flies easily pick up the scent released when the roots are disturbed. Similarly, it makes sense to dig up all your mature carrots at the same

Carrot-fly

Looks: Dark, slender fly to 5 mm; grubs creamy white

Food: Carrots, parsnips, parsley, celery

When: Adult spring to autumn: larva all year, but usually dormant in winter

Where: Britain and Continental Europe

A larva of the Carrot-fly nibbling out a groove on the surface of a carrot. Although this does not affect the flavour of the rest of the carrot, the grooves and tunnels look unsightly and affected carrots are useless for the market.

time. If you do need to thin the crop or harvest it piece-meal, it is worth covering the remaining plants with horticultural fleece to keep the flies away. Delaying sowing your carrots until late spring also helps because the first generation of Carrot-flies will already have gone by then. Some carrot varieties are less susceptible to Carrot-fly than others, so it is well worth choosing one of these more resistant strains, such as 'Resistafly'. Companion planting is also worth considering. The Carrot-fly is repelled or perhaps confused by the strong scent of onions and their relatives, and planting onions or leeks, or perhaps a colourful row of chives next to your carrots will give them a good deal of protection. In return, the carrots are believed to afford the onions some protection against the Onion-fly **(see below)**.

No insecticidal treatment is available for controlling the Carrot-fly. Dry sand sprinkled along the carrot rows may help by making it difficult for the flies to get at the roots, and if you sprinkle a few drops of paraffin at intervals along the row it might work even better – perhaps by masking the smell of the carrots. Yesterday's gardeners used crushed mothballs instead of paraffin. They might have had good crops, but we don't know what they tasted like! Because the Carrot-fly does not fly more than a few centimetres above the ground, it is also possible to reduce infestations by surrounding the carrot rows with low fences of fleece or plastic sheeting.

ONION-FLY

Delia antiqua

This small greyish fly attacks leeks and onions. It spends the winter in the pupal stage in the soil and adults emerge to lay their eggs on or around the plants in spring and early summer. The little white grubs or maggots damage the roots, often causing young plants to turn yellow and die, but onions grown from sets do not suffer quite as badly as those grown from seed. Fully grown grubs are 0.8–1 cm long and they pupate in the soil. New adults emerge later in the summer and lay more eggs, the grubs from which tunnel into the bulbs as well as nibbling the roots. Infested bulbs become soft and often rot away as a result of secondary fungal infection. Affected bulbs should be removed and burned. No insecticides are available for use against the Onion-fly, but growing onions and related crops under horticultural fleece will keep most of the flies off them.

TOP TIP

• Growing a row of carrots on each side of the onion patch can help.

• Never plant onions on freshly manured ground, as Onion-fly seems to be attracted by the smell of manure.

• Always rake the ground thoroughly before planting

Onion-fly

Looks: Small, greyish fly; white grubs

Food: Leeks, onions

When: Adult and larva spring and summer

Where: Britain and Continental Europe

An adult Cabbage Root-fly enjoying a meal of nectar.

CABBAGE ROOT-FLY
Delia radicum

This fly is a major pest of cabbages and most other brassica crops, including swedes and turnips as well as cauliflowers and broccoli. Wallflowers may also be affected, while fields of rape are important habitats from which the flies can invade our gardens. The adult flies resemble small, grey house-flies and are on the wing from late spring until well into the autumn. Winter is spent in the pupal stage in the soil, and the first adults appear when the soil warms up in the spring. The females lay their eggs close to the host plants, on or just below the soil surface, and the resulting white grubs tunnel into the roots and stems. Affected plants soon wilt, especially in the sunshine, and the leaves often take on a bluish tinge, while the roots turn black. Seedlings and recently transplanted plants may be killed: established plants may survive, but become stunted and fail to produce decent yields. The grubs are fully grown in about three weeks and then they pupate in the soil. New adults appear about a week later and start the cycle again, and a third generation may appear in late summer.

No insecticide is available to combat the Cabbage Root-fly. Regular cultivation of the ground prior to planting will bring many pupae to the surface where they will be eaten by birds, and covering young plants with horticultural fleece will keep the adult flies away. Sowing seeds in pots and not

TOP TIP

• *Regular cultivation will expose pupae and larvae so that they can be picked off and squashed.*

• *Horticultural fleece will protect plants against the adult flies.*

Cabbage Root-fly larvae boring into a root.

planting them out until their root systems are well developed also reduces the risk of serious damage, and you can reduce the amount of egg-laying by the adult flies by placing discs of plastic or cardboard around the stems. The discs should be about 15 cm across. Plants that do become infected should be removed and burned, and it is advisable not to plant brassicas in the same ground for two or three years. Recent research suggests that planting birds-foot trefoil among the cabbages can deter Cabbage Root-fly, and the nitrogen-fixing activities of the trefoil's root-nodules will also give the cabbages a boost.

The Cabbage Root-fly is particularly susceptible to a fungus called *Entomophthora muscae* and flies killed by the fungus sometimes cover the vegetation in the autumn. Masses of white spores can be seen bursting from the swollen abdomens of the corpses, and it is interesting that infected flies tend to climb upwards before they die, with the result that the spores are exposed to the breeze and have the best chance of being blown away to reach new host insects.

Cabbage Root-fly

Looks: Adults resemble small grey house flies; grubs are white

Food: Cabbages and other brassicas; wallflowers, rape

When: Adult and larva late spring to autumn

Where: Britain and Continental Europe

A cluster of Cabbage Root-flies killed by the fungus *Entomophthora muscae*. This is a common sight in fields and gardens in late summer and autumn.

The Bean Seed-fly resembles a small and rather bristly house-fly. You can avoid the worst of its effects by not sowing your beans too early.

BEAN SEED-FLY
Delia platura

Many gardeners have been disappointed to find that French beans and, less often, runner beans sown in the open ground often fail to appear above the surface, or come up seriously damaged. Slugs often get the blame, but the real culprit here is usually the Bean Seed-fly, closely related to and similar to the Onion-fly and the Cabbage Root-fly. After spending the winter as pupae in the soil, the flies emerge in the spring and lay their eggs close to the germinating seeds. Maggots hatching from the eggs attack the seeds and seedlings, chewing the leaves and leaving ugly brown marks on the young shoots. Some seeds and seedlings may be completely destroyed before they get above ground level. Those that do make it usually recover eventually, although growth is generally slow. Gardeners like to encourage their beans by planting them in well-manured ground, but the Bean Seed-fly is strongly attracted to fresh manure so it is best to fill the bean trenches in the autumn, giving the manure a chance to rot before the beans are sown. Early sowings, which take a while to germinate in the cool soil, are much more at risk than later sowings, so it is wise not to sow too early in the open ground. Seeds sown in June in Britain have a much better chance of survival because they germinate much more quickly in the warm soil. Alternatively, sow your seeds in pots in a frame or greenhouse and put the plants out when their first few leaves are well developed. No insecticides are

TOP TIP

Sow later when placing beans in open ground to avoid the seedling being destroyed by Bean Seed-flies before they even reach ground level.

Bean Seed-fly

Looks: Small greyish fly; white maggots

Food: Beans including French and runner beans

When: Adult and larva spring and early summer

Where: Britain and Continental Europe

available for treating the Bean Seed-fly. Beans that appear above ground only to disappear a few hours later are probably taken by mice – or by birds that mistake the arched white shoots for worms or grubs!

The adult Carnation-fly gets its nectar from a wide range of flowers, although its grubs have a more restricted diet.

CARNATION-FLY
Delia cardui

Sweet williams and all kinds of carnations and pinks are attacked by the Carnation-fly. Eggs are laid on the leaves in the autumn and the resulting larvae tunnel through the leaves and stems throughout the winter, leaving pale streaks and patches (leaf mines) to indicate their progress. Whole shoots and even complete plants may be killed by a heavy infestation. Mature grubs are about 1 cm long and they pupate in the soil in the spring. Although new adults start to appear in the middle of the summer, they do not lay their eggs until the autumn, when there is plenty of fresh growth. The pest can be controlled by spraying the plants with a systemic insecticide.

Carnation-fly

Looks: Greyish fly; white grubs to 1 cm

Food: Carnations, pinks, sweet williams

When: Adult in summer: larva autumn to spring

Where: Britain and Continental Europe

BEET LEAF MINER
Pegomya hyoscyami

Also known as the Spinach Leaf Miner, this insect damages both beet and spinach, including the various forms of chard or spinach beet. It lays its eggs on the undersides of the leaves and its larvae produce large, pale, blotchy mines **(see p. 21)** as they munch their way through the tissues between the upper and lower leaf surfaces.
Mature plants are rarely permanently harmed, even if large areas of leaf are killed, although the growth of younger plants may be somewhat restricted. Mature larvae pupate in the soil or, less frequently, in the leaf, and there may be several generations in a year. Larvae of the final generation pupate and overwinter in the soil. New adults, about 6 mm long, emerge in the spring. Systemic insecticides based on pyrethroids can be sprayed on the young plants, but it is better simply to cut out or squash the mined parts of the leaves as soon as you see them. Remove and destroy all old leaves, and use horticultural fleece over seedling rows to reduce the number of flies reaching them.

TOP TIP

Cut out or squash the mined parts of the leaves as soon as they are spotted to avoid having to use insecticides.

Beet Leaf Miner

Looks: Adult to 6 mm; larvae pale

Food: Beetroot, chard, spinach

When: Adult and larva spring to autumn

Where: Britain and Continental Europe

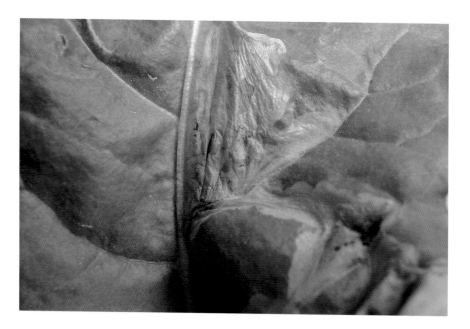

Beet Leaf Miner and damage: the orange body in the centre is a pupa

IRIS-FLY
Cerodontha iridis

Iris leaves that develop unsightly pale streaks and blotches are usually playing host to the larvae of the Iris-fly. The larvae are leaf-miners and they spend their lives tunnelling in the leaves during the summer. Heavily infested leaves turn white and then brown as the grubs consume the living tissues and leave only the outer skin. The grubs pupate in the lower parts of the leaves and tiny, black adult flies emerge in late summer although, with a wingspan of no more than about 6 mm, the insects are rarely seen. The fly's natural host is the yellow flag iris, so cultivated plants are most likely to be attacked if there is a nearby pond or stream, or maybe even a garden pond containing this plant. Only rhizomatous irises seem to be attacked. Yellow flag irises may also be attacked by the very similar ***Cerondontha ireos*** but this species, which has yellow 'knees' on all legs, does not seem to care for other irises. Spraying the plants with a systemic insecticide as soon as the mines are noticed will prevent further damage, but do not use anything with pyrethrins or pyrethroids in it as this will harm anything living in the water. It is better to squash the mines and their contents by running a finger and thumb up and down the leaves.

Iris-fly

Looks: Adult flies are tiny and black; grubs pale

Food: Iris plants

When: Adult summer; larva spring and summer

Where: Britain and Continental Europe

LEFT: Iris leaves mined by the Iris-fly. The pale patches are the mines – tunnels where the fly grubs have removed all the nutritious tissues between the two leaf surfaces.

ABOVE: Iris-fly pupae revealed by peeling the skin from the lower part of a leaf.

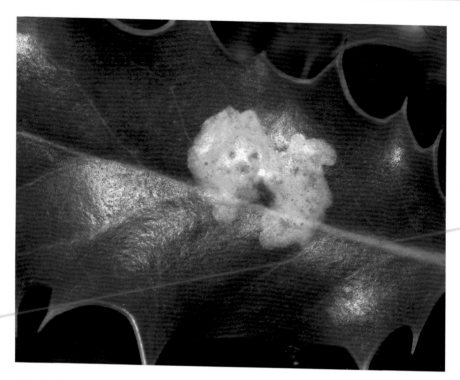

A blotch mine on a holly leaf caused by the Holly Leaf Miner. These mines are extremely common, but seem to do no harm to the trees.

HOLLY LEAF MINER
Phytomyza ilicis

This miner is responsible for the yellowish blotches that disfigure many garden holly trees and bushes throughout the year. In fact, it is quite rare to find a holly without any such blotches. The adult insect resembles a small house-fly, with a wingspan of only about 6 mm, and it is on the wing for much of the spring and summer. Egg are laid on the underside of young leaves in late spring and early summer and the larvae spend the next few months chewing their way through the nutritious tissues between the upper and lower leaf surface. The blotches, which are true leaf mines, show where the insects have been at work and often form a noticeable bulge on the upper surface. The grubs remain in their mines during the winter and pupate there in the spring. New adults escape through holes in the underside of the leaf. Remove and burn affected leaves if you are bothered by the blotches, but the insects do not seriously damage the holly trees and no treatment is really necessary or successful.

Holly Leaf Miner

Looks: Adult looks like small house-fly – to 6 mm; pale grubs

Food: Holly leaves

When: Adult spring and summer: larva can be found in mine much of the year

Where: Britain and Continental Europe

CHRYSANTHEMUM LEAF MINER
Chromatomyia syngenesiae

A wide range of plants in the daisy family, including lettuces and marigolds, as well as chrysanthemums are prey to this miner. The larvae tunnel through the leaves, producing pale winding mines that usually start near the leaf margin and gradually get wider as they approach the mid-rib and the enclosed larvae get bigger. The mines are clearly visible on both sides of the leaf. Mature larvae pupate in the mines and soon turn into tiny, dark adult flies no more than about 3 mm long. Several generations can be produced in the summer, and breeding can go on throughout the year in the greenhouse. The insect is best controlled by squashing the mines or by removing and destroying affected leaves as soon as the mines are detected. There is no effective insecticidal treatment, but some tiny parasitic wasps may provide good control in the greenhouse.

Chrysanthemum Leaf Miner

Looks: Tiny dark flies up to 3 mm; pale maggots

Food: Chrysanthemums, lettuces, marigolds

When: Adult and larva all year in greenhouses: summer and autumn out of doors

Where: Britain and Continental Europe

TOP TIP

Squash the mines or remove and destroy affected leaves as soon as you know that the leaves are being mined.

Typical mines on a chrysanthemum leaf.

TOP TIP

• *Remove and destroy the areas which have been affected by miners.*

• *Or squash with your fingers to destroy the larvae.*

Celery-fly

Looks: Adult has wings patterned with lines and spots; pale larvae

Food: Celery, celeriac, parsnips

When: Adult spring to autumn: larva in mines summer and autumn

Where: Britain and Continental Europe

CELERY-FLY
Euleia heraclei

Pale blotches on the leaves of celery and celeriac are usually the work of the grubs of the Celery-fly. Parsnips are also attacked by this leaf-mining pest. The adult, an attractive little insect with intricate patterns of dark lines and spots on its wings, lays its eggs on the leaves in the spring and the grubs then eat their way through the succulent tissues between the upper and lower surfaces of the leaves. The mined areas are cream at first, but soon turn brown and dry. Mature larvae leave their mines and pupate in the soil. New adults emerge in the summer and lay more eggs. The larvae from these eggs may pupate in the leaves or in the ground. Some adults may emerge in the autumn, but most remain in their pupae until the spring. The leaf stalks (sticks) of affected celery plants may become bitter and stringy, and a heavy infestation results in stunted plants. Infestations can be controlled by removing and destroying the mined areas – this does no great harm to the plants – or you can simply squash the mines with your fingers to crush the larvae. Destroying all old leaves after harvest will reduce the number of insects available to infest the following year's crop, but don't put the leaves on the compost heap! Covering newly planted crops with horticultural fleece will keep many adult flies away, although it gives no protection against flies emerging from the surrounding soil.

The Celery-fly belongs to a group known as picture-winged flies, on account of their beautifully patterned wings. It is a tiny insect, with wings no more than 5 mm long.

OLIVE FRUIT-FLY
Bactrocera oleae

One of the most serious olive pests in southern Europe, the adult fly, only 4–5 mm long, is largely black and white and rather shiny, and it lays its eggs in the young olive fruits. The resulting grubs destroy much of the olive flesh and render the fruits useless. There are up to four generations in a year, with grubs of the final generation leaving the fruit to pupate in the soil, where they remain throughout the winter. Other generations generally pupate in the fruits.

MEDITERRANEAN FRUIT-FLY
Ceratitis capitata

Probably the most destructive fruit pest in the world, the Mediterranean Fruit-fly originated in tropical Africa but now occurs nearly all over the globe and is known to attack over 250 different kinds of fruit. The adult insect is only about 5 mm long, with patterned wings and purplish eyes that exhibit a beautiful green iridescence. It is on the wing throughout the year in southern Europe, where there may be four or five generations in a year. Apples, pears, cherries and plums are all seriously damaged by this fly, with citrus fruits, peaches and apricots being added to the list in southern Europe. Eggs are laid just under the skin of the fruit, usually as it begins to ripen, and the resulting larvae quickly destroy the flesh. In warm areas the larvae are ready to leave the rotting fruit and pupate within a week, and new adults can be on the wing just two weeks after the eggs are laid. The fly frequently arrives in the British Isles in consignments of fruit and, although not yet found in the wild, it could well become established as a result of climate change.

Olive Fruit-fly

Looks: Adult up to 5 mm is black and white and shiny; pale grubs

Food: Olive trees

When: Adult and larva spring to autumn

Where: Southern Europe

TOP TIP

Insecticides are of little use in the battle against the Mediterranean Fruit-fly, but recent work in Spain suggests that we may eventually be able to control it biologically with an environmentally friendly product based on bacteria.

Mediterranean Fruit-fly

Looks: Adult up to 5mm; iridescent purple eyes and patterned wings; pale grubs

Food: Apples, pears, cherries, plums, citrus fruit, apricots, peaches

When: Adult and larva all year

Where: Mainly southern Europe. Often imported into Britain and parts of central and northern Europe

The Mediterranean Fruit-fly is another of the picture-winged flies and, in common with many of its relatives, it has beautiful iridescent eyes that range from green to purple according to the angle at which they are seen.

Cherry Fruit-fly

Looks: Dark fly with bright yellow patch on thorax; white larvae

Food: Cherries

When: Adult and larva spring and summer

Where: Much of Europe; grubs arrive in Britain in imported fruit

CHERRY FRUIT-FLY
Rhagoletis cerasi

This is a somewhat darker relative of the Mediterranean Fruit-fly that attacks cherries in many parts of Europe. It can be distinguished from several other flies with decorated or pictured wings by the bright yellow patch at the rear of its thorax. It is not resident in the British Isles, although its plump white larvae frequently arrive in imported fruit.

LARGE NARCISSUS-FLY
Merodon equestris

Also called the Large Bulb-fly, this one of the few hover-flies that do not do the gardener any favours. Although the adult may help with a bit of pollination, its grubs wipe out any benefit by destroying the bulbs of daffodils, hyacinths, lilies, tulips and many other garden flowers. Bluebells are major host plants in the wild. The adult fly is on the wing from late spring until well into the summer. It is very hairy and looks rather like a small bumblebee, although it flies more rapidly than a bumblebee and often hovers over the vegetation while giving out a high-pitched whine. Some individuals are completely black, while others have varying amounts of brown and grey, allowing them to mimic several different kinds of bumblebee. The female flies lay their eggs on or near the leaf bases, especially when the leaves start to die down and splay out at the base. The resulting grubs tunnel into the bulbs and gradually eat them away from the inside. Many of the affected bulbs rot away: some manage to survive and send up spindly leaves in the following spring, but they do not flower. There is normally only one grub in each bulb and, with a length of about 1.5 cm when mature, it almost fills the bulb. The grubs spend the winter in the bulbs and then leave to pupate in the soil.

Large Narcissus-fly

Looks: Adult hairy, can be black, brown or grey and resembles small bumblebees; pale larvae

Food: Daffodils, tulips, hyacinths, lilies and other bulbs

When: Adult spring and early summer: larva in bulbs summer to spring

Where: Britain and Continental Europe

The Large Narcissus-fly looks very much like a small bumble bee, but it has only two wings and its antennae are very much shorter antennae than those of bumble bee – they are not much more than a couple of bristles on the front of the head.

LESSER BULB-FLY
Eumerus tuberculatus

This is another hoverfly that attacks daffodils and narcissi and if your daffodil and narcissi bulbs contain several grubs, this species is the most likely culprit. Much smaller and less hairy than the previous species, the adult fly is rarely noticed, although it is common in many gardens.

CLUSTER-FLY
Pollenia rudis

Not strictly a garden pest, unless it qualifies as one because its grubs are parasites of earthworms, the Cluster-fly is a considerable nuisance in and around the house, especially in autumn and spring. The adult flies congregate on sunny walls in autumn and make their way into roof spaces and wall cavities where they spend the winter asleep. They are even more of a problem when they wake in spring: lofts may be full of them, and they get down into bedrooms through the smallest cracks. The flies are sluggish at this time and crawl everywhere. Windows become covered with them as they try to escape. Although harmless, they leave drops of excrement on the walls and windows and their dead bodies soon accumulate on floors and window-sills if they can't escape. Opening the windows to let them out as soon as they appear in the spring is the best remedy, but severe loft infestations can be dealt with by using smoke cones – as long as you are prepared to sweep up the carcases afterwards. Tell your neighbours and the fire brigade what you are up to first!

Lesser Bulb-fly

Looks: Smaller and less hairy than Large Narcissus-fly; pale larvae

Food: Daffodils, narcissi, and other bulbs

When: Adult spring to autumn: larva in bulbs summer to spring

Where: Britain and Continental Europe

Cluster-fly

Looks: Larger than a House-fly with gold hairs and chequered abdomen

Food: Grubs are parasites of earthworms

When: All year, but most often seen in spring and autumn: dormant in winter, often in houses

Where: Britain and Continental Europe

A little larger than a House-fly, the Cluster-fly is readily recognised by its golden hairs and the chequer-board pattern on its abdomen.

WASPS

The black and yellow wasps that buzz around our tea tables and picnics and deliver the occasional sting are the commonest and most conspicuous of our wasps. They live in large colonies and are known as social wasps. In many people's eyes they are pests, and the gardener who watches his ripe plums disappearing into the wasps' jaws will certainly agree. A single wasp is capable of demolishing an entire greengage in a morning, so the population of a nest can quickly destroy a whole crop. Grapes, pears and apples are equally acceptable to the wasps in our gardens.

But these wasps are not all bad. As youngsters they are fed almost entirely on animal food, and that food consists largely of chewed-up caterpillars, flies and other insects that are detrimental to the garden and a nuisance in the house. A single colony can rear over 20,000 wasps during the summer and it has been estimated that to reach maturity the young wasps would need to eat something in the region of 250,000 other insects between them! So perhaps we should look more kindly on our garden wasps. They do not usually sting unless provoked – although merely crossing a flight path close to the nest may be sufficient provocation – and for much of the summer they are far too busy to bother us. Collecting food for themselves and for the grubs is a full-time job. Although the grubs are fed on meat, including carrion as well as insects, the adults feed largely on energy-giving nectar, and while feeding they pollinate a wide range of flowers.

Thousands of relatives

Wasps belong to a huge group of insects called the Hymenoptera, along with bees and ants, sawflies (see p. 286), and a vast range of parasitic insects. There are over 40,000 different kinds of hymenopterans in Europe alone and it is hard to give a definition of the group as a whole because they are so varied. Most species have two pairs of wings, of which the hind ones are small and often difficult to see, but many have no wings at all. Many females can sting, but males have no stings because the stinging apparatus is actually the much-modified egg-laying equipment. Many of the parasites help us with pest control in the garden.

A Common Hornet enjoying a meal of grapes. The queen of this species is about 3 cm long, but the species is generally less aggressive than its smaller cousins. Gardeners in southern Europe, however, may meet a much larger and nastier beast – the Asian Giant Hornet, which reaches lengths of 5.5 cm. It has more extensive brown bands on the abdomen and a deep orange head. A relatively new species to Europe, it has a very powerful and dangerous sting. Just a few of these hornets can completely destroy a Honey Bee colony.

A Common Wasp worker using its powerful jaws to strip wood fibres from a fairly soft piece of timber.

RIGHT: The Common Wasp can be distinguished from other garden species by the black anchor-shaped mark on its face. The yellow streaks on its thorax are narrow and parallel-sided.

BELOW RIGHT: Part of the covering or envelope of the nest of a Common Wasp. Each coloured band is formed from a load of wood pulp brought in by a single wasp.

Common Wasp

Looks: Vivid black and yellow pointed abdomen: face with black anchor mark

Food: Eats a wide range of other insects, carrion, and fruit

When: Spring to late summer, only the dormant young queens surviving the winter. Nests in various cavities

Where: Britain and Continental Europe

German Wasp

Looks: Vivid black and yellow pointed abdomen; yellow legs. Usually has 3 black dots on the face

Food: Eats a wide range of other insects, carrion, and fruit

When: Spring to late summer, only the dormant young queens surviving the winter. Nests in various cavities

Where: Britain and Continental Europe

Several species of social wasps live in Europe, commonly visiting gardens and often settling down to nest in them. Apart from the hornets, which are brown and gold, they are not easy to distinguish from each other without looking them in the face – and this is something that few gardeners will want to do. As far as British gardens are concerned, the two commonest species are the **Common Wasp** (*Paravespula vulgaris*) and the **German Wasp** (*Paravespula germanica*). Both species nest in cavities of some kind. These may be underground, often in hedgebanks, or in wall cavities and hollow trees. The insects are also happy to build their homes in our attics and garden sheds as long as they can approach through a fairly narrow entrance. The nests, like those of all our social wasps, are constructed of paper, which the wasps make by chewing up wood. You can often see, and even hear the wasps scraping particles from fence posts and other timbers. The Common Wasp uses fairly rotten wood, which gives its nests a yellowish colour and a very fragile texture. The German wasp goes for sounder timber and its nests are much greyer in colour and less fragile.

Life in a wasp colony

Each colony is generally ruled by a single queen, who is the mother of all the other colony members. She starts the colony in the spring by building a few paper cells and laying an egg in each one. She carries on building and within a couple of weeks or so the nest is about the size of a golf ball, consisting of about 20 cells wrapped in a paper envelope. The first eggs have hatched by this time and the queen divides her time between building and collecting food for her grubs. These grubs grow into worker wasps, which are all sterile females and noticeably smaller than the queen. The queen then retires from domestic chores and devotes herself to laying eggs, leaving the workers to continue the building work. They also have to feed the queen and the new grubs – their younger sisters who will eventually join the workforce. A mature nest may be as large as a football and contain 10,000 cells in several tiers. The queen carries on laying eggs throughout the summer, but the workers do not live for more than a few weeks and, although a colony may rear over 20,000 of them during the summer, there are rarely more than about 3,000 wasps in the colony at any one time.

Wasps on a mission

Towards the end of the summer some of the eggs develop into new queens and others produce male wasps. The latter are larger than the workers and can be recognised by their very long antennae or feelers. Their only function is to mate with the new queens. When these males and new queens have appeared, the old queen gradually stops laying eggs and, with no more work to do, the workers spend their last few weeks in the unadulterated pursuit of ripe fruit and other sweet foods. This is when they make their presence felt, by circling exposed food, darting in to grab mouthfuls of jam or other sugary substances. It is difficult to ignore them, but this is the best approach: waving your arms around in an attempt to chase them away is more likely to attract the wasps' attention and lead to your being stung. If the wasps really are a nuisance, try tempting them to another part of the garden with some jam or squashed fruit. It does not always work, but it is worth a try and a bit of jam can be looked on as a reward for all their hard work earlier in the year! If you want to get

A nest of the Common Wasp opened at an early stage to show the six-sided paper cells and the surrounding envelope. The white cells in the centre are covered with silk caps produced by the mature larvae and now contain pupae, while the outer cells contain eggs or growing larvae.

There are several species of paper wasps in southern Europe. They are particularly common around houses and they build simple nests consisting of a few dozen cells without any envelope.

rid of them for good, try the old-fashioned trap – a jam jar half full of water with some jam or honey, or even beer, in which they will happily immerse themselves and drown!

The workers and males all die along with the old queens in the autumn, leaving only the newly mated queens to survive the winter. These queens hide away in various places, including hollow trees, sheds and attics and other relatively undisturbed places. The folds of curtains in the spare room are commonly used as sleeping quarters, and it is always wise to examine clothes that have not been worn for a while: a sleepy queen hiding in a sleeve can deliver a painful sting. Take care when bringing logs into the house as well, for queens often pass the winter in log-piles.

The queens wake as temperatures rise in the spring and seek energy-providing nectar from cotoneasters, sallow catkins and a wide range of other flowers: they are also regular visitors to currant and gooseberry bushes and seem to do a good job of pollinating the flowers while lapping up the nectar. After a few good feeds, the queens begin searching for nest sites to start the cycle again. Although they may use the same sites, they do not use their old nests. In fact, there is usually little left of the old nests by this time for they have usually been wrecked by an assortment of scavengers, including beetles and fly grubs, which chew their way through the nests and quickly reduce them to dust. The availability of suitable sites is the critical factor determining the wasp population in the summer, so killing a few hibernating wasps has little effect. Far more wasps go into hibernation in the autumn than can ever establish nests in the spring.

What to do about wasp nests

Many people dash for the aerosol as soon as they see a wasp but, unless a nest is sited close to a regularly used path or doorway or near an area where children play, there is absolutely no need to destroy it. But if destruction is necessary, you can usually achieve it by spraying the entrance hole with an insecticidal spray or dust in the evening or early in the morning when the wasps are tucked up inside. They will pick up the poison as they leave. If you can't manage the job yourself, then call in a pest control company or your local council – it's probably safer.

TOP TIP

A new idea for deterring wasps, although not for controlling them, is to hang artificial nests in the garden in the spring. Available from garden centres, these balloon-like structures really do seem to dissuade the Norwegian Wasp and other species that nest in the open from taking up residence in the vicinity, although they are less likely to work against the hole-nesting species.

The Bee-killer Wasp's yellow abdomen is commonly marked with small black triangles. Having been caught by the wasp, in flight or on a flower, a Honey Bee is slung under the wasp's body as shown here and carried off to the wasp's nest, usually in a sandy bank. Although the Bee-killer has a sting for paralysing its victims, it rarely stings people unless handled.

Solitary wasps

In terms of species, our social wasps are far outnumbered by solitary wasps, many of which are called digger wasps because they excavate nesting burrows in the ground or in dead wood. The solitary wasps have no workers: each female makes one or more small nests and lays her eggs in them and, with a few exceptions, she has no contact with her offspring. Before leaving, she stocks her nests with insects or spiders that she has paralysed with her sting. Because they are not dead, the victims remain fresh and are gradually eaten by the wasp grubs. Weevils, caterpillars, flies and aphids are commonly taken by the solitary wasps, with each species having its preferred targets. One species even plucks frog-hopper nymphs from their cuckoo-spit. The solitary wasps, although not numerous and not often noticed, are therefore quite useful in the garden. There is one notable exception, however – the **Bee-killer Wasp** (*Philanthus triangulum*). Also known as the 'bee-wolf', this wasp preys almost entirely on the Honey Bee and can be a problem for bee-keepers on the continent. It is uncommon in the British Isles, but has been increasing its numbers in recent years and is now widely distributed in the south and east of England.

Bee-killer Wasp

Looks: Bright yellow abdomen usually with small black triangles

Food: Preys on Honey Bees

When: Adult summer

Where: Continental Europe; increasing in British Isles

Bee or wasp?

The fundamental difference between bees and wasps is that the bees, whether solitary or social, feed their young on pollen and nectar whereas young wasps are all reared on a diet of animal flesh – usually some kind of insect. Visually, however, the most obvious difference is that bees are generally much hairier than the wasps. They use their hairy coats as an aid to gathering pollen. Many bees also have pollen baskets on their hind legs. These are made of stiff hairs and are used to carry the pollen back to their nests. But not all bees are very hairy. Some of the smaller species have little hair at all, and there are also a number of hairless cuckoo bees. These lay their eggs in the nests of other species like the cuckoos of the bird world and, because they gather no food for their offspring, they need no hairs for gathering pollen. Hairiness is thus a useful, but not an infallible guide when trying to separate bees from wasps.

Red-tailed Bumblebee with full pollen basket.

BEES

The bees, of which we have about 250 different kinds in the British Isles, are essentially our friends. Without the Honey Bee we would have no honey but, far more importantly, without the vital pollinating activities of the numerous bee species, we would lose most of our fruit and vegetable crops and many of our garden flowers as well. Nevertheless, there are a few bees that are sometimes a little bit naughty. Our bumblebees have tubular tongues ranging from about 6 mm to 1.4 cm in length, and only those with the longest tongues can reach the nectar in deep-throated flowers such as sweet peas. Those with shorter tongues usually confine themselves to flowers with more accessible nectar, but they sometimes resort to 'stealing' nectar from sweet peas, and also from runner bean flowers, by chewing through the bases of the petals. This means that they bypass the stamens and stigmas and fail to perform their pollination duties in return for the nectar.

This bumblebee is 'stealing' nectar by biting through the base of a flower. Its tongue is not long enough to reach the nectar by the proper route that takes its past the stamens and stigma.

LEAF-CUTTER BEES

Leaf-cutter bees live up to their name by cutting pieces from the leaves of roses and other plants. The bees use these leaf sections, which are mostly semi-circular, to construct their nests in various cavities. They occasionally remove sections from petals but, although their depredations may be unsightly and annoy some gardeners, they do no real harm to our plants. The adults are active throughout the summer, but the youngsters remain tucked up in their nests until the following spring. The commonest of several similar species is the Common Leaf-cutter Bee (***Megachile centuncularis***). In common with most of our bees, the leaf–cutters are solitary creatures. Only the bumblebees and the Honey Bee lead social lives and live in colonies.

ABOVE: This Common Leaf-cutter Bee, displaying the brick-coloured pollen brush on the underside of its abdomen, is using its jaws to cut a section from a leaf. It will take only a few seconds to cut out a perfect semi-circle.

LEFT: With the leaf section clasped firmly under its body, the bee flies back to its nest cavity. Several such leaf fragments will be needed to construct each of the six or seven cigar-shaped cells that make up the nest.

This female Red Mason Bee, about 1.2 cm long, is displaying her large jaws and the spade-like horns that she uses in her building work.

RED MASON BEE
Osmia rufa

This rather rounded bee is named for the reddish or gingery hairs on its abdomen. It sometimes alarms people by nesting in house walls in the spring, but it is not usually a problem. It cannot burrow into sound mortar and its presence may well indicate that the mortar is already soft and crumbling. It is a solitary species, with each female building her own little nest or nests, although where the conditions are right there may be lots of nests in close proximity. The bee actually prefers to nest in pre-existing cavities and often uses old nail holes in walls and fences. Each nest contains up to 10 cells, which the female stocks with 'bee bread' – a mixture of pollen and nectar – before laying an egg in each one and sealing it up. The cells are built with mud, which the female manipulates partly with a pair of stout horns on her head. The young bees remain in their nests for nearly a year and do not leave until early spring. Large numbers of males can be seen flying around the nesting sites at this time as they wait for the females to emerge, and this is when the insects may cause unnecessary alarm, or even panic. They are harmless and will not sting, and they actually help us by pollinating many of our fruit crops.

Red Mason Bee

Looks: Plump, rounded with reddish hairs on abdomen

Food: Eats pollen and nectar. Burrows in and builds nests in walls

When: Spring

Where: Britain and Continental Europe

Amazing mimics

Many bees and wasps have bold patterns, known as warning colours because they warn birds and other predators to keep away. It is believed that once a predator has tried eating these insects and been stung – or merely repelled by a foul taste – it remembers the pattern and thereafter leaves the insects alone. We tend to do the same once we have discovered that bees and wasps can sting! Many harmless insects, including numerous flies and sawflies and a few moths and beetles, benefit by having colour patterns similar to those of various bees and wasps. These similarities have evolved through countless generations of natural selection and today we can see some truly amazing examples of mimicry – many of them in our own back yards. So not every black and yellow insect that you see is a wasp!

Many of the solitary wasps have their mimics, few of which are better than the wasp beetle (Clytus arietis). Although structurally very different from the wasps, it scuttles over tree trunks and other vegetation in a very wasp-like fashion and its pattern is sufficiently like that of the wasps to make birds and lizards hesitate and allow the beetle to escape. Behaviour is obviously a very important component of mimicry, for even the best colour or pattern match would be useless without the right kind of flight or resting attitude.

Bee hawkmoths are excellent bumble bee mimics, although their flight is swifter and more darting than that of the bees and they hover in front of the flowers while feeding. Although rarely seen in British gardens, they are common visitors to buddleias and other flowers on the continent.

ABOVE LEFT: The Broad-bordered Bee Hawkmoth. ABOVE RIGHT: The Wasp Beetle. LEFT: A sawfly. RIGHT: A hover-fly. All are harmless mimics of bees and wasps.

ANTS

Looking at an ant, it can be hard to realise that it belongs to the same large group as the bees and wasps. It resembles them in having a 'wasp waist', but that's about it as far as physical appearances are concerned. Ants are a good deal smaller than the familiar bees and wasps and have little or no hair, and the worker ants, which make up the bulk of every colony, are wingless. The ants are all social insects, living in colonies ranging in size from a few hundred to several thousand individuals. Large colonies may have several egg-laying queens. There are carnivorous ants and herbivorous species, but most ants, including the familiar garden species, are omnivorous.

BLACK GARDEN ANT
Lasius niger

Black Garden Ant

Looks: Small, black

Food: May feed on fruit

When: Most of year, but dormant in coldest months

Where: Britain and Continental Europe

One of the commonest garden ants, it nests under garden paths and patios and even under buildings and town pavements. Each colony is ruled by a single queen and may contain over 5,000 workers. The snaking galleries connecting the various chambers of the nest are often seen when lifting paving slabs or large stones in the garden. Eggs, larvae and pupae can be seen in the chambers and at first sight there seems to be pandemonium among the workers as they rush to carry the brood to safety, but the activity is well co-ordinated and the brood is quickly carried down to the lower levels of the nest. These ants eat lots of smaller insects, both living and dead, but are very fond of sweet things, especially the honeydew exuded by aphids and other bugs.

Ants will guard clusters of aphids and encourage them to exude honeydew by stroking them. This process is often called 'milking' and the aphids are sometimes referred to as the ants' 'cows'. The ants regularly 'farm' the aphids by moving them around on the aerial parts of the plants and carrying them to the most succulent shoots. They also install the aphids on roots passing through their nests, and sometimes use soil to build little 'cow-sheds' to protect the aphids feeding around the bases of the stems. These are red ants (see opposite).

The closely related **Yellow Ant (Lasius flavus)** occurs mainly in those gardens with areas of undisturbed grass – under trees, for example – where it usually builds low mounds. It stays mainly in the mounds or under the ground, feeding on small insects and tending aphids on roots.

RED ANTS

The chestnut-brown ants *Myrmica ruginodis* and *Myrmica rubra* are both generally known as 'red ants'. They are hard to tell apart, like to nest under stones and are not uncommon in rockeries. Their colonies are smaller than those of the Black Garden and Yellow Ants, with no more than a few hundred workers, although they do have several queens. They are largely carnivorous and are just as likely to eat the aphids as to milk them. Unlike the Black Garden and Yellow Ants, the red ants can sting.

Red ant

Looks: Chestnut brown

Food: May eat seeds and disperse weeds; aphid feeding can affect plant roots

When: Most of the year but dormant in coldest months

Where: Britain and Continental Europe

LEFT: An ant 'cow-shed', constructed with soil particles to keep the aphids safe as they feed on the lower parts of a stem.

BELOW: Red ants and their larvae. If you disturb a nest and expose the larvae, the workers quickly set to and carry the larvae to safer quarters.

The odd ant problem

Ants do not do much direct harm to our garden plants, and actually do some good by aerating the soil and removing some of the pests. They can be a problem on rockeries, however, by swamping low-growing plants with excavated soil. Removal of soil from around the roots can also lead to wilting and death of the plants. The ants like to nest on rockeries because the stones absorb and retain a good deal of the sun's heat and this helps to keep the ants' nests warm. They also enjoy the extra warmth found in raised beds and, as on rockeries, the insects can damage our plants by removing soil from around their roots. Another, rarely serious, problem stems from the ants' liking for oil-rich seeds, which they may steal from seed-beds and trays. Primula and viola seeds are particularly vulnerable in this respect. The seeds of several common weeds, including fumitory, deadnettles and some speedwells, are also attractive to ants. These seeds have oily outgrowths and are eagerly sought by the ants. The outgrowths are removed and taken to the ants' nests and the actual seeds are scattered along the way. Ants are thus responsible to some extent for dispersing some of our garden weeds. The main problem with ants, however, is connected with the aphids that they guard. Large populations of aphids feeding on the roots can cause wilting and possibly death of the plants, and then it may be necessary to take some action. Several dusts and sprays, mostly based on some kind of pyrethroid, are marketed specifically for ant control. Sugary baits containing an insecticide are also very effective and are particularly useful when ants get into the house. The insects lap up the bait and take it back to their nests, where they share it among their sisters with fatal results. You can also wage biological warfare against the ants with the help of a parasitic nematode worm.

Despite their huge numbers and constant activity, the ants keep a fairly low profile for most of the time and come to most people's notice on just one or two days in the year. This is when the males and young queens embark on their 'marriage flights'. Having been reared by their worker sisters, these 'flying ants', as they are commonly known, wait patiently in the nests and are not allowed out until the weather is just right. Warm, humid afternoons are ideal for flight and when the workers are satisfied with the conditions they open the nest entrances and allow the winged ants to pour out. Black

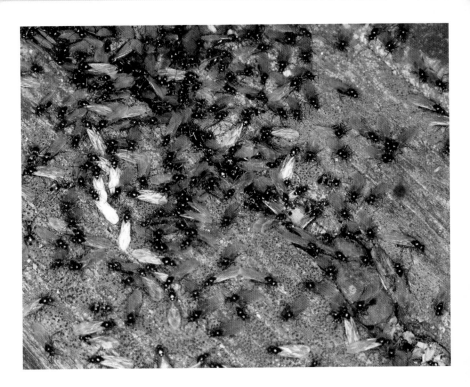

Garden Ants usually emerge in late July or August and, with all the nests in an area erupting at the same time, they blacken the ground and the surrounding plants and then rise into the air like wisps of smoke. They can be a nuisance when they get into hair and houses, but do no harm. The birds have a great time for a few hours, and spider webs trap huge numbers of the insects. Relatively few ants achieve their objective and manage to pair up. Mating takes place either in the air or when the insects have landed and the males die soon afterwards. Mated females break off their wings and each one seeks a retreat in which it can eventually begin a new nest. Other ant species may fly at different times of the year, and mated queens may enter existing nests instead of starting new nests from scratch.

Individual worker ants live for just a few weeks during the summer months, but the queen is a very long-lived insect and has been known to survive for more than 20 years in some colonies. Activity in the nest dies down as autumn approaches and air temperatures fall. The queen stops laying eggs and all the ants gather together in the lower regions of the nest where they pass the winter in a dormant state.

Black Garden Ants usually embark on their mating flights in July or August, and then large areas of the ground and vegetation may be blackened with the swarming insects. The winged individuals are accompanied by hordes of wingless workers.

SAWFLIES

The sawflies belong to the same large group as the bees and wasps, although they differ in having no 'wasp-waist'. Their name comes from the saw-like egg-laying apparatus possessed by most of the females. It is used to cut slits in leaves and stems in which the eggs are then concealed. Adult sawflies are mostly sluggish insects and much less active than the bees and wasps, many simply slinking deeper into the vegetation when disturbed and not attempting to fly away. Most species feed mainly on pollen, with a few being at least partly carnivorous. Sawflies have no stings and are quite harmless to us, although several species are excellent mimics of bees and wasps (**see p. 281**). The larvae are all vegetarians, chewing leaves or tunnelling inside stems. Free-living larvae are rather like the caterpillars of butterflies and moths, but they have more legs: whereas caterpillars never have more than five pairs of fleshy legs on the rear half of the body, the sawfly larvae have at least six pairs. Sawfly larvae or grubs living inside stems have no abdominal legs. Relatively few sawflies bother us in the garden, but several species are serious pests of agriculture and forestry.

This small sawfly could be mistaken for a true fly, but it has four wings and much longer antennae than most flies.

BANDED ROSE SAWFLY
Allantus cinctus

This common pest of roses attacks both wild and cultivated forms, although it does not do a huge amount of damage. It is one of several species in which the adult has a broad white band towards the rear of the abdomen. The adults are active throughout the summer but they are rarely noticed and, as with all our sawfly pests, it is the larvae that do the damage. The larvae are olive green on the top and pale green below and they usually feed on the undersides of the leaves. When fully grown they tunnel into the stems, often by way of cut ends, and pupate there. Although some new adults may appear later in the summer and produce fresh batches of larvae, most individuals remain in the stems until the following year. Affected plants can be sprayed with contact insecticides, but the sprays do not always reach larvae feeding underneath the leaves and hand-picking is probably the best way to control these sawfly pests.

Banded Rose Sawfly

Looks: Adult has broad white band on abdomen: larva is olive green above and paler green below

Food: Wild and garden roses

When: Adult in summer: larva summer and autumn

Where: Britain and Continental Europe

TOP TIP

The most effective control method is hand removal of the larvae.

The larva of the Banded Rose Sawfly is up to 2 cm long but hard to spot among the rose leaves unless it exposes its orange head.

ROSE SLUG SAWFLY
Endelomyia aethiops

This sawfly gets its name because its grubs look rather like green slugs, although close examination will reveal that they do have short legs. They feed on both wild and cultivated roses, stripping the tissues from either the upper or lower surface and leaving just the veins and the epidermal layer on the opposite side. Affected leaves thus look as if they have numerous small windows in them. Up to 1.5 cm long, the larvae can be found throughout the summer, with two generations each year. They pupate in the soil and those that pupate in late summer remain in the soil until the following spring. The adult insects are about 5 mm long and almost completely black. Males are very rare and the females nearly all lay fertile eggs without mating. Squashing the larvae as soon as they are seen is the best way to control the pest, although contact insecticides and insecticidal soaps are very effective. Regular hoeing under the roses is also advisable, as it disturbs the pupae.

TOP TIP

• *Squash larvae as soon as you see them.*

• *Hoe regularly around roses to disturb pupae.*

Rose Slug Sawfly

Looks: Adults black, up to 5 mm; larvae resemble green slugs

Food: Leaves of wild and cultivated roses

When: Adult late spring and summer: larva summer and early autumn

Where: Britain and Continental Europe

Larvae of the Rose Slug Sawfly do look somewhat like green slugs. Their presence can usually be detected by the 'windows' that they create as they strip the surface tissues from the leaves.

CHERRY-SLUG SAWFLY
Caliroa cerasi

Also called the Pear-slug Sawfly, it has slimy black larvae that really do look like slugs, although close examination will reveal their tiny legs. They are commonly called 'slug-worms'. Up to 1.5 cm long, these larvae usually feed by scraping away the upper layers of the foliage and leaving just the translucent lower skin and a few veins. There are two generations in a year and the larvae can be found throughout the summer and early autumn. Pupation takes place in the soil. The adult sawflies are small, black and shiny. As well as damaging the leaves of cherries and pears, the pest attacks rowan and hawthorn, but it is easily controlled by spraying with a contact insecticide. Light infestations can be dealt with simply by removing affected leaves and their occupants and destroying them.

Cherry-slug Sawfly

Looks: Black shiny adult; black larvae look like slugs

Food: Cherries, pears, hawthorn and rowan

When: Adult all summer; larva summer and early autumn

Where: Britain and Continental Europe

Cherry Slug Sawfly larva with damaged leaf.

TOP TIP

Remove and destroy affected leaves and the larvae on them to control a light infestation.

These rolled-up rose leaflets have been galled by the Leaf-Rolling Sawfly. The rolls feed and shelter the sawfly grubs, but not all of the rolls actually contain grubs: gall-formation begins as soon as the female sawfly prods the leaf with her ovipositor, even if she decides not to lay an egg there.

LEAF-ROLLING SAWFLY
Blennocampa phyllocolpa

Tightly rolled leaves on your rose bushes are usually the work of the Leaf-rolling Sawfly. This is a tiny black beast, only about 4 mm long, but just a few individuals can certainly spoil the look of the rose bushes. The adult insects emerge from their subterranean pupae in the spring and, although rarely seen, they remain active for much of the summer. The females use their ovipositors to slice into the rose leaflets and lay their eggs in the wounds. The edges of affected leaves quickly roll downwards, converting the leaflets into slender tubes in which the sawfly grubs live and feed. The rolled leaflets are thus true galls. Towards the end of the summer the fully grown grubs leave the galls and burrow into the soil, where they spend the winter in a dormant state before pupating early in the spring. Infestation by this sawfly does not have much effect on the flowering abilities of the roses because the leaves can still photosynthesise to some extent, but the rolled leaves do not enhance the appearance of the bushes and it is wise to remove affected leaflets as soon as you notice them. This is the best way to control the pest, for insecticidal sprays have little effect on the grubs tucked up inside their galls. Roses with fairly small leaflets, including wild dog roses and other climbers, seem to suffer most, while those with large shiny leaves tend to avoid attack.

Leaf-rolling Sawfly

Looks: Tiny black fly to 4 mm; grey-green grub

Food: Roses

When: Rolled leaves can be found at most times of the year, but they are occupied by larvae only during the summer months

Where: Britain and Continental Europe

Arge pagana and *Arge ochropus*

If the young shoots of your roses turn black and collapse they have probably been visited by a species of large rose sawfly – either **Arge pagana** or **Arge ochropus**. These two insects are both about 9 mm long with an orange or yellow abdomen, but they can be distinguished because *A. ochropus* has a clear yellow collar just behind the head and *A. pagana* has a largely black collar. The adults appear in mid-summer and the females slit open the rose stems and lay their eggs in the slits. Affected stems die back from the tip, but the grubs move off and feed on other shoots and young leaves. Greenish-yellow with orange heads and numerous dark spots on the body, they feed communally and can strip roses of their leaves in a very short while. They usually cling to the edges of the leaves while feeding, and when disturbed they raise their rear ends in unison – a display that is quite enough to frighten most predators. When fully grown, they go down and pupate in the soil, producing a second brood of adults in the autumn. The offspring of this second generation pass the winter as dormant larvae in the soil and pupate in the spring. Although both species are widely

Arge ochropus

Looks: Orange or yellow abdomen; clear yellow collar behind head; greenish-yellow grubs with orange heads

Food: Roses

When: Adult in summer and autumn: larva summer to spring but dormant in ground in winter

Where: Britain and Continental Europe

Arge pagana

Looks: Orange or yellow abdomen; largely black collar; greenish yellow grubs with orange heads

Food: Roses

When: Adult in summer and autumn: larva summer to spring but dormant in ground in winter

Where: Britain and Continental Europe

TOP TIP

Remove damaged shoots before the eggs have a chance to hatch to control both of these species.

A female sawfly (*Arge pagana*) laying her eggs in a rose stem.

Arge pagana larvae tucking in to a rose leaf.

Croesus septentrionalis

Looks: Adult has broad red band on abdomen; larva is pale green with black spots and black head

Food: Birch, hazel

When: Adult in summer and autumn: larva summer to spring but dormant in ground in winter

Where: Britain and Continental Europe

Larvae of the sawfly *Croesus septentrionalis* in typical alarm position on the edge of a hazel leaf. Many sawfly larvae adopt this pose, and some release pungent odours at the same time.

distributed on the Continent, British populations of these sawflies are confined to the southern half of England. Removal of damaged shoots before the eggs hatch is the surest way to control these pests. Alternatively, squash the larvae on the leaves or spray them with a contact insecticide. The larvae of **Croesus septentrionalis**, often abundant on birch and hazel, differ from those of the *Arge* species in having black heads. The adult, in common with several other species, has a broad red band on the abdomen.

BARBERRY SAWFLY
Arge berberidis

Barberry bushes and hedges that suddenly lose a large proportion of their leaves are likely to have been targeted by the Barberry Sawfly. This species ravages a wide range of barberry cultivars as well as the native *Berberis vulgaris* and will also attack mahonia bushes. The adult insects, which can be found on and around barberry bushes in spring and summer, are about 8 mm long with deep blue or black shiny bodies and dark wings. The females lay small batches of eggs in the undersides of the leaves and the resulting larvae are dirty white with black and yellow spots. They reach lengths of about 1.8 cm and can be found munching their way through the barberry leaves from spring until well into the autumn. There are two or three generations in a year and populations can build up rapidly, with the result that garden hedges can be completely defoliated. Winter is passed in the pupal stage in the soil. Although widely distributed on the continent, the Barberry Sawfly was unknown in the British Isles until 2002, when it was discovered in several gardens in the London area. It is now firmly established in many parts of England. Removing the larvae by hand is possible where only small bushes are involved, but the prickly nature of the plants can make this a painful process and spraying is the only option for larger bushes and hedges. A systemic insecticide such as thiaclo-prid and contact insecticides containing pyrethroids provide good control, although spraying needs to be carried out as soon as the larvae are noticed in the spring if defoliation is to be kept to a minimum.

TOP TIP

Spraying with a systemic or contact insecticide is the most effective control method on the prickly bushes that the Barberry Sawfly favours.

Barberry Sawfly

Looks: Adults to 8 mm with deep blue or black shiny bodies; larvae dirty white with black and yellow spots

Food: Barberry, mahonia

When: Adult and larva spring to autumn

Where: Britain and Continental Europe

BELOW: An adult Barberry Sawfly INSET: Barberry Sawfly larvae can be recognised by their conspicuous black and yellow spots.

Larvae of the Solomon's Seal Sawfly live gregariously and can rapidly reduce the leaves to skeletons.

TOP TIP

Remove and squash larvae as soon as they are spotted.

SOLOMON'S SEAL SAWFLY
Phymatocera aterrima

This creature is responsible for reducing the leaves of Solomon's Seal to skeletons in early summer. The adult insect is about 9 mm long and shiny black. Even the wings are black. The insects emerge from their subterranean pupae in the spring and the females lay rows of eggs in the young stems. Pink or purplish streaks up to 2.5 cm long reveal the position of the eggs. The resulting larvae are pale grey with small black heads and they munch away at the leaf tissues until only a few unsightly veins are left. When mature, the larvae tunnel into the ground to pupate and they remain there throughout the winter. Spraying with a pyrethroid-based insecticide provides good control of the pest, but the best remedy is to squash the larvae as soon as you see them. Although widely distributed on the Continent and in many parts of England, the insect does not seem to have reached Scotland or Ireland.

Solomon's Seal Sawfly

Looks: Shiny black adult to 9 mm; larvae pale grey with black heads

Food: Solomon's Seal

When: Adult in spring and early summer: larva summer

Where: Southern and central England; Continental Europe

The adult Solomon's Seal Sawfly is one of several closely related species with shiny black bodies and dark wings.

AQUILEGIA SAWFLY
Pristiphora aquilegiae

The leaves of aquilegias or granny-bonnets commonly suffer the same fate as Solomon's Seal leaves and young leaves may disappear altogether, although it is not easy to spot the cause of their disappearance. The culprits are the larvae of the Aquilegia Sawfly, which are pale green and blend beautifully with the leaves. They grow to about 1.8 cm in length and then pupate in the soil. The adults resemble those of the Solomon's Seal Sawfly but are only about 6 mm long and they have clear wings. There are several generations in a year and constant vigilance is necessary to keep the pest in check. Pluck the larvae from the plants if you can find them, or else spray the plants with a pyrethroid-based insecticide when you see the damage.

Aquilegia Sawfly

Looks: Adults black and shiny to 6 mm; larvae pale green

Food: Aquilegia leaves

When: Adult and larva spring to autumn

Where: Britain and Continental Europe

Larvae of the Aquilegia Sawfly often resemble twisted stems and are very difficult to spot on the leaves.

TOP TIP

As the larvae are hard to spot on leaves, spraying with a pyrethroid-based insecticide is probably the most effective method of control.

APPLE SAWFLY
Hoplocampa testudinea

This sawfly attacks our apples in the spring, as soon as they start to develop in the pollinated flowers. The female sawflies lay their eggs in the flowers as they open and the resulting grubs tunnel into the tiny fruitlets. They remain just under the skin for a short while and then burrow into the centre, hollowing out the fruitlets and destroying the developing seeds. Having wrecked its first home, each grub usually moves on to a second fruitlet and possibly a third one before reaching its full size of about 1.5 cm. Affected apples fall to the ground – usually in June or July – and the pale cream grubs nibble their way out and burrow into the soil, where they pupate and produce new adults in the following spring. Many grubs, however, die before reaching the centre of the fruit and then the apples can continue to grow and ripen more or less normally, although they may be malformed and exhibit meandering scars showing where the grubs had tunnelled just under the skin. Small apples falling as a result of attack by the sawfly should not be confused with those of the 'June drop' – a normal process by which the trees get rid of excess fruit. Exit holes, often oozing with orange mush, indicate a sawfly problem, although by the time you find the holes the grubs will probably be safely tucked up in the soil! You can minimise the problem for future years by gathering and destroying the fallen fruit on a regular basis – every day if possible – to reduce the numbers of grubs entering the soil. Or let your chickens do the job **(see p. 255)**. Damage can also be reduced by spraying the little fruit clusters with a contact insecticide as soon as the petals have fallen. This will kill the grubs as they explore the fruitlets before tunnelling into them. Cooking apples seem to be less affected by the Apple Sawfly than eating varieties.

COMMON GOOSEBERRY SAWFLY
Nematus ribesii

Gooseberry bushes are regularly stripped of their leaves in the summer by clusters of sawfly larvae, the commonest of three rather similar species being the Common Gooseberry Sawfly. Red and white currants are also attacked by this pest. The adults of this species are largely golden-yellow and they emerge from their subterranean pupae in the spring. Eggs are then laid in the lower surfaces of the leaves. The

---

TOP TIP

Regular collection and destruction of any damaged fruit will help to control Apple Sawfly infestations in future years.

Apple Sawfly

Looks: Adults black; grubs are pale cream

Food: Apples

When: Adult in spring: larva spring and early summer

Where: Britain and Continental Europe

resulting larvae are light green with numerous black spots and a small black head. They feed communally for a few weeks and can quickly reduce the leaves to skeletons. They pupate in the soil when fully grown. Two more generations appear during the summer and continue to defoliate the bushes. Magpie Moth caterpillars **(see p. 201)** cause similar damage but are much more colourful and not likely to be confused with the sawfly larvae. Hand picking of the larvae is an effective means of control, but it can be painful because the pests live deep in the gooseberry bushes. Most gardeners prefer to get out the insecticide. Use a quick-acting contact insecticide as soon as you notice the larvae and you should have no serious damage, but make sure you do not use it too close to harvest-time – read the instructions.

Common Gooseberry Sawfly

Looks: Golden-yellow adults; light green larvae have black spots and head

Food: Gooseberries, red and white currants

When: Adult and larva in spring and summer

Where: Britain and Continental Europe

TOP TIP

You might prefer to try a traditional remedy. One of these recommends steeping a bunch of elder leaves in a bucket of water for a few hours and then spraying the water over the gooseberries. Mixing some soap with it is said to make it even better!

ABOVE: The adult Common Gooseberry Sawfly is abundant in many gardens, feeding on pollen from a wide range of flowers in the spring.

LEFT: The larva of the Common Gooseberry Sawfly is sometimes confused with the caterpillar of the Magpie Moth (see p.201), but the latter is much more colourful and has fewer legs. Both insects can defoliate your gooseberry bushes.

The adult Turnip Sawfly.

TURNIP SAWFLY
Athalia rosae

The adult resembles the Gooseberry Sawfly in colour but has much shorter and stouter antennae and a conspicuous dark streak along the front edge of its wings. Its gregarious, dull green larvae damage a wide range of cruciferous plants, not just turnips, and, in common with many other sawfly larvae, they can rapidly turn the leaves into skeletons. The larvae pupate in the soil and there are two or three generations in a year. Adults are warmth-loving insects, flying only when the temperature reaches about 18°C, so the species is most troublesome in the warmer parts of Europe. It was actually quite rare in the British Isles in the middle of the 20th century, but it is now widely distributed and quite common in the southern half of England. Climate change may be partly responsible, but the expansion of oil-seed rape cultivation has undoubtedly played some role in the increase of this pest. Pyrethroid-based contact insecticides can be used to treated any infestation.

Turnip Sawfly

Looks: Golden adult with stout antennae and dark streak on wings; larvae are dull green

Food: Turnips and other cruciferous plants

When: Adult and larva spring to autumn

Where: Southern Britain; warmer parts of Continental Europe

Pontania proxima

Anyone with willow trees in the garden, especially the narrow-leaved species and varieties, is likely to meet the willow bean gall. This is an oval swelling or gall caused by this little black sawfly. The gall starts to swell when the female sawfly lays an egg in the leaf **(see p. 24)**. When the egg hatches the grub starts to nibble the gall tissue and the gall eventually becomes little more than a hollow shell, 5–10 mm long, containing the mature grub. The latter then leaves to pupate in the soil. There are two generations each year and galls can be found on the leaves from mid-summer onwards. In common with most galls, the bean galls do not seem to harm the trees in any way. Red specimens can be quite attractive and, although some gardeners may dislike them, there is really no need to remove them.

Pontania proxima

Looks: Small black adult; larvae induce galls that start off green and then become red

Food: Willows

When: Galls can be found from mid-summer until leaf fall

Where: Britain and Continental Europe

Willow Bean galls, induced by the sawfly *Pontania proxima*. Each 'bean' is home to one sawfly larva.

Hawthorn Sawfly

Looks: Adult resembles a bee but has clubbed antennae; larva pale blue-green

Food: Hawthorn leaves

When: Adult in spring: larva in summer

Where: Uncommon in Britain and Continental Europe

RIGHT: The adult Hawthorn Sawfly is one of relatively few sawfly species with clubbed antennae. Look for it around hawthorn hedges.

BELOW LEFT: Mature Hawthorn Sawfly larvae spin tough, fibrous cocoons on the twigs and pupate inside them. The cocoons are quite easy to spot in the winter. The adult insect emerges in the spring by slicing off the top of its cocoon with its strong jaws, as seen here.

BELOW RIGHT: The Hawthorn Sawfly larva is not easy to see among the hawthorn foliage in the summer.

HAWTHORN SAWFLY
Trichiosoma lucorum

Rarely common enough to be called a pest, the larvae of the Hawthorn Sawfly can certainly strip the leaves from small stretches of hawthorn hedge in the summer. These larvae are solitary and, being pale bluish-green, they blend quite well with the undersides of the leaves. They pupate in tough, sausage-shaped cocoons which are quite conspicuous on the bare branches in winter. The adult insect audibly saws the top off the cocoon with its strong jaws in the spring. It looks very much like a bee and even buzzes like a bee in flight, but it is quite harmless.

ENJOY YOUR GARDEN

A cursory glance through this book might give one the impression that gardening is a mug's game, in view of all the creepy-crawlies lurking among the flowers and vegetables or hiding in the trees and shrubs. Some of them certainly do compete with us, but a more leisurely look at the preceding pages will reveal that not all of our garden residents are eager to devour our precious plants. Many of them are actually on our side, protecting our plants by removing a variety of the more harmful species. Spend a bit of time learning which ones are which: ask questions first and then take action if necessary, rather than putting the boot in first and doing the research afterwards. You will find that most of your guests are pretty harmless, and that even the most voracious of pests can be kept under control fairly easily. Intervene and attack the pests when necessary, but a garden is for enjoyment and you don't have to be working all the time. Grow as wide a variety of plants as your garden can accommodate and then enjoy the birds and other wildlife that the plants attract. The numerous residents will keep each other in check, so diversity can actually enhance productivity without the need for expensive pesticides. There is no reason why a garden should not be a haven for wildlife and still keep you in food, so take time to sit back and enjoy your private outdoor space. Appreciate the scents and colours of your flowers – and if you can enjoy a meal of fresh fruit and vegetables at the same time so much the better.

INDEX